Foreword

Evangelical Christian Doctrine. The very words have a negative connotation for many people, conjuring up thoughts of dull, boring, religious theory and study. That's an unfortunate association. Doctrine – that which is believed and taught – is important because it provides a basis for faith, revealing what traditional Evangelical Christians believe and the biblical basis for that belief.

A study of doctrine can answer questions such as these:
- Who is Jesus Christ?
- Why did Jesus die? Is He alive today?
- Is Jesus coming back to earth in the future?
- What happens after we die?
- Is Hell a real place?
- How do I know I can trust the Bible?
- Did God create the world? Why?
- Is Satan a real person?
- How can I live a life that pleases and honors God?
- What are apostles and prophets? Do they exist today?
- What is a "dispensation"?
- What will we do for eternity?

Doctrine is important also because what you believe affects the way you live and how you relate to others. Holding incorrect doctrine or misinterpreting correct doctrine can result in negative consequences.

This book begins with the seventeen-point Biblical Ministries Worldwide (BMW) Doctrinal Statement and builds on that foundation, expanding and explaining each of the points. The BMW Doctrinal Statement was selected from the many excellent doctrinal statements available because it is comprehensive and orthodox – true to the Bible.

Each of the seventeen numbered sections in this book is a "study note" that was initially written for a small-group Bible study. The study notes are not – and are not intended to be – deep theological treatises. Entire books have been written on many of the doctrines addressed in the BMW Statement.

Note that quoting a given author in the study notes does not necessarily imply agreement with his or her position on all doctrinal matters!

Disclaimer: This Survey book was not commissioned by BMW, nor is the author affiliated with BMW.

The following abbreviations are used in this document:

AB	Amplified Bible "Scripture quotations taken from the Amplified® Bible, Copyright © 1954, 1958, 1962, 1964, 1965, 1987 by The Lockman Foundation, Used by permission."
BMW	Biblical Ministries Worldwide, Lawrenceville, GA
CRI	Christian Research Institute, Charlotte, NC
ESV	English Standard Version "Scripture quotations marked ESV are from The Holy Bible, English Standard Version® (ESV®), copyright © 2001 by Crossway, a publishing ministry of Good News Publishers. Used by permission. All rights reserved."
HCSB	Holman Christian Standard Bible "Scripture quotations marked HCSB are taken from the Holman Christian Standard Bible®, Copyright © 1999, 2000, 2002, 2003, 2009 by Holman Bible Publishers. Used by permission."
ICR	Institute for Creation Research, Dallas, TX
KJV	King James Version Scripture quotations marked KJV are from the Holy Bible, King James Version. Scripture quotations not otherwise identified are from the KJV.
NASB	New American Standard Bible "Scripture quotations marked NASB are from the New American Standard Bible®, Copyright © The Lockman Foundation 1960, 1962, 1963, 1968, 1971, 1972, 1973, 1975, 1977, 1995. Used by permission."
NDSB	New Defender's Study Bible (King James Version)
NIV	New International Version "Scripture quotations marked NIV are from the Holy Bible, New International Version®, © 1973, 1978, 1984, 2011 by Biblica, Inc. Used by permission. All rights reserved worldwide."
NKJV	New King James Version "Scripture quotations marked NKJV are from the New King James Version®. © 1982 by Thomas Nelson, Inc. Used by permission. All rights reserved."
NLT	New Living Translation "Scripture quotations marked (NLT) are taken from the Holy Bible, New Living Translation, copyright © 1996, 2004, 2007 by Tyndale House Foundation. Used by permission of Tyndale House Publishers, Inc., Carol Stream, Illinois 60188. All rights reserved."

A Survey of

Major

Biblical

Doctrines

Based on the

Biblical Ministries Worldwide

Doctrinal Statement

Written By
Malcolm W. Howard

Seventh Edition

ISBN 978-1-329-66252-0

Preface To The Second Edition

Why release a Second Edition so soon after the First Edition? Short answer: To add content.

As I reviewed the First Edition of this document, I saw the need for ancillary material – and incorporated it. For example, in the study note entitled *The Eternal State*, I integrated brief comments regarding soul sleep, prayer for the dead, purgatory, and what will Christians do in Heaven for eternity. In *The Ministry and Spiritual Gifts*, I addressed the topic of the roles of men and women in the church. Etc.

Writing a survey-type document is difficult in the sense that the author has to perform a balancing act between document size and adequate content. There's always more that can be said about a given subject, but how much is enough? The answer would seem to be the same as that given by the wealthy man who, when asked how much money was enough, replied, "Just a little more."

So it is with this Second Edition – I've added "just a little more" explanatory content to many of the seventeen topics discussed in this Survey document.

Preface To The Third Edition

Solomon, reportedly the wisest man who ever lived, stated, *of making many books there is no end…* Ecclesiastes 12:12 (KJV). That appears to be applicable to this Third Edition.

Here's a partial list of the new and embellished topics in this edition and an indication of the doctrinal points to which they apply:

- Foreknowledge, Predestination, and Election (5)

- Salvation, Justification, Sanctification, and Glorification (6)

- Occultism (12)

- Jewish Temples (13)

Also in this edition is additional information regarding the Old Testament Sacrificial System, physical healing, and a description of the unholy trinity.

Please remember that this is a survey document; coverage of the included subjects is purposely broad, not deep.

Preface To The Fourth Edition

As was true for previous editions, this Fourth Edition was produced to add new material and augment existing material. Below is a list of some topics that meet that criteria. The numbers in parenthesis are the affected points of the BMW Doctrinal Statement.

- Biblical inerrancy (1)

- Sufficiency of Scripture (1)

- Preexistence of souls (2)

- Mary, mother of the Savior (3)

- Sin (4)

- Salvation (6)

- Victory over sin (6)

- Works-based salvation (6)

- The proper motive for inviting the Lord Jesus Christ into your life (6)

- Saints of the Church Age (7)

- Priests / priesthood (7)

- Paganism, pantheism, polytheism, universalism (9)

- Angels (12)

- New Age Movement (12)

- Heaven (14)

- Resurrection bodies (14)

My purpose in writing this book has always been twofold: First and foremost, to present sound Evangelical doctrine – which I believe is lacking in many churches today, and, secondly, to expose and refute some of the aberrant teaching found in Christendom and other religious traditions.

This Fourth Edition is the first to incorporate a comprehensive Scripture Index. For ease of reference, especially for those who are less familiar with the Bible, the Index is in normal alphabetical sequence, not the sequence of the Old and New Testaments.

Preface To The Fifth Edition

Doctrine is critically important to the Church and to the individual believers who constitute the Church, the body of Christ. Here's a quote from Dr. John MacArthur:

"Simply put, doctrine is divine truth, nothing more, nothing less. Doctrine is the absolute representation of the divine character and will of God, worthy of every believer's most diligent study and demanding total acceptance and obedience. As a result, there's nothing more practical and life transforming than doctrine. What we believe to be true about God, Satan, man, salvation, the world, and the church always finds its way into our attitudes, actions, words and worship. You don't get more practical than doctrine." From the September 16, 2013, letter to supporters of the Grace to You ministry.

To be useful and practical, doctrine must be correct. By that I mean true to God's Word, the Bible. That's why one of the goals of this book is to expose aberrant doctrine as well as teach correct doctrine.

This Fifth Edition continues the trend of adding material to the discussion of the BMW Doctrinal Statement. Thirteen of the seventeen doctrinal point discussions have been augmented in this edition.

This edition also incorporates some new material. Here's a partial list of the new topics and an indication of the doctrinal points to which they apply:

- Who is qualified to properly interpret Scripture? (1)

- Are church traditions and pronouncements of church leaders equal in authority with the Bible? (1)

- Can a man become a god? (2)

- Was Christ's death a ransom paid to Satan to purchase man's freedom? (3)

- Is the biblical doctrine of Election unfair? (5)

- What are "canonization" and "veneration"? (6)

- Is it acceptable to pray to "saints"? (6)

- Is sinless perfection possible in this life? (6)

- Can clergymen (priests) forgive sins? (6)

- What is transubstantiation? (8)

- What is baptismal regeneration? (8)

- What is "mysticism"? (9)

- Are the first-century extraordinary spiritual gifts still operational today? (10)

- Are there genuine apostles today? (10)

- What is the "abomination of desolation" spoken of in the books of Daniel and Revelation? (13)

- Creation and Science (15)

Preface To The Sixth Edition

Dr. John Munro, Senior Pastor of Calvary Church in Charlotte, North Carolina, made the following statement regarding the importance of doctrine:

> "Doctrine is essential, otherwise the church becomes like the world, prizing innovation, creativity, conformity to the pop culture rather than faithfulness to Christ and His Word, also we will be able to repudiate false doctrine so that the church is stable and is not characterized by error or by the latest church fad or gimmick or movement." Back To The Bible radio program, February 4, 2014

Some of the new and augmented material in this Sixth Edition is described below. The numbers in parenthesis indicate the doctrinal points to which the material applies.

Although we can never document all the attributes of God – because He is infinite in being – this edition adds some new definitions and augments others. (2)

A substantial amount of new material has been added to the discussion of the importance to us of the resurrection of the Lord Jesus Christ. (3)

Regarding salvation, two new topics have been added:
* What about those who have never heard the Gospel? (6)
* Infant salvation (6)

A description of the "last days," (almost) always a subject of general interest, has been added to the discussion of the second advent of Christ (13).

This is the first edition to incorporate a General Index. It replaces the Topical Index found in previous editions. The new index will make it easier to find desired information more quickly.

The new General Index encompasses all the subjects from the previous Topical Index and many more.

Preface To The Seventh Edition

Sean McDowell, Author, Conference Speaker, Youth Minister, wrote the following regarding the importance of doctrine:

> "There is a trend in the church today to elevate unity above truth. Many are willing to set aside essential doctrines for the sake of harmony. … As shown in the Sermon on the Mount, Jesus saw the value in dividing over essential doctrine because it saves people from the consequences of false teaching.

> "True unity (in our churches) comes not when we sacrifice true doctrine, but when we focus on the core truths of the Gospel. Thus, the real question is not if we teach doctrine, but what doctrines do we teach, how do we teach them, and do we live them out in our relationships. For the sake of our youth and the vitality of the church, we must not cave in to the pressure to stop teaching doctrine. The proper response to the attack on doctrine is

not to retreat, but to march forward with an even greater resolve, unity, and love." From *The Doctrine Debate: Why Doctrine Matters More Than Ever*, printed in the *Christian Research Journal*, Volume 31 Number 1. The complete article can be accessed at http://www.equip.org/article/the-doctrine-debate/

This Seventh Edition includes a considerable amount of new information. Here's a brief description of that material. The number in parenthesis indicates the associated doctrinal point.

Biblical inspiration, inerrancy, and infallibility (1).

The apocryphal books (1).

The hermeneutical Principle of Recurrence (1).

The process of Textual Criticism (1).

The illuminating ministry of the Holy Spirit (4)

Foreknowledge, predestination, and election (5).

Mankind's sinful nature (5).

Characteristics of a disciple (9).

The Lake of Fire (14).

The Dominion Mandate (14).

The Glory of God (15).

Sexual sin (16).

Evaluating activities (17).

The General Index, which appeared for the first time in the Sixth Edition, has been substantially augmented to facilitate finding desired information.

To further assist you, an additional navigation aide has been included at the beginning of each doctrinal point study note: An index of the major topics discussed in that note.

Contents

Commentary on the Doctrinal Statement Points

Our Beliefs

There are two things on the earth that will last forever: the Word of God and the souls of people. Christians have been called to bring the two together.

BMW is committed to scriptural integrity and doctrinal purity as expressed in our doctrinal statement. We seek to hold these beliefs in the spirit of love and humility.

Our Doctrinal Statement

The Holy Scriptures

We believe in the verbal and plenary inspiration of the Scriptures, consisting of 66 books which constitute the Old and New Testaments, the Word of God, inerrant in the original writings, the complete and unalterable special revelation of God, and our final authority. We believe in the normal, literal, and consistent interpretation of the Scriptures; and a dispensational understanding of God's progressive revelation. (Matthew 5:18; John 16:12-13; 2 Timothy 3:16-17; 2 Peter 1:20-21)

The Godhead

We believe in the one triune God, eternally existing in three persons – Father, Son, and Holy Spirit – co-eternal in being, co-identical in nature, co-equal in power and glory, and having the same attributes and perfections. (Deuteronomy 6:4; 2 Corinthians 13:14)

The Person and Work of Christ

We believe the Lord Jesus Christ, the eternal Son of God, became man, without ceasing to be God, having been conceived by the Holy Spirit and born of the virgin Mary, and lived a sinless life. He came that He might reveal God and redeem sinful man. (Luke 1:35; John 1:1-2,14)

We believe the Lord Jesus Christ accomplished our redemption through His death on the cross as a representative, vicarious, substitutionary sacrifice sufficient for the sins of the whole world, and our justification is verified by His literal, physical resurrection from the dead. (Romans 3:24-25; Ephesians 1:7; Hebrews 2:9; 1 Peter 1:3-5; 2:24; 1 John 2:2)

We believe the Lord Jesus Christ ascended to heaven and is now exalted at the right hand of God where, as our High Priest, He fulfills the ministry of Representative, Intercessor, and Advocate. (Acts 1:9-10; Romans 8:34; Hebrews 7:25; 9:24; 1 John 2:1-2)

The Person and Work of the Holy Spirit

We believe the Holy Spirit is the person of the Godhead who in this present age convicts the world of sin, righteousness, and judgment; who regenerates and baptizes into the body of Christ those who believe; and who indwells and seals them unto the day of redemption. (John 16:8-11; Romans 8:9; 1 Corinthians 12:12-14; 2 Corinthians 3:6; Ephesians 1:13-14)

We believe the Holy Spirit is the Divine Teacher who guides believers into all truth; and it is the privilege of believers to be filled with, and their duty to walk in, the Holy Spirit. (John 16:13; Galatians 5:16; Ephesians 5:18; 1 John 2:20, 27)

The Total Depravity of Man

We believe man was created in the image and likeness of God; in Adam's sin the race fell, inherited a sinful nature, and became alienated from God; and man is totally depraved and unable to remedy his lost condition. (Genesis 1:26- 27; Romans 3:22-23; 5:12; Ephesians 2:1-3, 12)

Salvation and Security

We believe the Lord Jesus Christ died for our sins according to the Scriptures as a representative and substitutionary sacrifice for all people and all who trust Him are saved by grace through faith on the grounds of His shed blood, accepted in the beloved, kept by God's power, and thus secure in Christ forever. (John 1:12; 6:37-40; 10:27-30; Romans 8:1,38-39; 1 Corinthians 1:4-8; Ephesians 1:7; 2:8-10; 1 Peter 1:5,18-19)

We believe every saved person is a new creation with provision made for victory over sin through the power of the indwelling Holy Spirit. The sin that is present in us is not eradicated in this life. (2 Corinthians 5:17; Romans 6:13; 8:12-13; Galatians 5:16-25; Ephesians 4:22-24; Colossians 3:10; 1 Peter 1:14-16; 1 John 3:5-9)

We believe it is the privilege of believers to rejoice in the assurance of their salvation through the testimony of God's Word, which, however, clearly forbids the use of Christian liberty as an occasion to the flesh. (Romans 13:13-14; Galatians 5:13; Titus 2:11-15; 1 Peter 2:13-20)

The Church

We believe the Church, which began with the baptizing work of the Holy Spirit on the day of Pentecost, is the body and bride of Christ. It is the spiritual organism made up of all born-again persons of the present age. (Acts 2:1-36; 1 Corinthians 12:13-14; 2 Corinthians 11:2; Ephesians 1:22-23; 5:25-27)

We believe the establishment and continuance of local churches is clearly taught and defined in the New Testament Scriptures. (Acts 14:27; 20:17, 28-32; 1 Timothy 3:1-13; Titus 1:5-11)

Ordinances

We believe the Lord Jesus Christ established two ordinances for the Church in this present age. These are believer's water baptism, practiced by immersion, and the Lord's Supper, observed as a memorial of His death. (Acts 8:12, 35-39; 10:47-48; 1 Corinthians 1:14; 11:23-34)

Missions

We believe that Christ commissioned individuals in the church to make disciples from among all nations, to baptize them in the name of the Father, the Son, and the Holy Spirit, and to teach them to observe all things whatsoever He has commanded. (Matthew 28:18-20; Acts 1:8; 2 Corinthians 5:19-20)

The Ministry and Spiritual Gifts

We believe the Lord Jesus Christ gives the Church evangelists and pastor-teachers. These gifted men are to equip the saints for the work of the ministry. (Ephesians 4:7-14)

We believe the Holy Spirit bestows spiritual gifts upon believers for Christian service and the edification of the Church. (Romans 12:3-8; 1 Corinthians 12:4-11; 1 Peter 4:10-11)

We believe the church age was initiated through the ministry of the apostles and prophets accompanied by sign gifts to confirm their message. These sign gifts gradually ceased by the time of the completion of the New Testament. (1 Corinthians 12:28-31; 13:8-10; 14:1-28; 2 Corinthians 12:12; Ephesians 2:19-22; Hebrews 2:3-4)

We believe God hears and answers prayer in accord with His own will for healing of the sick and afflicted. (John 14:13-14; 15:7; 1 John 5:14-15)

Dispensationalism

We believe the Scriptures interpreted in their natural, literal sense reveal divinely determined dispensations, which define man's responsibility in successive ages. A dispensation is not a way of salvation, but a divinely-ordered stewardship by which God directs man according to His purpose. (John 1:17; 1 Corinthians 9:17; 2 Corinthians 3:9-18; Galatians 3:13-25; Ephesians 1:10; 3:2-10; Colossians 1:24-25; Hebrews 7:19; Revelation 20:2-6)

We believe salvation is always by grace through faith regardless of the dispensation in which the believer may have lived. God's purpose of salvation by grace through faith alone has always been based upon the substitutionary atonement of our Lord Jesus Christ upon the cross. (Ephesians 2:8-10; Hebrews 11:6; 1 Peter 1:10-12)

The Personality of Satan

We believe Satan is a created being, the author of sin, the tempter in the fall, the declared enemy of God and man, and the god of this age. He shall be eternally punished in the lake of fire. (Job 1:6-7; Isaiah 14:12-17; Matthew 4:2-11; 25:41; Revelation 20:10)

The Second Advent of Christ

We believe in the personal, imminent, pretribulational and premillennial coming of the Lord Jesus Christ for His redeemed ones. We believe that at the end of the seven-year tribulation He will return to earth with the saints in power and glory to reign for a thousand years. (Zechariah 14:4-11; 1 Thessalonians 1:10; 4:13-18; 5:9; Titus 2:13; Revelation 3:10; 19:11-16; 20:1-6)

The Eternal State

We believe in the bodily resurrection of all men, the saved to eternal life and the unsaved to judgment and everlasting punishment. (Matthew 25:46; John 5:28-29; 11:25-26; Revelation 20:5,6,12-13)

We believe the souls of the redeemed are, at death, absent from the body and present with the Lord, where in conscious bliss they await the first resurrection when spirit, soul, and body are reunited and glorified to be forever with the Lord. (Luke 23:43; 2 Corinthians 5:8; Philippians 1:23; 3:21; 1 Thessalonians 4:16-17; Revelation 20:4-6)

We believe the souls of unbelievers are, at death, absent from the body and in conscious misery until the second resurrection, when with soul and body reunited they shall appear at the Great White Throne Judgment and shall be cast into the lake of fire, not to be annihilated, but to suffer everlasting conscious punishment. (Matthew 25:41-46; Mark 9:43-48; Luke 16:19-26; 2 Thessalonians 1:7-9; Jude 6-7; Revelation 20:11-15)

Creation

We believe the triune God, by a free act and for His own glory, without the use of existing materials or secondary causes, brought into being - immediately and instantaneously in six literal days by the word of His mouth - the whole visible and invisible universe. (Genesis 1:1-27; Exodus 20:8-11; Nehemiah 9:6; Psalm 104:25-26; Isaiah 40:21-31; John 1:1-5; Colossians 1:16-17)

Human Sexuality

Sexual intimacy is a wonderful gift of God that is only to be expressed between a man and a woman within the love and bonds of marriage. Therefore, we believe that any other form of sexual intimacy is both immoral and a perversion of God's gift. (Genesis 2:24-25; Proverbs 5:18; 1 Corinthians 7:5; 1 Thessalonians 4:3-5; Hebrews 13:4; Leviticus 18:1-30; Proverbs 6:32; 1 Corinthians 6:18; Romans 1:26-27)

Separation and Unity

We believe the saved should be separated unto the Lord Jesus Christ, necessitating holy living in all personal and ecclesiastical associations and relationships. We believe we are responsible to identify false teaching and dangerous movements where they relate to the conduct of the Mission's ministries. We believe separation is required in those instances where people, groups, and organizations whose doctrinal position is the same as the Mission's engage in contradictory practices which compromise the faith. (Romans 12:1-2; 14:13; 1 Corinthians 6:19-20; Titus 2:14; James 4:4-5; 1 Peter 2:9; 1 John 2:15-17; Matthew 18:15-17; Romans 16:17; 1 Corinthians 5:7-11; 2 Corinthians 6:14-18; Ephesians 4:1-6; 2 Thessalonians 3:11-14; 2 Timothy 3:1-5; Titus 3:10; 2 John 9-11)

(Scripture verses are representative, and not to be considered exhaustive.)

1.   The Holy Scriptures

*"We believe in the **verbal and plenary inspiration** of the **Scriptures**, consisting of 66 books which constitute the Old and New Testaments, the Word of God, **inerrant** in the original writings, the **complete and unalterable special revelation** of God, and our **final authority**. We believe in the **normal, literal, and consistent interpretation** of the Scriptures; and a **dispensational** understanding of God's **progressive revelation**. (Matthew 5:18; John 16:12-13; 2 Timothy 3:16-17; 2 Peter 1:20-21)"*

The words appearing in **bold** text in the paragraph above are explained in this study note. Here's where to find those words – and more – in this note:

Scripture

Simply stated, Scripture is God's verbal revelation to us. When Scripture speaks, God speaks!

The word "Scripture" (Greek *graphe*) means "a written document." In evangelical Christianity, "Scripture" is used interchangeably with "Bible." Both terms refer to the 66 books that comprise the Old and New Testaments.

Other religious traditions have a wider definition of "Scripture," incorporating writings they consider authoritative. While some of these writings may be inspiring, they are not inspired by God. God's revelation to man was complete when the book of Revelation was finished (c. A.D. 96).

Inspired

"Inspiration" is from a Latin word meaning "to breathe into." When used to refer to Scripture, "inspired" means "God-breathed" (Greek *theopneustos*: *theo* = God + *pneuma* = breath, air).

We believe the Holy Spirit revealed the mind of God to the minds of the original authors of Scripture. This refutes any idea of human inspiration, such as a poet or musician might claim.

> *... for prophecy never came by the will of man, but holy men of God spoke as they were moved by the Holy Spirit.* 2 Peter 1:21 (NIV)

"In the New Testament, the word 'inspiration' is reserved solely for God's Word. The Bible was written by special men, under special conditions and the canon is closed. There are no songs, no books, no visions, no poems, no sermons that are inspired today." Excerpted from Dr. John MacArthur's book, *Why Believe The Bible?*

Dr. Woodrow Kroll of Back to the Bible Ministries explained inspiration thusly:

> "The Bible came from the mouth of God to the minds of men – not dictation – they didn't write down what they heard, God overwhelmed them by the Spirit of God so that what they wrote down in their own words were exactly the words that came from the mind of God."

Here's Dr. MacArthur's description of "inspiration":

> "As those godly men (the human authors of Scripture) were carried along by the Holy Spirit, He superintended their words and used them to produce the Scriptures. As a sailing ship is carried along by the wind to reach its final destination, so the human authors of Scripture were moved by the Spirit of God to communicate exactly what He desired. In that process, the Spirit filled their minds, souls, and hearts with divine truth – mingling it sovereignly and supernaturally with their unique styles, vocabularies, and experiences, and guiding them to a perfect, inerrant result." From *Strange Fire: The Danger of Offending the Holy Spirit with Counterfeit Worship*

Additional insights from Dr. MacArthur's book *Why Believe The Bible?* :

> "Inspiration is God's revelation communicated to us through writers who used their own minds, their own words, and yet God had so arranged their lives and their thoughts and their vocabularies, that the words they chose out of their own minds were the very words that God determined from eternity past that they would use to write His truths."

Regarding the authors of Scripture:

> "God made them into the kind of men whom He could use to express His truth and then God literally selected the words out of their lives and their personalities, vocabularies and emotions. The words were their words, but in reality their lives had been so framed by God that they were God's words. So, it is possible to say that Paul wrote the book of Romans and to also say that God wrote it and be right on both counts."

Verbal and Plenary Inspiration

The inspiration extends to the very words themselves (verbal inspiration), not just concepts or ideas; and the inspiration extends to all parts of Scripture and all subject matters of Scripture (plenary inspiration). "Plenary" means "full, complete in every respect."

"When Paul sat down and wrote (an epistle), the Spirit of God took control of him. The Spirit of God breathed into Paul's mind what God wanted said and then Paul used his own vocabulary and his own personal experience to write Scripture. The Bible is not only God's Word, it is God's *words.*" (Italics in original.) From *Why Believe The Bible?* by Dr. John MacArthur

Inerrant

"Inerrant" means "without error" – there are no errors in the original autographs (*autographa*, manuscripts, documents) that comprise Scripture. This, of course, means there are also no genuine contradictions in Scripture. Difficulties and phenomena we cannot explain are not errors!

"Inerrancy means that when all the facts are known, the Scriptures in their original autographs and properly interpreted will be shown to be wholly true in everything they teach, whether that teaching has to do with history, science, geography, geology, or other disciplines or knowledge." James Montgomery Boice at the International Council on Biblical Inerrancy

The Bible is flawless because it was authored (inspired) by a God Who is flawless. *The law of the Lord is perfect* (Psalm 19:7).

The Bible doesn't tell us everything there is to know, but what it does tell us is truth. Because it comes from the God of truth, we would expect Scripture to be true. And that's exactly what it claims for itself:

The words of the Lord are pure words, like silver refined in a furnace on the ground, purified seven times (Psalm 12:6 – ESV)

But you are near, O Lord, and all your commandments are true (Psalm 119:151 – ESV)

The sum of your word is truth, and every one of your righteous rules endures forever (Psalm 119:160 – ESV)

We don't have the original Scripture autographs. Yes, there are minor discrepancies between manuscript copies. Even the earliest and best manuscripts have scribal errors: miscopying numbers, misspelling proper names, omitting words. But we have thousands of early copies, in many languages, and we can compare them with each other. Comparing manuscripts to determine the original meaning is known as "textual criticism." Using this method, we can arrive at an accurate translation of the text.

How reliable and trustworthy are our biblical source texts? We have Old Testament manuscripts that predate Christ. Shortly after it was written, the New Testament was copied rapidly into various languages throughout the known world, and all of these translations corroborate one another. In fact, if we didn't have a single bit of the Greek New Testament (which we do, with thousands of complete manuscripts and many thousands of manuscript fragments), we would be able to reliably piece the Greek text back together from these other languages.

In addition, there are 10,000 manuscript copies in Latin and 9,000 manuscript copies of the New Testament in other languages – and more copies are being unearthed by archaeologists.

Within the early centuries of the Christian church a number of scholars quoted the New Testament. Amazingly, they quoted the New Testament so much that every verse of all 27 books of the New Testament is quoted by these scholars with the exception of only 11 verses, all within a few hundred years of the beginning of the Church.

Much of the New Testament was written within just a few decades of the death and resurrection of Christ. The book of First Corinthians, for instance, dates from the 50s – only twenty years or so after the death and resurrection of Christ. This is important because 1 Corinthians 15 contains key elements of the gospel message, emphasizing the importance of Christ's resurrection, and claiming that more than 500 people had seen the risen Christ. People who would still have been alive at the time of the writing of 1 Corinthians would have been around to corroborate or criticize the claims made in the letter.

Claiming the Bible is inspired but not inerrant – as is fashionable in some theological circles today – is to deny that God is omniscient (He didn't have sufficient knowledge to produce a text without error), omnipotent (He couldn't protect His Word from error), good (He did something that wasn't right).

In his sermon, *Let God Be True!*, Dr. Richard Strauss emphasized the importance of inerrancy:

"To weaken the biblical doctrine of inerrancy is to set us adrift on a sea of human speculation and rob the Christian message of its uniqueness and power.

"If parts of the Bible are true and parts are false, what criteria can we use for determining which parts we can accept as correct? Who will make that decision? The parts that are false cannot be from God since He is the God of truth, so they must be of human origin. Yet Scripture claims to be from God in its entirety. If we are the ones who determine what is true and what is false, then we are elevating ourselves above Scripture, and ultimately above God Himself.

"If the Bible is not true in its historical facts, then we cannot be sure it is true when it speaks about eternal salvation or daily responsibility. We are left with no sure word from God. We cannot be certain that anything about the biblical message is true, and we are free to follow the spirit of our age."

How do we know the Bible is true?

- Archaeological finds consistently verify the accuracy of the Bible's text.

- Internal consistency and coherence. The 66 books of the Bible were penned by more than 40 different authors over a period of approximately 1500 years, written in three different languages, written in many countries by men in every plane of social life. In order for this Book to be inerrant it had to have been inspired, and it had to have only one Author – the Holy Spirit.

- Fulfilled prophecy. The Bible contains more than 1000 prophecies. To date, more than 500 have been fulfilled exactly as written. That gives us confidence that the others will be likewise fulfilled just as precisely!

Infallible

Not only does the Bible have no errors, it's *incapable* of having error. Because God the Holy Spirit wrote the Book, there's not even the possibility of error – because God never makes a mistake!

From Dr. John MacArthur:

"As God's perfect revelation, the Bible reflects the glorious character of its Author. Because He is the God of truth, His Word is infallible. Because He cannot lie, His Word is inerrant. Because He is the King of kings, His word is absolute and supreme. Those who wish to please Him must obey His Word. Conversely, those who fail to honor the Scriptures above every other truth-claim dishonor God Himself." From *Strange Fire: The Danger of Offending the Holy Spirit with Counterfeit Worship*

Here's a synopsis of the words "infallible" and "inerrant," from *The Chicago Statement on Biblical Inerrancy*:

"*Infallible* signifies the quality of neither misleading nor being misled and so safeguards in categorical terms the truth the Holy Scripture is a sure, safe, and reliable rule and guide in all matters. Similarly, *inerrant* signifies the quality of being free from all falsehood or mistake and so safeguards the truth that Holy Scripture is entirely true and trustworthy in all its assertions."

Complete and Unalterable Special Revelation

God's revelation to mankind was complete when the book of Revelation was finished, circa A.D. 96. Many cults attempt to alter God's revelation by adding to or subtracting from God's Word, the Bible.

Revelation 22:18-19 tells us that God has not given any new revelation since A.D. 96. Dreams, visions, so-called "words of prophecy," and the like that relate to new revelation do not have a divine origin. Everything God wants us to know about Himself, the future, etc., is already in His Book. We are not to seek or participate in extra-biblical revelation.

In his October 6, 1872, sermon entitled "The Paraclete," Charles Spurgeon made these candid remarks:

"Whatever is to be revealed by the Spirit to any of us is in the word of God already – He adds nothing to the Bible, and never will. Let persons who have revelations of this, that, and the other, go to bed and wake up in their senses. I only wish they would follow the advice, and no longer insult the Holy Ghost by laying their nonsense at His door."

Dr. Lewis Sperry Chafer, founder and long-time president of Dallas Theological Seminary, stated that while the Holy Spirit may lead believers in matters of conduct, He does not do so "in the formulating of doctrine which might be superimposed upon the Word of God." In other words, the Holy Spirit is not giving new revelation. All we need is already in the Book!

Special Revelation and General Revelation

Revelation from God falls into two categories: general and special.

General revelation is non-written revelation. It includes the knowledge of Himself and His law that God has written in our hearts (Romans 2:15), and what can be known about God through nature.

> *The heavens declare the glory of God, the skies proclaim the work of His hands …* (Psalm 19:1 – NIV).

> *For since the creation of the world God's invisible qualities – His eternal power and divine nature – have been clearly seen, being understood from what has been made, so that men are without excuse.* (Romans 1:20 – NIV)

General revelation is sufficient to make man aware of God and His nature, and to convict man of his sinfulness, but is not sufficient to give him the knowledge of how to be saved from sin. That requires special revelation – the Gospel presented in God's Word, the Bible.

General revelation has been defined as "the revelation of God to all people, at all times, and in all places, that reveals that God exists and that He is intelligent, powerful and transcendent."

Special revelation is how God has chosen to reveal Himself through miraculous means. Special revelation includes physical appearances of God, the written Word of God, and most importantly, the Lord Jesus Christ, Who is the living Word of God.

Final Authority / Sole Authority

The Bible is our sole and final authority for doctrine (what we believe and teach) and practice (how we live). When there is a dispute, the Bible is the last word, it trumps everything; what it says is true.

Some religious traditions have other authorities which, for them – and to their detriment – supersede the Bible. They are trading man's wisdom for God's wisdom.

Some religions teach that their church tradition and the pronouncements of their leaders have equal authority with the Bible. Neither is true. Only the Bible is inspired by God – it's the only book He ever wrote – and the church leaders and their pronouncements are not infallible. Only God is.

Normal, Literal, And Consistent Interpretation

"This is sometimes called the *grammatical-historical* interpretation since the meaning of each word is determined by the grammatical and historical considerations. The principle might also be called *normal* interpretation since the literal meaning of words is the normal approach to their understanding in all languages. It might also be designated *plain* interpretation so that no one receives the mistaken notion that the literal principle rules out figures of speech. Symbols, figures of speech, and types are all interpreted plainly in this method and they are in no way contrary to literal interpretation. After all, the very existence of any meaning for a figure of speech depends on the reality of the literal meaning of the terms involved. Figures often make the meaning plainer, but it is the literal, normal or plain meaning that they convey to the reader." *Dispensationalism* by Dr. Charles C. Ryrie

"If one takes God at His Word, accepting the meaning of words and sentences as determined by grammar and context, *one reads* (not interpreting) God's Word literally. Taking God literally means, of course, that the parables are taken as parables, poetry as poetry, visions as visions, metaphors as metaphors, figurative language as figurative language, commandments as commandments, and history as history. The foundational belief of the literalist is that the Bible is God's revelation, a revealing of Himself, so God wants to speak clearly, and be clearly understood, by those who accept Him with the trusting faith and the desire to learn of a loving child." *After Eden: Understanding Creation, the Curse, and the Cross* by Dr. Henry M. Morris III

"When the plain sense of Scripture makes common sense, seek no other sense; therefore, take every word at its primary, ordinary, usual meaning unless the facts of the immediate context, studied in light of related passages and axiomatic and fundamental truths, indicate clearly otherwise." *The Golden Rule of Interpretation* formulated by Dr. David L Cooper

"In determining what the God-taught writer is asserting in each passage, we must pay the most careful attention to its claims and character as a human production. In inspiration, God utilized the culture and conventions of his penman's milieu, a milieu that God controls in His sovereign providence; it is misinterpretation to imagine otherwise. So history must be treated as history, poetry as poetry, hyperbole and metaphor as hyperbole and metaphor, generalization and approximation as what they are, and so forth. Differences in literary conventions in Bible times and in ours must be observed ... Non-chronological narration and imprecise citation were conventional and acceptable and violated no expectations in those days … Scripture is inerrant, not in the sense of being absolutely precise by modern standards, but in the sense of making good its claims and achieving that measure of focused truth at which its authors aimed." From *The Chicago Statement on Biblical Inerrancy.*

Some religious traditions teach that only those in their church hierarchy can properly interpret the Bible. That's the opposite of what the Bible itself teaches! God's Holy Spirit, Who indwells every born-again Christian, enables us to understand the message of the Bible (John 14:16-17). The Apostle Paul admonished Timothy to be diligent in studying God's Word (2 Timothy 2:15). The Christians in Berea were commended for using the Scriptures to verify what they were taught (Acts 17:11). Let's be Bereans!

Dispensationalism / Dispensations

Dispensationalism is one way of classifying the different methods (economies, modes) God has been using to relate to mankind through the ages. Dispensationalism sees God as dealing with mankind differently at various stages of history. For example, God's governance was different with Adam than with Abraham, etc.

God has a plan for the ages and He's working it out according to His will and His timetable. That plan has been in place since eternity past and is invariant. God doesn't make up His game plan as He goes along. Dispensationalism is simply one way of viewing the outworking of God's plan for the ages. God reveals and administers (dispenses) His plan in stages over time. Those stages are called *dispensations*.

We'll explore Dispensationalism in more detail in *Dispensationalism*, the study note for point eleven of the BMW Doctrinal Statement.

Progressive Revelation

God's revelation to man is progressive. In each successive dispensation, God reveals more of His plan for man's redemption.

> *Surely you have heard about the administration of God's grace that was given to me for you, that is, the mystery made known to me by revelation, as I have already written briefly. In reading this, then, you will be able to understand my insight into the mystery of Christ, which was not made known to men in other generations as it has now been revealed by the Spirit to God's holy apostles and prophets.* Ephesians 3:3-5 (NIV)

> *Now to him who is able to strengthen you according to my gospel and the preaching of Jesus Christ, according to the revelation of the mystery that was kept secret for long ages but has now been disclosed and through the prophetic writings has been made known to all nations, according to the command of the eternal God, to bring about the obedience of faith— to the only wise God be glory forevermore through Jesus Christ! Amen.* Romans 16:25-27 (ESV)

See also 1 Peter 1:10-12.

It's important to note that Progressive Revelation doesn't mean that God's requirements for man's salvation have changed over time, from dispensation to dispensation. Throughout all time, there has been only one way to be saved, and that is by the power of God, made possible through the sacrifice of the Lord Jesus Christ.

Canon of Scripture

"Canon" comes from the root word for "reed." A reed was used as a measuring rod, and came to mean "rule" or "standard." In early Christian usage, the word "canon" came to mean "rule of faith." As applied to Scripture, "canon" means "an officially accepted list of books." Thus, the "canon of Scripture" refers to the 66 books that comprise our Bible.

"Canon" describes the books that are divinely inspired and therefore belong in the Bible. The difficult aspect of determining the biblical canon is that the Bible does not give us a list of the books that belong in the Bible. Determining the canon was a process, first by Jewish rabbis and scholars, and then later by early Christians. Ultimately, it was God who decided what books belonged in the biblical canon. A book of Scripture belonged in the canon from the moment God inspired its writing. It was simply a matter of God convincing His human followers which books should be included in the Bible.

The Septuagint (Greek translation of the Old Testament) was completed around 250 B.C. It contained all 39 books we recognize as canonical.

The first recognized "canon" was the Muratorian Canon, which was compiled in A.D. 170. The Muratorian Canon included all the New Testament books except Hebrews, James, and 3 John. In A.D. 363, the Council of Laodicea stated that only the Old Testament (along with the Apocrypha*) and the 27 books of the New Testament were to be read in the churches. The Council of Hippo (A.D. 393) and the Council of Carthage (A.D. 397) also affirmed the same 27 New Testament books as authoritative.

A Survey of Major Biblical Doctrines – The Holy Scriptures

* *Apocrypha* is from the Greek word *apokruptein* meaning "to hide away." In Latin, *Apocrypha Scripta* means "hidden writings" implying they were not approved for public reading. The Apocrypha is the 14 books included as an appendix to the Old Testament in the Septuagint and the Vulgate (fourth-century Latin version of the Bible promulgated by the Roman Catholic Church) but not included in the Hebrew canon. They are not printed in Protestant versions of the Bible.

Other meanings of *apocrypha* include "esoteric," "spurious," "of questionable authenticity," and "Christian texts that are not." The true authors of many of the apocryphal writings are unknown.

In the New Testament, the Lord Jesus Christ quoted or alluded to the Old Testament 64 times. He never quoted or alluded to any apocryphal works.

John MacArthur said this about the apocryphal books:

> "These books were never accepted by the general church consciousness because it was apparent they were not inspired. They are filled with historical error. In other words, their datings and so forth are wrong, inconsistent with what we know to be historical. They are filled with theological error. They are filled with spiritual and moral error. It is apparent to the most cursory reader of those books that they don't match up. And so the church never recognized them at all." From *Bible Questions and Answers Part 12*

The canon of Scripture is closed. Books cannot be added or removed.

Constantine, and the Council of Nicea (A.D. 325), for that matter, had virtually nothing to do with the forming of the canon. It was not even discussed at Nicea. The council that formed an undisputed decision on the canon took place at Carthage in A.D. 397, sixty years after Constantine's death.

How were books selected for inclusion in the canon of Scripture? One writer said the books …

> "… were written by an apostle or prophet of God (Ephesians 2:20), they were confirmed by the acts of God (Hebrews 2:4), they told the truth about God (1 John 4:6), they came with the power of God (Hebrews 4:12), and they were immediately collected by the people of God (2 Peter 3:15-16)." *Reasons For Our Hope: Why We Can Trust The Bible*, Norman L. Geisler, *Decision* Magazine, July-August, 2006

Hermeneutics / Hermeneutical Principles

Hermeneutics is the art and science of interpreting a passage, making it clear. The word "hermeneutics" comes from a Greek word meaning "interpretation."

Bible interpretation "is a science because it is guided by rules within a system; and it is an art because the application of those rules is by skill, not by mechanical imitation." Bernard Ramm, *Protestant Biblical Interpretation*

The *goal* of biblical hermeneutics is to point us to the correct interpretation which the Holy Spirit has already inspired into the text. The *purpose* of biblical hermeneutics is to protect us from improperly applying a Scripture to a particular situation.

Exegesis is part of the process of hermeneutics. "Exegesis" literally means "lead out." (Greek *ex* = out + *hegeisthai* = to lead, guide). Exegesis is approaching a passage with an open mind, asking God to show us the true meaning, the meaning He put into the passage. It's reading God's meaning out of a passage. It is properly interpreting a passage. A person who practices exegesis is called an *exegete*.

Exegesis is described in the NASB as *handling accurately the word of truth*; the KJV translates this passage as *rightly dividing the word of truth* (2 Timothy 2:15). "Rightly dividing" (Greek *orthotomeo*) means "cutting straight." We are to read the Word of Truth, the Bible, exactly as it is written, unless the writer himself makes it evident that he is using symbolic language or a figure of speech.

The opposite of exegesis is eisegesis. "Eisegesis " is reading our desired meaning into a passage. It's approaching a passage with a preconceived idea and trying to make the passage say what we want it to say. (Greek *eis* = into.) Someone has likened eisegesis to a would-be marksman shooting holes in a blank target then drawing a bulls-eye around the holes!

A given Bible verse or passage has one correct meaning but may have many applications.

Some people approach a verse or passage with a theological preunderstanding – a doctrinal opinion he or she has formed. The danger for Bible interpreters is that their interpretations easily can be biased by their theological preunderstanding.

The Principle of Double Reference states that a prophetic passage can have a partial fulfillment at one time and a complete fulfillment at a later date; a "near" fulfillment and a "far" fulfillment. Stated differently, "double reference" says that a passage can have one meaning for the immediate hearers and one meaning for future hearers.

The Principle of First Mention holds that the first time some important idea is mentioned in the Bible, you'll often find a special measure of insight in the passage surrounding it. This insight can help in interpreting other passages where the idea appears.

The Principle of Recurrence exists throughout the Scriptures as an event documented in two or more places. In such cases, frequently a story is told very generally, and then told again from the beginning but providing additional detail. Not only is recurrence frequently used in Scripture, it is in fact the technique by which Scripture itself presents the account of creation.

The Principle of The Analogy of Faith is commonly stated as "Scripture interprets Scripture." When we say that, we must realize that not every Scripture is interpreted by another Scripture. This principle can also be stated as "all Scripture is in agreement and will not contradict itself." The principle assumes the unity and harmony of teaching throughout the Bible.

The Reformers formulated the *analogia scriptura* principle which states that if an interpretation of a particular verse contradicts a truth taught elsewhere in Scripture, the interpretation of the verse cannot be correct. When multiple passages say something about a topic (either explicitly or implicitly), then what those passages say about that topic will be consistent and will not be contradictory.

We should interpret unclear passages in light of clear passages, not the other way around! When a passage is unclear to us, we can and should go to other passages that address the same topic more clearly in order to help us understand the unclear passage.

Certainty of Fulfillment

The Lord Jesus Christ Himself guaranteed that all that is written in the Bible will come to pass:

Think not that I am come to destroy the law, or the prophets: I am not come to destroy, but to fulfill. For verily I say unto you, Till heaven and earth pass, one jot* or one tittle** shall in no wise pass from the law, till all be fulfilled. Matthew 5:17-18 (KJV)

> * "Jot" is a translation of the Greek word *iota*. The NIV translates this as "smallest letter." It would be roughly equivalent to the dot above the letter "i" in English.
>
> ** A "tittle" is a mark that distinguishes between Hebrew letters. The NIV translates this as "stroke." It would be roughly equivalent to the diagonal line (the stroke) that distinguishes an "R" from a "P" in English.

Profitable

God's Word is profitable for every aspect of our Christian life:

All scripture is given by inspiration of God, and is profitable for doctrine, for reproof, for correction, for instruction in righteousness: That the man of God may be perfect (adequate, sufficient for the destined purpose, completely qualified) thoroughly furnished (equipped) unto all good works. 2 Timothy 3:16 - 17 (KJV)

In his book, *Be Faithful*, Warren Wiersbe explained the verse above thusly:

"They (all scriptures) are profitable for doctrine (what is right), for reproof (what is not right), for correction (how to get right), and for instruction in righteousness (how to stay right). A Christian who studies the Bible and applies what he learns will grow in holiness and avoid many pitfalls in the world."

Sola Scriptura

Sola scriptura literally means "Scripture only." This Latin phrase was coined by the sixteenth-century Reformers to indicate their belief that Scripture is the sole source of written revelation.

The following four paragraphs were obtained from *The Cambridge Declaration*, available at www.monergism.com/thethreshold/articles/topic/fivesolas.html

"Scripture alone is the inerrant rule of the church's life, but the evangelical church today has separated Scripture from its authoritative function. In practice, the church is guided, far too often, by the culture. Therapeutic technique, marketing strategies, and the beat of the entertainment world often have far more to say about what the church wants, how it functions and what it offers, than does the Word of God. Pastors have neglected their rightful oversight of worship, including the doctrinal content of the music. As biblical authority has been abandoned in practice, as its truths have faded from Christian consciousness, and as its doctrines have lost their saliency, the church has been increasingly emptied of its integrity, moral authority and direction.

"Rather than adapting Christian faith to satisfy the felt needs of consumers, we must proclaim the law as the only measure of true righteousness and the gospel as the only announcement of saving truth. Biblical truth is indispensable to the church's understanding, nurture and discipline.

"Scripture must take us beyond our perceived needs to our real needs and liberate us from seeing ourselves through the seductive images, clichés, promises and priorities of mass culture. It is only in the light of God's truth that we understand ourselves aright and see God's provision for our need. The Bible, therefore, must be taught and preached in the church. Sermons must be expositions of the Bible and its teachings, not expressions of the preacher's opinions or the ideas of the age. We must settle for nothing less than what God has given.

"The work of the Holy Spirit in personal experience cannot be disengaged from Scripture. The Spirit does not speak in ways that are independent of Scripture. Apart from Scripture we would never have known of God's grace in Christ. The biblical Word, rather than spiritual experience, is the test of truth."

Sufficiency of Scripture

All scripture is given by inspiration of God, and is profitable for doctrine, for reproof, for correction, for instruction in righteousness: That the man of God may be perfect*, thoroughly furnished (equipped) *unto all good works.* 2 Timothy 3:16-17 (KJV)

> * Adequate, sufficient for the destined purpose, completely qualified, competent, capable of doing everything one is called to do, proficient

The fact that God the Holy Spirit tells us that Scripture furnishes us, equips us, for every good work bespeaks the sufficiency, the adequacy, of Scripture. It also indicates that the canon of Scripture is closed, that no more revelation is to come from God. If more revelation is yet to come, then the canon of Scripture is not sufficient to completely equip the man of God, and we have no standard by which to judge false teachers.

The Bible contains all the information we need to be saved and live a godly life (sanctification). We don't need – and in fact, God is not providing – additional (extra-biblical) revelation in the form of dreams, visions, non-canonical writings, and experiences.

In his book, *Strange Fire: The Danger of Offending the Holy Spirit with Counterfeit Worship*, Dr. John MacArthur addresses this topic:

"Preoccupied with mystical encounters and emotional ecstasies, Charismatics* seek ongoing revelation from heaven – meaning that, for them, the Bible alone is simply not enough. Within a Charismatic paradigm, biblical revelation must be supplemented with personal 'words from God,' supposed impressions from the Holy Spirit, and other subjective religious experiences. That kind of thinking is an outright rejection of the authority and sufficiency of Scripture (2 Timothy 3:16-17)."

* "Charismatic" is from the Greek word *charismata*, meaning "grace gifts." In general, Charismatics believe that all the spiritual gifts given by the Holy Spirit to the first-century church are operational today. Most Evangelicals do not subscribe to this view. For more information, refer to *The Ministry and Spiritual Gifts*, point nine of the BMW Doctrinal Statement.

2. The Godhead

*"We believe in the **one triune** God, **eternally existing** in **three persons** – Father, Son, and Holy Spirit – co-eternal in being, co-identical in nature, co-equal in power and glory, and having the same **attributes and perfections**. (Deuteronomy 6:4; 2 Corinthians 13:14)"*

The words appearing in **bold** text in the paragraph above are explained in this study note. Here's where to find those words – and more – in this note:

Godhead

"Godhead" refers to the divine Trinity – Father, Son, and Holy Spirit, one God manifested in three Persons*. The word "Godhead" itself does not mean "trinity," but simply "Godhood" – the nature of God, God as He has revealed Himself. But that's the point – He has revealed Himself as a triune God. The three persons of the Trinity exist simultaneously today, and always have.

> *   A person is self-aware, can speak, has a will, can love, hate, etc. Each of the three persons in the Trinity demonstrates these qualities.

God's Existence

How do we know God exists? The existence of God is taken for granted in the Bible. There is nowhere any biblical argument to prove it. It is assumed to be true. The person who disbelieves this truth is spoken of as a "fool," one devoid of understanding (Psalm 14:1). Romans 1:21 tells us that when a person rejects God's revelation of Himself, that person's heart is "darkened" (deprived of light) and he or she becomes a fool (verse 22).

The arguments generally offered by theologians in proof of the being of God are described below.

- The *a priori* (prior to) argument, which is the testimony afforded by reason, independent of experience, verification or testing.

  (a) The chief *a priori* argument is the ontological* argument. It states that God exists because our conception of Him exists and nothing greater than God can be conceived of. Stated differently, if we can conceive of the greatest possible being, then He must exist.

> * Ontology (*onto* = being + *logia* = study, science, theory) is the study of the nature of being, reality, and substance.

Anselm, eleventh-century Christian apologist (defender), stated that when a fool says in his heart that there is no God (Psalm 14:1), he demonstrates that he understands what is meant by the term "God," namely "that than which nothing greater can be conceived."

- The *a posteriori* (posterior to, occurring at a time after something else) argument, by which we proceed logically from the facts of experience to causes. These arguments are

(a) The cosmological*, by which it is proved that there must be a First Cause of all things, because every effect must have a cause. There cannot be an infinite regress (going back) of causes; therefore, there must be an uncaused cause: God.

> * Cosmology (*cosmos* = universe + *logia*) is the study of the origin and nature of the universe.

The cosmological argument starts with the existence of the universe (*cosmos*) and reasons to the existence of God as the best explanation of the universe.

(b) The teleological*, or the argument from design. We see everywhere the operations of an intelligent Cause in nature. A Designer must exist since the universe and living things exhibit marks of design in their order, consistency, unity, and pattern.

> * Teleology (*teleo* = end, goal, result + *logia*) is the study of final causes, results.

(c) The moral argument, called also the anthropological* argument, based on the moral consciousness and the history of mankind, which exhibits a moral order and purpose which can only be explained on the supposition of the existence of a transcendent Being (God) Who imbues mankind with an innate moral compass.

> * Anthropology (*anthropos* = man, human + *logia*) is the study of humanity.

One (God)

God is one in both number and in unity.

Not only is there only one God, but His nature renders impossible the existence of more than one. No more than one God can embody the attributes of God, of originating all and sustaining all completely and independently. Every attribute is found completely and uniquely perfectly in

God alone. God is unique overall but this does not need to mean that a plurality of persons in one being is excluded.

Speaking of Himself, God told the Israelites,

> *Before me no god was formed, nor shall there be any after me. I, I am the Lord, and besides me there is no savior.* Isaiah 43:10b-11 (ESV)

Some religious traditions teach that there are many gods, and that man can become a god. This contradicts the Bible's teaching that there is only one God, Who is a trinity of three divine Persons: Father, Son, and Holy Spirit.

Psalm 82, quoted by the Lord Jesus Christ in John 10:34, is cited as proof that man can become a god. Here are verses 6-8 of this Psalm:

> *I* (God) *have said, Ye are gods; and all of you are children of the most High. But ye shall die like men, and fall like one of the princes. Rise up, O God, judge the earth, for all the nations are your inheritance.* (KJV).

The teaching that man can become a god is a classic example of taking verses out of context! Psalm 82 describes human judges ("gods" – Hebrew *Elohim*) who are urged to act with impartiality and true justice (verses 2-5) because they too must some day stand before God, the ultimate Judge.

Psalm 82 is saying that God has appointed men to positions of authority in which they are considered as gods among the people. They are to remember that even though they are representing God in this world, they are mortal and must eventually give an account to God for how they used that authority.

Calling a human magistrate a "god" indicates three things: (1) that he has power over other human beings, (2) the power he wields as a civil authority is to be feared, and (3) he derives his power and authority from God Himself, Who is pictured in verse 8 as judging the whole earth.

Conclusion: Psalm 82 and John 10:34 cannot be used to prove that a man can become a god. Nor can any other passage.

Triune / Trinity / Three Persons

The holy Trinity is comprised of God the Father, God the Son, and God the Holy Spirit. Thus, the Trinity is a tri-unity: one "what" (substance, essence) and three "who's" (persons).

There is only one true God and He exists as three distinct persons, each with a different ministry. The teaching that there is one God who manifests* Himself in three ways, not that there are three distinct persons in the Trinity, is simply wrong because it doesn't agree with clear biblical doctrine.

> * The erroneous teaching, known as *Modalism*, is frequently that God sometimes manifests Himself as the Father, sometimes as the Son, sometimes as the Holy Spirit.

Modalism was condemned by the Synod of Smyrna (A.D. 200). The Nicene and Athanasian Creeds also condemn Modalism.

The following two paragraphs are excerpted from an article available at http://www.gotquestions.org/Godhead.html

"What does it mean that God exists as the Trinity? It is a basic principle of our biblical faith that there is only one God. 'Hear, O Israel! The LORD our God, the LORD is one!'. The unity of the Godhead cannot be questioned. God does not consist of parts. He is one. But Scripture reveals that there are, in that one divine essence, three eternal distinctions. Those distinctions seem best described as *Persons*, known as the Father, the Son, and the Holy Spirit. All three have identical attributes, however, and therefore they are one—not merely one in mind and purpose, but one in substance. To possess all the same attributes is to be one in essential nature. The three Persons of the Godhead possess identical attributes. They are one in substance and one in essence, and therefore they are one God.

"The reality of the triune Godhead cannot be denied. Those outside of Christ may object to it, but their objections arise primarily because they seek to understand the Creator in terms of the creature, to see God as merely a bigger and better version of man when in reality He is a totally different kind of being, an infinite being whom our finite minds cannot fully comprehend. We believe in the Godhead not because we understand it, but because God has revealed it. It is not incidental or unimportant. It is the very essence of His being, the way He is."

William Romaine, an eighteenth-century English cleric, provides this insight into the Trinity:

"The Scripture makes no difference between the divine Persons, except what is made by the distinct offices (Father, Son, Holy Spirit). The Persons are each equal in every perfection and attribute; none is before or after another, none is greater or less than another; but the whole three Persons are co-eternal together and co-equal. And consequently, Christ, Who was from eternity co-equal with the Father, did not make Himself inferior, because He covenanted to become a Son, nor did the Holy Spirit, who was from eternity co-equal with the Father and the Son, make Himself inferior because He covenanted to make the spirits of men holy by his grace and influence." Excerpted from *The Self-Existence of Jesus Christ*

There are many passages that name the three Persons of the Trinity. Here are five from the New Testament.

*The next day John seeth **Jesus** coming unto him, and saith, Behold the Lamb of God, which taketh away the sin of the world. This is he of whom I said, After me cometh a man which is preferred before me: for he was before me. And I knew him not: but that he should be made manifest to Israel, therefore am I come baptizing with water. [32]And John bare record, saying, I saw the **Spirit** descending from heaven like a dove, and it abode upon him. [33]And I knew him not: but **he that sent me to baptize with water** (the Father), the same said unto me, Upon whom thou shalt see the Spirit descending, and remaining on him, the same is he which baptizeth with the **Holy Ghost**. [34]And I saw, and bare record that this is the **Son of God**.* John 1:29-34 (KJV)

*Go ye therefore, and teach all nations, baptizing them in the name of the **Father**, and of the **Son**, and of the **Holy Ghost**: Teaching them to observe all things whatsoever I have commanded you: and, lo, I am with you alway, even unto the end of the world. Amen.* Matthew 28:19-20 (KJV)

*But when the **Comforter** is come, whom **I** will send unto you from the **Father**, even the **Spirit of truth**, which proceedeth from the **Father**, he shall testify of **me**:* John 15:26 (KJV)

*(We are) Elect according to the foreknowledge of **God the Father**, through sanctification of the **Spirit**, unto obedience and sprinkling of the blood of **Jesus Christ**: Grace unto you, and peace, be multiplied.* 1 Peter 1:2 (KJV)

*The grace of the **Lord Jesus Christ**, and the love of **God**, and the communion of the **Holy Ghost**, be with you all. Amen.* 2 Corinthians 13:14 (KJV)

All three members of the Trinity were / are involved in many divine activities. Here are a few:

- Creating the world

- The incarnation (Christ's first advent)

- Revealing the Messiah to Israel (at Christ's baptism)

- Providing redemption

- Proclaiming salvation

- Sending the Holy Spirit into the world

- Indwelling believers

- Baptizing believers

- Providing a believer's access to God

Eternally Existing

Simply stated, the Godhead has always existed and will always exist. The Godhead will never cease to be.

John 1:2 tells us that Jesus, the Word of God, existed before the creation of the universe, extending without an initial beginning into eternity past (some theologians label this "eternal generation").

With our finite minds, we can't fully comprehend eternity, much less eternal existence – yet every soul will live eternally.

> "As creatures, we must reckon in terms of the past and future, but to the Creator of time, all is present. He is transcendent to (above, beyond) time as well as space." Note from *New Defender's Study Bible* on Exodus 3:14

Ephesians 1:4 tells us that we were *chosen in (Christ) before the foundation of the world* – before God established time – but we didn't exist physically until conception. Did our souls exist before time? No, there is no biblical support for this teaching. In fact, Scripture teaches the opposite. In Genesis 2:7, we read

The Lord God formed the man of dust from the ground and breathed into his nostrils the breath of life, and the man became a living creature. (ESV)

In this passage, "creature" is the Hebrew word *Nephesh*, meaning the seat of both our life and our personhood.

In his book, *The Glory of Heaven*, Dr. John MacArthur comments on this verse:

"It was not until God was finished with creation that Adam *became* a living soul. There is no room for any sort of preexistence of human souls in the biblical account. ... Scripture nowhere suggests that our human souls existed prior to our conception – in fact, all the biblical data argues otherwise (cf. Psalm 51:5)." (Emphasis in the original.)

God's Word tells of other things that happened before the foundation of the world. Here's a partial list:

1. John 17:5, 24 speak of the love of the Father for the Son before the world was created.

2. Jesus, the sacrificial Lamb of God, was slain before the world was created (1 Peter 1:20, Revelation 13:8). We think of Jesus as being slain 2000 years ago, but, to God, Jesus was slain before the foundation of the world. (God inhabits all time simultaneously.)

3. The elect, the ones God predestined to be saved, were called and saved by grace before creation (2 Timothy 1:9).

4. Before creation, God promised eternal life to His children (Titus 1:2).

5. True wisdom, centered in Christ, existed in the heart of God before the world began (1 Corinthians 2:7).

6. All God's works were known and planned before creation (Acts 15:18). No event on earth takes God by surprise.

Attributes (qualities, characteristics) and Perfections of God

An attribute of God is anything that is true of Him.

Only what God has chosen to reveal about Himself can be known. God reveals His character to us in the Bible for the purpose of knowing Him.

Note that the list below is not exhaustive. God has an infinite number of attributes!

- Eternal – has always existed, He had no beginning and will always exist. Refer to *Self-existent* below.

- Faithful – trustworthy.

- Forgiving – willing to forgive our sins on the basis of Christ's substitutionary death on our behalf.

- Good – always does what is right and best.

- Gracious – gives us what we don't deserve. *By grace are ye saved …* (Ephesians 2:8-9).

   Grace is a demonstration of God's love.

- Holy – without sin, totally separated from all moral defilement and hostile toward it.

   "Holiness is the preeminent attribute of God. Everything God does is subject to the unchangeable rock of God's holy nature. Even the love that drove Him to become man and die a substitutionary death for our sins is driven by the holiness that demands justice for the horrible rebellion against that very holiness." From the article *Genesis and the Character of God* by Dr. Henry Morris III, accessed at http://www.icr.org/article/6755/

   "God is absolute, transcendent purity. He does not conform to the standard (of purity), He *is* the standard. Since God is Holy, all His other characteristics or attributes are also holy. Thus, when God speaks, He will not and cannot lie. He never deceives, neither does He distort or misrepresent what He says or does. Lying is against His nature." From *Knowing God* by J. I. Packer

- Immanent

   God is present in all of creation, while remaining distinct from it. There is no place where God is not. His sovereign control extends everywhere simultaneously. Transcendence (God exists outside of space and time) and immanence (God is present within space and time) are both attributes of God. Refer to *Transcendent*.

- Immutable – never changes.

   God does not change because He cannot change. If God could change He could then cease to be God, which is impossible. He truly cannot deny Himself. God never differs from Himself.

   God acts consistent with His character at all times. While God cannot change, He can apply His character differently to different people and even to the same people at different times. These changes in God's choices do not represent a change in His being.

   Because God does not change, His promises are sure and can be completely trusted. What God has promised He will fulfill. God will not change His mind about His promises. He will not change His plan or His purposes.

   God's immutability is a comfort to Christians because we know His love and mercy will never change, but His immutability is fearful for the unbeliever because it means his judgment on sin and sinners is unchanging.

- Incomparable – there is no one like Him!

- Infinite – free from all limitations except for self-imposed limitations.

God is infinite with respect to time, space, and being.

God is infinite in time in that He is immortal and eternal. God is the Creator of time, pre-dating and post-dating all of creation. All events are equally present to God; in His timelessness, there is no succession of moments. Therefore, God can communicate all about future and past events with equal certainty and the prophetic Word of God is sure.

God is immortal in that He can never die. He is eternal in that He always was and always will be, without both beginning and ending.

God is infinite in His being also regarding His perfection. Every communicable attribute* of God exists perfectly (without defect) in God. Since God's being is perfect, all His ways are flawless as well and can be completely trusted.

> * Communicable attributes are those that we are commanded to imitate.

- Inscrutable – incomprehensible, unfathomable and unsearchable as far as understanding Him completely.

- Longsuffering – patient and kind.

- Loving – desiring the highest good for us, the objects of His love.

  This love is not shown by giving us what we desire, but by giving us what He deems we need. Love is the motivating plan behind all that God does in saving a soul.

- Merciful – doesn't give us what we deserve.

  Mercy moved God to provide a Savior for the unsaved.

- No respecter of persons – doesn't show favoritism.

- Omnipotent – all powerful.

  In His omnipotence, God is sovereign over all. All things happen as a result of God's sovereign will. God can change situations but in His wisdom He may choose not to. Bad things happen under God's sovereignty because God has, for His good purposes, allowed the world to be ruled by the evil one. One day, God will exercise His power and bring about the restoration of all His creation. It is not God's power that brings this delay, it is God's sovereign wisdom.

- Omnipresent – everywhere present at all times with total consciousness.

  "God is omnipresent Spirit (John 4:24). God is not nature. God is not the universe. God is not a cosmic consciousness or a force of mystery. God is not man—He is greater than man (Job 33:12) and does not change His mind (Numbers 23:19)." From the article *Genesis and the Character of God* by Dr. Henry Morris III, accessed at http://www.icr.org/article/6755/

There is no place where God is not. His sovereign control extends everywhere simultaneously. Refer to *Immanent*. God permeates the world in sustaining creative power, shaping and steering it in a way that keeps it on its planned course.

- Omniscient – all knowing (*omni* = all + *science* = knowledge).

    There is nothing God does not know. God has always known everything. He has never learned anything – who would be His instructor? (Romans 11:34)

    Because God is all knowing, we can trust His Word on every subject it touches (plenary inspiration). We do not need to question who is correct when man's ideas and God's ideas are in conflict. God's omniscience renders man's wisdom foolishness and we must defer to God's knowledge in all things.

    "God cannot be progressively aware. God's knowledge is immediate. God is free from imperfection. God knows all there is to know. God's purpose and order flow from His omniscience. His decisions are unchangeable and without confusion. God's specific will and pleasure are always implemented." Dr. Henry Morris III, http://www.icr.org/article/6755/

- Reliable – can be trusted to do what He says.

- Righteous – cannot and will not pass over wrongdoing; He is just.

- Self-existent – God is distinctly independent from everything.

    God's being is in no way dependent on anything outside Himself and exists forever in Himself alone. He alone can give life because life is in Him. He does not need anything and can do as He pleases.

    God is distinct from His world, does not need it, and exceeds the grasp of any created intelligence that is found in it.

    "The most personal name that God reveals is 'I AM'—the One who exists by the right and nature of who He is." Dr. Henry Morris III, http://www.icr.org/article/6755/

- Sovereign – Supreme Ruler of the universe.

    God is under no external restraint whatsoever. He is the Supreme Dispenser of all events. All forms of existence are within the scope of His dominion.

    "Unlimited in power, unrivalled in majesty and not limited by anything outside Himself, our God is in complete control of all circumstances, causing or allowing them for His own good purposes and plans to be fulfilled exactly as He has foreordained." http://www.blogos.org/christianlifeandgrowth/in-charge-1-sovereignty-of-God.php

- Spirit – God is not dependent on matter and cannot be discerned by the bodily senses.

  Because God is spirit, we do not need to be at a certain place to worship Him. The Scripture often describes God with bodily parts but these are unquestionably anthropomorphic* figures of speech. God as spirit is invisible and no created person, while on earth, has ever seen God.

  > * An anthropomorphism (Greek: *anthropos* = man, human + *morphe* = form, shape) is an attribution of human forms or qualities to entities which are not human.

  The truth that God is spirit is behind the second commandment (Exodus 20:4) to not make any image of God. It is impossible for man to picture God as similar to His creation without dishonoring Him.

  God as a spiritual being possesses life in Himself. He is self-conscious and self-determining as a distinct personality, with intellect and will. As spirit and life, He is able to impart spirit and life to man.

- Transcendent

  God is distinct from His world, does not need it, and exceeds the grasp of any created intelligence that is found in it (transcendence); while on the other hand He permeates the world in sustaining creative power, shaping and steering it in a way that keeps it on its planned course (immanence).

- Truthful – always speaks the truth.

  At least four times in Scripture we are assured that God does not lie (Numbers 23:19, 1 Samuel 15:29, Titus 1:2, Hebrews 6:18).

- Wise – makes due use of knowledge; discerns and judges soundly.

Some theologians classify God's attributes as communicable, (i.e.) those which can be imparted in degree to his creatures: goodness, holiness, wisdom, etc.; and incommunicable, those which cannot be so imparted. A simple way to look at this distinction is that God's incommunicable attributes are those that are completely unique to God alone, and God's communicable attributes are those that we are commanded to, and have been given the ability to, imitate. Keep in mind that none of God's attributes are completely communicable to us. For this reason, we can never become completely like God.

Some of the information above regarding God's attributes was obtained from
http://www.valleybible.net/Adults/ClassNotes/TheologySurvey/God/AttributesOfGod.pdf

3. The Person And Work Of Christ

*"We believe the **Lord Jesus Christ**, the **eternal Son of God**, became man, without ceasing to be God, having been **conceived by the Holy Spirit** and born of the virgin Mary, and lived a sinless life. He came that He might **reveal God** and **redeem sinful man**. (Luke 1:35; John 1:1-2,14)*

*"We believe the Lord Jesus Christ accomplished our redemption through His death on the cross as a **representative, vicarious, substitutionary sacrifice** sufficient for the sins of the whole world, and our **justification** is verified by His literal, physical **resurrection** from the dead. (Romans 3:24-25; Ephesians 1:7; Hebrews 2:9; 1 Peter 1:3-5; 2:24; 1 John 2:2)*

*"We believe the Lord Jesus Christ ascended to heaven and is now exalted at the right hand of God where, as our **High Priest**, He fulfills the ministry of **Representative, Intercessor, and Advocate**. (Acts 1:9-10; Romans 8:34; Hebrews 7:25; 9:24; 1 John 2:1-2)"*

The words appearing in **bold** text in the paragraphs above are explained in this study note. Here's where to find those words – and more – in this note:

The Lord Jesus Christ

Lord   is a title. It means "master." Jesus Christ is my Master. By choice I am His bond servant (literally, His slave – He owns me).

Jesus   is the Savior's human name. Before the birth of Jesus, an angel appeared to Joseph and said

> *you shall call his name 'Jesus' for He shall save his people from their sins.* Matthew 1:21 (KJV)

Why did the angel tell Joseph to "call His name Jesus"? The verse tells us: "for (because) He shall **save** His people from their sins." The key word here is "save."

The Hebrew word for "Jesus" is *Yehoshua* (that's Hebrew for *Joshua*) which means "The Lord (Jehovah*) saves" or "the Lord is salvation." *Yehoshua* is frequently shortened to *Yeshua*.

The names "Jesus" and "Joshua" are essentially the same. There are places in the New Testament where the names are used interchangeably (Acts 7:45, Hebrews 4:8), depending on which translation you're reading (ESV uses "Joshua," KJV uses "Jesus").

> *   *Jehovah* (the Lord) is a translation of the Hebrew word *Yahweh* (the tetragrammaton YHVH or YHWH – the Jewish name for God).

Christ   means "Messiah" or "Anointed One." It's a title representing His threefold office as Prophet, Priest, and King.

In the New Testament, the Savior is sometimes addressed as "Jesus Christ" and sometimes as "Christ Jesus." "Jesus" speaks of His humanity. "Christ" speaks of His deity. Changing the order of the names changes the emphasis.

Eternal Son of God

The Lord Jesus Christ existed before His birth at Bethlehem. He claimed to be preexistent when He said, *before Abraham was* (came to be) *I am* (John 8:58). He is declared to be the Creator Who *is before* (predates) *all things* and by Whom *all things consist* (Colossians 1:16-17). Micah 5:2 also teaches the eternality of the Son – His *goings forth have been from eternity*.

Jesus Christ, as a Member of the divine Trinity, is God today, has always been God, and will always be God. Every member of the Trinity is today what He has always been and will always be. Jesus Christ is as holy today as He was in eternity past and as He will be in eternity future.

Jesus Christ is the same yesterday and today and forever. Hebrews 13:8   (NIV)

The Lord Jesus Christ is the unique (one and only) Son of God – the King James Version describes Him as "the only begotten of the Father" (John 1:14). Here's a quote from Vine's *Expository Dictionary of New Testament Words* relative to the phrase "only begotten":

> "the phrase … indicates that as the Son of God, He was the sole representative of the Being and character of the One who sent Him … the word 'begotten' does not imply a beginning of His Sonship. It suggests relationship indeed, but must be distinguished from generation as applied to man."

In his dissertation, *The Self-Existence of Jesus Christ*, William Romaine, an eighteenth-century English cleric, describes the eternality of Christ and provides a comprehensive overview of His ministry:

> "The whole economy and government of the world, from the time of its creation to the final dissolution, was put into (Christ's) hands; and therefore the Scripture expressly assures us

that He created it, that He governs it by His providence, that He redeemed His people by His blood, and that He is to come again at the last day, in all His glory, to judge it. And He, Who was almighty to create all things, Who was all-wise to govern all things, Who had infinite merit to redeem His body the Church, and Who is to be … the Judge of all at the last great day, certainly this almighty, this all-wise, this meritorious and divine Judge, must be self-existent. And being possessed of these offices, He might truly say, I AM; because He could not but have necessary existence in Himself, Who was the First Cause, and Who gave existence to every other being and thing."

He Became Man – The Hypostatic Union

"Hypostatic union" is the term used to describe how God the Son, Jesus Christ, took on a human nature, yet remained fully God at the same time. Jesus always had been God (John 8:59, 10:30,), but at the incarnation He also became a human being (John 1:14). With the addition of the human nature to the divine nature, Jesus became the God-man – one Person, fully God and fully man.

> "[The] union of undiminished deity and perfect humanity forever in one Person is called the doctrine of the hypostatic union (that is, the union of two hypostases or natures) and this is the uniqueness of Jesus Christ.

> "The uniqueness of Christianity is the person, Jesus Christ, and the distinctiveness of Christ is the fact that He is the God-man. In other words, He is a divine-human Being, something unique in time and eternity." *A Survey of Bible Doctrine* by Charles C. Ryrie

Jesus' two natures, human and divine, are inseparable. Jesus will forever be the God-man, fully God and fully human, two distinct natures in one Person. Jesus' humanity and divinity are not mixed, but are united without loss of separate identity. Jesus sometimes operated with the limitations of humanity (John 4:6, 19:28) and other times in the power of His deity (John 11:43, Matthew 14:18-21). In both, Jesus' actions were from His one Person. Jesus had two natures, divine and human, both sinless, but only one personality.

Without Ceasing to be God – The Kenosis

Kenosis is from the Greek word *kenos* meaning "empty." At the incarnation, when the Son came to earth, He voluntarily, temporarily, set aside some of His privileges and glory in order to take the form of a servant to ultimately die for our sins. Philippians 2:5-11 describes the *kenosis*, the self-emptying of the Son of God. Note that the kenosis did not involve giving up any divine attributes. He was still fully God although He chose not to use some of His divine attributes.

Miraculous Conception

God the Son was divinely conceived by the Holy Spirit in Mary's womb (Matthew 1:18-20; Luke 1:35). As a result, He didn't inherit a sinful human nature, as did all of us who have human parents. He took to Himself a human nature, but not sinfulness or weakness (1 Peter 2:21-24; 1 John 3:5).

Because of the curse that God pronounced on the physical earth as a result of Adam and Eve's sin (Genesis 3:17), both Joseph's and Mary's bodies were contaminated with the "bondage of corruption" (decay and death) described in Romans 8:21-22. The cell placed in Mary's womb by the Holy Spirit was a direct creation of God so there was no genetic connection with either

Joseph or Mary. (A genetic connection with Joseph or Mary would have resulted in Jesus inheriting the sinful nature of Adam which is transmitted through physical parentage.)

Reveal God

The Lord Jesus Christ is the visible manifestation of the eternal God.

One of the reasons why the Lord Jesus Christ came to earth was to make the Father known, to reveal God to man. We can know what God is like by examining the person of Jesus Christ. He is God in flesh.

Redeem

In the New Testament, "redeem" means "a loosing away" or "loosing from bondage," particularly by paying a price. Before something can be loosed, it must be bound. Before a person is born into God's spiritual family by personally inviting the Lord Jesus Christ to be his or her Savior from sin, they are in bondage:

- Bondage to the dominion and curse of sin (Ephesians 2:1-5)

    Before our conversion to Christ, we were slaves to sin; it had dominion over us.

- Bondage to Satan (John 8:44)

    When we accept the Lord Jesus Christ as Savior, we are loosed from Satan's domination, we get a new master.

- Bondage to death as the penalty for sin (Romans 6:23)

Christ's death on the cross redeemed us from the forms of bondage described above.

Note that the Lord Jesus Christ is the only Redeemer of fallen mankind.

Some religious traditions teach that Mary, the human mother of our Savior, is a "co-redemptrix" with Christ, that she somehow participated in our redemption. This teaching has no biblical support.

The angel Gabriel told Mary that she was "highly favored" and "blessed among women" (Luke 1:28 – KJV) because she had been given the privilege of bearing the Savior. Mary's relative, Elizabeth, mother of John the Baptizer, also declared of Mary, "Blessed are you among women" (Luke 1:42 – KJV). None of these accolades warrant our worshiping Mary as the "Mother of God."

Mary herself acknowledged that she was a sinner, in need of a Savior (Luke 1:47).

Bottom line: Redemption is through the sacrificial blood of Christ alone (Colossians 1:14; 1 Peter 1:18-19).

Representative, Vicarious, Substitutionary Sacrifice

The BMW Doctrinal Statement informs us that the Lord Jesus Christ was a

- Representative Sacrifice

- Vicarious Sacrifice

- Substitutionary Sacrifice

He was also a Willing Sacrifice – He voluntarily laid down His life for me (John 10:18) – and a Perfect Sacrifice – the Father accepted the death of His Son as the full and final payment for the sins of the whole world (1 Timothy 2:5-6).

Representative Sacrifice

Christ's sacrificial death was representative – His death represented my death – spiritually, I died when He died (Galatians 2:20). The Lord Jesus Christ acted as my representative in His work of atonement. His life, death, resurrection, and continuous intercession accrue to my benefit. He did it for me, on my behalf.

Vicarious Sacrifice

"Vicarious" means "acting on behalf of" or "representing another" or "instead of" and is used to describe something performed or suffered by one person with the results accruing to the benefit or advantage of another. In His vicarious death, Christ suffered on my behalf. The result: the penalty due for my sins has been paid, making it possible for me to be saved through personal faith in the Lord Jesus Christ.

Christ was our substitute, our Vicar. My favorite definition of *vicar* is "one who represents and suffers for the benefit of another at great personal cost to themselves" – what a great description of the Lord Jesus Christ!

Substitutionary Sacrifice

The Lord Jesus Christ was a substitutionary sacrifice. On the cross He paid the penalty I should have paid for my sins. I should be eternally punished for my sins, but the Lord Jesus Christ willingly stood in my place, as my substitute, and bore the full wrath of His Father against my sins.

Note that some religious traditions reject the doctrine of the substitutionary atonement of Christ and teach instead that His death was a ransom paid to Satan to purchase man's freedom and release him from enslavement to Satan.

"Ransom Theory," as it is called, is unbiblical for at least three reasons:

- God, not Satan, is the One Who requires a payment for man's sin.

- Satan is not as powerful as the Ransom Theory views him. He's a created being, he's not divine, he's not omnipotent, omniscient, or omnipresent. But he is our archenemy. Satan has only as much power as God allows (Job 1).

- Ransom Theory downplays our personal sinfulness. We are not victims of rebellious spiritual powers, we are guilty sinners before God. If we are held captive by evil powers, it is our fault; it is because of choices we have made.

Because of the sacrifice Christ made for us, we are admonished to present our bodies, our entire lives, to God as holy, acceptable (to God), living sacrifices (Romans 12:1-2). In the same passage, the Apostle Paul tells us not to be conformed (molded) to the ways of the world, but to be transformed (changed) by the renewing of our minds – and that can only be achieved by studying God's Word.

Atonement

Literally, a covering. In the New Testament, "atonement" refers to Christ's covering our sins by the shedding of His own blood as our substitute. He has *washed us from our sins in His own blood* (Revelation 1:5b).

The BMW Doctrinal Statement indicates that Christ's sacrificial death was "sufficient for the sins of the whole world." This is known as "unlimited atonement." There are others – principally, proponents of Reformed Theology – who believe in "limited atonement"; that is, that the Lord Jesus Christ died only for those He chose to be His own, those who He elected to be saved.

Both positions, limited atonement and unlimited atonement, have scriptural support, but regardless of which position we subscribe to, we can rest in the fact that Christ's death was sufficient to cover the sins of all who desire to trust Him as their Savior!

Justification

Being judicially (God is the Judge) declared "not guilty" of my sin and "righteous" (in right standing with God) because of my relationship with the Lord Jesus Christ. Justification occurs at the instant of salvation (Galatians 2:16).

Justification is by grace alone (*sola gratia*) through faith alone (*sola fide*) because of Christ alone (*solus Christus*). This is the article by which the church stands or falls.

Resurrection

Bringing a physically dead person back to life. Resurrection is the opposite of physical death.

The Lord Jesus Christ was crucified for our sins, died physically, was placed in a grave, and three days later resurrected His own dead body; He came back to life. He is now alive forevermore (Revelation 1:18).

Those who have received the Lord Jesus Christ as their Savior from sin are serving a risen, living Savior! All other men, even the greatest men and the holiest men, have died. Buddha, Mohammed, Zoroaster, Confucius, Caesar, Marx—men who made a profound impact on the world in one way or another—are all dead. But Jesus Christ is alive!

The bodily resurrection of Jesus Christ from the dead is the crowning proof of Christianity. If the resurrection did not take place, then Christianity is a false religion. If it did take place, then Christ is God and the Christian faith is absolute truth.

The resurrection of Christ

- Proves that He is God

- Means that He can be trusted absolutely

- Means that our sins have been forgiven

- Means that Satan has been defeated

- Guarantees our resurrection to eternal life

Let's look at these points individually.

Christ's resurrection proves that He is God

From *The Bible Knowledge Commentary:* "The authentication of Christ's person and work was His resurrection."

Christ Jesus ... was declared with power to be the Son of God by His resurrection from the dead Romans 1:4 (KJV)

In his address to the Athenian philosophers on Mars Hill, the Apostle Paul said

[God] ... has appointed a day, in which he will judge the world in righteousness by that man* whom he has ordained; whereof he has given assurance [proof] *unto all men, in that he has raised him from the dead.* Acts 17:31 (KJV)

> *   A reference to the Son of Man, the Lord Jesus Christ, from Daniel 7:13-14.

The resurrection of Christ, the fact that God *has raised him from the dead,* also proves that the Lord Jesus Christ is the Creator of life. Here's an explanatory note from the *New Defender's Study Bible:*

"Death has always been man's greatest, and finally victorious, enemy, and only the Creator of life, the Judge who imposed the sentence of death because of sin, can conquer death. The founders and leaders of all other religions and philosophies eventually die, but Jesus Christ is alive! His tomb is empty, and He has ascended in His resurrection body to the Father in heaven. His bodily resurrection, which can be shown to be the best-proved fact of Biblical history, is the certain assurance that He is the Creator and Judge of all."

Christ's resurrection means that He can be trusted absolutely

Jesus promised His disciples that He would be crucified, would die, then rise again (Matthew 16:21, 17:23, 20:19; John 10:17-18). His resurrection means, among other things, that His word can be trusted.

If Jesus has spoken truthfully with respect to this – the greatest of all miracles – then we can be sure that all his other teachings are reliable.

Christ's resurrection means that our sins have been forgiven

The resurrection means Christ's sacrifice for sin has been accepted by God. The Lord Jesus Christ would still be in the tomb if that were not true.

In the Old Testament, the high priest went into the "Holy of Holies" (the holiest place in the Tabernacle/Temple) once a year, on the Day of Atonement, to make sacrifice for the sins of the people. If God accepted the sacrifice, the priest was allowed to live, and reappeared before the people; if the sacrifice was not accepted, the priest's corpse was pulled out of the Holy of Holies by means of a rope tied around his ankle. (The rope was affixed in preparation for this priestly duty.) When Jesus rose the third day, His reappearance to His disciples proved that God had accepted His sacrifice for our sins.

Christ's resurrection means that Satan has been defeated

On the cross, Christ battled with the one who has the power of death, Satan, and was victorious (Luke 22:53; Hebrews 2:14). Christ has conquered all our enemies; we have nothing to fear.

Christ's resurrection guarantees our resurrection to eternal life!

The Lord Jesus Christ is alive, and He is the "firstfruits" of those who die in faith (1 Corinthians 15:20-23).

> God … *according to His great mercy, has caused us to be born again to a living hope through* [by means of] *the resurrection of Jesus Christ from the dead.* 1 Peter 1:3 (NASB)

I have the assurance (that's the meaning of "hope" in this passage) that because He lives I shall live also! The Christian's hope includes the hope of the resurrection of the body in perfection (1 Corinthians 15:51-54). Our hope is a living hope because the Lord Jesus Christ is our living Savior!

The resurrection of the Lord Jesus Christ is the reason, the basis, for our hope. If the Savior had not physically come out of the tomb, we would have no reason to hope.

Associated with the resurrection is the hope of heaven, our eternal home. God's promises of provision, protection, healing, etc., translate into the hope of heaven. We may not realize the fulfillment of those promises in this life, on this earth, but we will in heaven. God keeps His promises!

> *If only for this life we have hope in Christ, we are to be pitied more than all men.* 1 Corinthians 15:19 (NIV)

But, thank God, our hope is not for this life only – it is for eternity!

The Holy Spirit, writing through the Apostle Paul, answered this question in a very powerful and sobering passage: 1 Corinthians 15:12-23. The verse references below are to this passage.

... if Christ has not been raised, then our preaching is in vain and your faith is in vain (verse 14 – ESV)

- The apostle's preaching was vain (empty, useless).

  This also applies to Christians of all ages, of course. If Christ be not raised, then we really have nothing of value to offer others – there is no true Christian faith without the resurrection.

- Our faith is vain.

We are even found to be misrepresenting God, because we testified about God that he raised Christ, whom he did not raise if it is true that the dead are not raised. (verse 15 – ESV)

- We (the apostles) arc false witnesses – we've lied to you.

  That's also true of us as followers of Christ. If Christ be not raised, we've been lying to people.

... if Christ has not been raised, your faith is futile and you are still in your sins. (verse 17 – ESV)

- Your faith is futile (literally, "without results").

- You are still in your sins (because you don't have a Savior – the Lord Jesus Christ is not God if He be not raised).

Then those also who have fallen asleep in Christ have perished. (verse 18 – ESV)

- Those who have died "in Christ" have perished (gone to eternal ruin) – we will never see them again. And we too will perish – spend eternity in the Lake of Fire.

Before we leave 1 Corinthians 15, note verse 21:

For as by a man came death, by a man has come also the resurrection of the dead (ESV)

Note that *by a man came* death. There was no death before Adam and Eve sinned (Genesis 3; Romans 5:12). The teaching that there were long ages before man (evolution) is simply wrong!

Salvation and Resurrection

... if you confess with your mouth that Jesus is Lord and believe in your heart that God raised him from the dead, you will be saved. For with the heart one believes and is justified, and with the mouth one confesses and is saved. Romans 10:9-10 (ESV)

Why the requirement that to be saved you must believe that Christ is risen? Because ...

... if Christ be not raised, your faith is vain; ye are yet in your sins. 1 Corinthians 15:17 (KJV)

If Christ be not raised, then He is not God, and if He is not God, He cannot be the Savior.

Note that just saying the words "Jesus is Lord" and proclaiming that He rose from the dead is not salvific – it cannot secure salvation (cf Matthew 7:21-23, James 2:19). What matters is not just *saying* Jesus is Lord, but *making* Him lord of your life. That means repenting of sin, trusting Him for salvation, and submitting to Him as Lord.

High Priest

As our High Priest, Christ represents us to God, just as the High Priest represented the Israelites to God in Old Testament times.

In Israel, the Jewish High Priest was the only person who could go into the very presence of God once a year with a sacrifice for the sins of the people. (This was done in the "Holy of Holies," also known as "the Most Holy Place," in the Tabernacle, and later in the Temple.)

When Christ died as our perfect sacrifice, He entered the heavenly Tabernacle, the true Tabernacle, on our behalf (Hebrews 9:24). Christ is now in the presence of His Father, interceding for us on the basis of His blood, shed on the cross.

The BMW Doctrinal Statement indicates that "As our High Priest (Christ) fulfills the ministry of Representative, Intercessor, and Advocate." Let's look at those terms.

Representative

The Lord Jesus Christ represents us to His Father. Christ is our Representative in the heavenly realms. Who better to represent us!

The Apostle Paul reminded us that born-again Christians are representatives of our Savior (2 Corinthians 5:20). What a great privilege – and what an awesome responsibility!

Intercessor

As our great High Priest, Christ intercedes for us with the Father. Christ is the mediator, the intermediary, between us and God the Father.

Christ's continual intercession for us (Romans 8:34) guarantees our eternal security. This is discussed in more detail in *Salvation and Security*, the study note for point six of the BMW Doctrinal Statement.

Advocate

An advocate pleads the cause of another person, she or he helps that person by defending or comforting her or him. As our great High Priest, the Lord Jesus Christ is our advocate, He is One called alongside to help (literal meaning of *parakletos*, the Greek word for advocate). When we sin, it is the Lord Jesus Christ who, as our attorney, pleads with the Father on our behalf, on the basis of His own death in our stead.

My little children, these things write I unto you, that ye sin not. And if any man sin, we have an advocate with the Father, Jesus Christ the righteous: And he is the propitiation* for our sins: and not for ours only, but also for the sins of the whole world. (1 John 2:1-2 – KJV)

> * "Propitiation" (Greek *hilasterion*) means "sacrifice" or "satisfaction." In His sacrificial death, the Lord Jesus Christ satisfied the justice of a holy God Who must punish sin.

Jesus Christ Is The Only Way To God

Jesus said

I am the way, and the truth, and the life; no man comes to the Father but through me John 14:6 (NASB)

"He did not come to show us the way, teach us the truth, and give us the life, though He does all of this. He is the Way to God, the Truth of God, and the Life in God." Dr. Henry M. Morris in *The New Defender's Study Bible*

Speaking of the Lord Jesus Christ, the Apostle Peter said

And there is salvation in no one else; for there is no other name under heaven that has been given among men by which we must be saved. Acts 4:12 (NASB)

The Holy Spirit, writing through the Apostle John, made it very clear:

The one who believes in the Son has eternal life, but the one who refuses to believe in the Son will not see life; instead, the wrath of God remains on him. John 3:36 (HCSB)

Other religious traditions and cults recognize – and some claim to worship – Jesus Christ, but their Jesus is not the One revealed in the Bible, he is "another Jesus" as the Apostle Paul wrote in 2 Corinthians 11:4.

It's vitally important that we lean our eternal destiny on the real Jesus Christ. In the Olivet Discourse (the most detailed end-times discourse delivered by Christ), Jesus Himself warned against false christs (Matthew 24:24) – and there have been, and continue to be, many. To be saved from sin, your faith must be in the Jesus of the Bible. There is no salvation in worshipping a false christ. Only the Jesus of the Bible has the power to save.

Some cults teach that Jesus was "a god" created by God the Father. That's not the Jesus of the Bible. Some teach that Jesus was only a prophet. That's not the Jesus of the Bible. Some teach that Jesus was an Archangel who became a man. That's not the Jesus of the Bible. Some teach that Jesus was once a man who became God. That's not the Jesus of the Bible. Jesus is not a man who became God – He is God who became man. He became one of us that He might taste death for everyone and provide salvation for us (Hebrews 2:9).

Christ's future ministry includes at least these elements:

- His coming for His own in the rapture of the Church (1 Thessalonians 4:13-18)

- Pouring out His wrath on the earth during the tribulation period (Revelation 6:16-17)

- Returning to earth as King of kings and Lord of lords to rule the world with a rod of iron (Revelation 19:11-16)

- His everlasting reign, first over the Millennial Kingdom, then forever

4. The Person And Work Of The Holy Spirit

"We believe the Holy Spirit is the **person** *of the* **Godhead** *who in this present age convicts the world of* **sin,** **righteousness,** *and* **judgment;** *who* **regenerates** *and* **baptizes** *into the* **body of Christ** *those who believe; and who* **indwells** *and* **seals** *them unto the* **day of redemption**. *(John 16:8-11; Romans 8:9; 1 Corinthians 12:12-14; 2 Corinthians 3:6; Ephesians 1:13-14)*

"We believe the Holy Spirit is the **Divine Teacher** *who guides believers into all truth; and it is the privilege of believers to be* **filled with**, *and their duty to* **walk in**, *the Holy Spirit. (John 16:13; Galatians 5:16; Ephesians 5:18; 1 John 2:20,27)"*

The words appearing in **bold** text in the paragraphs above are explained in this study note. Here's where to find those words – and more – in this note:

Baptize   Page 57
Body of Christ   Page 57
Day of Redemption   Page 58
Divine Teacher   Page 59
Fill   Page 59
Godhead   Page 54
How to be filled with the Holy Spirit   Page 60
Indwell   Page 57
Judgment   Page 55
Other ministries of the Holy Spirit   Page 62
Person   Page 53
Regenerate   Page 55
Righteousness   Page 55
Seal   Page 58
Sin   Page 54
Walking in the Spirit   Page 61

Person

The Holy Spirit is a divine person, eternal, underived, possessing all the attributes of personality and deity, including intellect (1 Corinthians 2:10-13), emotions (Ephesians 4:30), will (1 Corinthians 12:11), eternality (Hebrews 9:14), omnipresence (Psalm 139:7-10), omniscience (Isaiah 40:13-14), omnipotence (Romans 15:19), and truthfulness (John 16:13).

When He returned to the Father after His resurrection, the Lord Jesus Christ sent the Holy Spirit to be with the believers, taking Christ's place in their lives – and ours (John 14:16).

From *Strange Fire: The Danger of Offending the Holy Spirit with Counterfeit Worship* by Dr. John MacArthur:

"The Holy Spirit is the power of God in a divine person acting from creation to consummation and everything in between (cf. Genesis 1:2; Revelation 22:17). He is wholly God, possessing all the attributes of God in the fullness that belongs to God. There is no sense in which He is God diminished. He participates fully in all of God's works. He is as holy and powerful as the Father and as gracious and loving as the Son. He is divine perfection in its fullness. Thus He is worthy of our worship as fully as the Father and as fully as the Son."

Godhead

The Divine Trinity: Father, Son, and Holy Spirit. Refer to *The Godhead*, the study note for point two of the BMW Doctrinal Statement.

Sin

What is sin? Here's a quote from Dr. John MacArthur, excerpted from the January, 2007, issue of *Decision* magazine:

> "Sin is any lack of conformity to the moral character of God or the law of God*. We sin by thinking evil, speaking evil, acting evil, or omitting good."

> *   Thus, sin is not being conformed to, not being aligned with, God's standards of right and wrong. Where are those standards revealed? In His Word!

Dr. MacArthur's concise definition of sin indicates that there are "sins of commission" – doing what we know is wrong – and "sins of omission" – failing to do what we know we should do. The Bible also speaks of "presumptuous sins." They are sins done willfully, knowingly, presuming on God's mercy and forgiveness – in effect, daring God to do something about our sin. ("Presumptuous" is from a Latin word meaning, "to dare.") In the Old Testament, the penalty for presumptuous sins was death (Numbers 15:30-31). No wonder King David asked God to keep him from presumptuous sins (Psalm 19:13)!

Dr. MacArthur also describes the nature of sin:

> "Sin is defilement. It is ugliness across the face of beauty. It is to the soul what scars are to a beautiful face; what a stain is to a white silk cloth.

> "Sin is rebellion. The sinner tramples on God's law, tramples on God's character, willfully crosses God's will, affronts God, mocks God.

> "Sin is ingratitude. Everything we have, everything we are, is from God. All the food the sinner eats, God gave him. All the air the sinner breathes, God gave him. All the joys the sinner experienced, God provided. The sinner eagerly embraces God's graces and mercy then betrays Him by being the friend of God's enemy, Satan."

The only sin that is unforgiveable (unpardonable) is described in Matthew 12:32b:

> *Whoever shall speak against the Holy Spirit, it shall not be forgiven him, either in this age or in the age to come.* (NASB)

The Holy Spirit is the One who convicts us of sin, and invites us to trust the Lord Jesus Christ as our Savior. The person who continues to reject those invitations, thus to "speak against the Holy Spirit," will die in his or her sins and spend eternity in the Lake of Fire.

Bottom line: The only unforgiveable sin is permanently rejecting Christ as Savior (John 3:18, 36). A genuine Christian cannot commit this sin because he or she has not rejected Christ. Just the opposite!

Historical Note: Who was the first sinner? Satan. 1 John 3:8 indicates that the devil, "has sinned from the beginning." When he was created, Satan was perfect (Ezekiel 28:12). He fell – sinned – when he rebelled against God. Satan was the original sinner. So there was sin in the angelic realm prior to Adam's sin. Adam became the vehicle Satan used to pass sin out of the angelic realm into the human realm.

Righteousness

"Righteousness" can be defined very simply as "right standing with God." Declaring you to be righteous is part of justification, what God does for us when we invite the Lord Jesus Christ into our lives as Savior.

The BMW Doctrinal Statement tells us that the Holy Spirit *convicts the world of … righteousness –* that is, the lack of righteousness. People without Christ, though they may be good people in the eyes of others, are not righteous from God's perspective, and the Holy Spirit convicts them, makes them aware of that fact.

Judgment

God's holiness and justice require that He judge sin and the sinner. All sin is an offense to God. There is no such thing as a "little sin" in God's view – sin is sin.

The unsaved – those who have never trusted the Lord Jesus Christ as Savior from sin – will stand before God at the Great White Throne Judgment (Revelation 20:11-13) and be sentenced to eternal punishment in the Lake of Fire.

For those who are saved,

> *There is therefore now no condemnation* (judgment for sins) *to them which are in Christ Jesus …* Romans 8:1 (KJV)

because Christ paid the penalty for their sins. Saved people will be judged regarding their works (1 Corinthians 3:11-15), but their salvation is secure in Christ.

The judgments are described in more detail in the study notes for points thirteen (*The Second Advent of Christ*) and fourteen (*The Eternal State*) of the BMW Doctrinal Statement.

Regenerate

"Regeneration" is re-generation – being generated (born) a second time. It is a spiritual rebirth. Regeneration is also known as "salvation," "the new birth," "being born again, "being born from above," and other terms. We'll use the terms "save" and "salvation." Note that regeneration is not reincarnation (being physically reborn, also known as "transmigration of the soul"). The latter is not biblical because

> *… it is appointed unto men once to die, but after this the judgment* Hebrews 9:27 (KJV)

Salvation is the state (condition) of being rescued (saved, delivered) from the power and penalty of sin. All three members of the Trinity are involved in saving a person who is lost.

From a biblical standpoint, the expressions "to be saved" and "getting saved" include at least the following:

- Having your sins forgiven on the basis of Christ's sacrificial death for you

- Being declared righteous (in right standing with God) and not guilty of your sins

- Being adopted into God's spiritual family; becoming a true child of God

- Being rescued from a future eternity in Hell – the Lake of Fire

In his book, *The Bible Has The Answer*, Dr. Henry Morris explains:

"The word 'saved,' in biblical terminology, means to be saved from sin, and death, and hell, and to be saved unto righteousness and heaven and eternal life."

God is the sole Operator in salvation. It is entirely His work. It cannot be earned; it is totally undeserved; it is a gift. Salvation is not attained by being a member of a particular church; it isn't attained by being baptized or doing good works; it's attained only by personally trusting the Lord Jesus Christ as your Savior.

He saved us, not because of righteous things we had done, but because of His mercy Titus 3:5 (NIV)

For it is by grace you have been saved, through faith – and this not from yourselves, it is the gift of God – not by works, so that no one can boast. Ephesians 2:8-9 (NIV)

For the wages of sin is death, but the gift of God is eternal life through Jesus Christ our Lord. Romans 6:23 (KJV)

Romans 6:23, the last verse quoted above, indicates that condemned sinners earn their eternal punishment by their sins. The most egregious of all sins is unbelief – failure to trust the Lord Jesus Christ as Savior (John 3:36). Unbelief is the only sin that will keep a person out of Heaven.

Note that a gift must be personally accepted before it becomes a possession. God made the gift of salvation available to us, but we have to receive it by a deliberate act of our will.

Being saved is the opposite of what the Bible refers to as *perishing*.

For God so loved the world that He gave His only begotten Son that whosoever believes in Him should not perish but have everlasting life John 3:16 (KJV)

For the Lord … is not willing that any should perish, but that all should come to repentance 2 Peter 3:9 (KJV)

"Perish" is such a sad word when applied to a person. There's a sense of finality to the word. As used in the Bible, "perish" means to go into eternal ruin. When something is ruined, it is irreparable, it cannot be fixed. Spiritual ruin is spending eternity in the place the Bible refers to as Hell – the Lake of Fire (Revelation 20:11-15). Yes, Hell is a real, physical place, not a state of mind.

For additional information regarding man's final destiny, refer to *The Eternal State*, the study note for point fourteen of the BMW Doctrinal Statement.

Regeneration is described in more detail in *Salvation and Security*, the study note for point six of the BMW Doctrinal Statement.

Baptize

Baptism is identification. The Bible speaks of two types of baptism: physical baptism (being immersed in water) and spiritual baptism. At the moment of salvation, the Holy Spirit spiritually baptizes the new believer into union with Christ (Romans 6:3) and into union with His spiritual body, the invisible, true Church (1 Corinthians 12:13).

Physical baptism is not required for salvation, but the Lord Jesus Christ commanded that believers be baptized as a demonstration that they have identified with the risen Christ (Matthew 28:19).

Some denominations teach that the baptism of the Holy Spirit is a "second blessing" that occurs subsequent to salvation (which they describe as the "first blessing"), and is something we must seek. Thus, it is not true of every believer. The Bible doesn't support this teaching.

For additional information regarding baptism, refer to study note entitled *Ordinances*, point eight of the BMW Doctrinal Statement.

Body of Christ

The "Body of Christ" is the true, invisible Church (Greek *ecclesia*) consisting of all who have accepted Christ as Savior during the current Church Age. For more information regarding the Body of Christ and the Church, refer to the study note entitled *The Church*, point seven of the BMW Doctrinal Statement.

"God's great master plan was to bring everything together (Ephesians 1:10) under Christ as Head (Ephesians 1:22-23); we, as the Body of Christ on earth, have a part in this plan and the Holy Spirit is the guarantee of God's promise (Ephesians 1:13-14)." From Ephesians introductory notes in the *Key Word Study Bible*

Indwell

When we accept the Lord Jesus Christ as our Savior from sin, we "receive" God the Holy Spirit (Galatians 3:2). The Apostle Paul wrote that our bodies are the temples of the Holy Spirit and that He dwells – resides – in us (1 Corinthians 3:16, 6:19).

The indwelling of the Holy Spirit is permanent – He never leaves the believer. (This wasn't true of saints in the Old Testament – Psalm 51:11.) When Christ promised to send the Holy Spirit to the disciples, He told them the Holy Spirit would be "with you and in you" (John 14:17). The Greek text of this verse suggests a permanent, uninterrupted residence.

God is one God, so all three members of the Godhead, through the Holy Spirit, indwell the believer. We don't each have a little piece of the infinite Holy Spirit, we all have His fullness! Our relationship with Him is intimate, our access to Him is immediate.

Seal

The Holy Spirit seals the new believer at the moment of salvation, the moment he or she trusts the Lord Jesus Christ to save them from their sins.

The sealing of the Holy Spirit reveals that

- Your salvation is a finished transaction (you are not on probation)

- You belong to the Lord Jesus Christ as His child

- Your salvation is secure

The sealing of the Holy Spirit also serves as an assurance and guarantee of our complete redemption when Christ returns – *it is the earnest of our inheritance* (the first installment of a guaranteed final purchase) that you will one day receive a new glorified redeemed body (Ephesians 1:13-14; Romans 8:23; 2 Corinthians 1:22).

The seal with which the Holy Spirit seals a believer isn't physical, of course, but spiritual. The Holy Spirit is Himself the seal according to Ephesians 1:13; 4:30. The latter verse (quoted below) also tells us how long we are sealed: *unto the day of redemption.* It is an eternal sealing!

> *And grieve not the holy Spirit of God, whereby ye are sealed unto the day of redemption.*
> Ephesians 4:30 (KJV)

Even grieving the Holy Spirit cannot destroy that seal.

> "While the Holy Spirit is grieved through the believer's sin and unwillingness to walk by faith, note that He is never grieved away. Ephesians 4:30 does not warn us, 'And grieve not the Holy Spirit of God whereby ye are sealed until you sin, backslide, apostatize, blaspheme, etc.' In fact, if the Holy Spirit seals you permanently and you could somehow lose your salvation, the Holy Spirit would then have to go to Hell forever with you. God forbid! The sealing of the Holy Spirit underscores for us the tremendous truth of eternal security."
> http://duluthbible.org/g_f_j/EternalSecurity10.htm

Day of Redemption

The Day of Redemption (Ephesians 4:30) is that glorious day when our redemption (our being loosed from bondage to sin and death) is complete – the day when we receive our glorified bodies and meet our Savior face-to-face.

The future resurrection of our bodies is so certain (because of the sacrifice of Christ), that our future glorification is spoken of in the past tense – it is already an accomplished fact in the mind and purpose of God:

> *... whom He did predestinate, them He also called: and whom He called, them He also justified: and whom He justified, them He also glorified**. Romans 8:30 (KJV)

> * Justification, Sanctification, and Glorification are described in detail in the Supplemental Information at the end of *Salvation and Security,* the study note for point six of the BMW Doctrinal Statement.

Divine Teacher

The following two paragraphs are from the book, *Strange Fire: The Danger of Offending the Holy Spirit with Counterfeit Worship,* by Dr. John MacArthur.

"Within the Trinity, the Holy Spirit functions as the divine agent of transmission and communication. He is the divine Author of Scripture, the One through whom God revealed His truth (1 Corinthians 2:10). Although the Spirit worked through many human authors, the resulting message is entirely His. It is the perfect and pure Word of God.

"Inspiration has given us the message inscribed on the pages of Scripture. Illumination inscribes that message on our hearts, enabling us to understand what it means, as we rely on the Spirit of God to shine the light of truth brightly on our minds (cf. 2 Corinthians 4:6)."

And from another MacArthur book, *Why Believe The Bible? :*

"The safeguard against misuse of the Bible is illumination from the Holy Spirit. No matter how religious he may be, the natural man can't understand the real message of Scripture. … The natural man may be able to read God's inspired revelation, but without the illumination of the Holy Spirit it won't make sense to him."

Fill

The Holy Spirit fills (controls) believers who yield to Him (Acts 2:4, Ephesians 5:18). Note that "indwelling" and "filling" are not the same.

Indwelling occurs at the moment of conversion and is a once-for-all-time action. The indwelling Holy Spirit never leaves the Christian; the relationship is never broken. Indwelling is unconditional; it does not depend on our actions.

As opposed to indwelling, the filling of the Holy Spirit is conditional; it occurs only when a believer voluntarily yields control of his life to the indwelling Holy Spirit.

In his book previously cited, Dr. John MacArthur points out that "(b)eing Spirit-filled starts with being Scripture-saturated; as believers submit themselves to the Word of Christ, they simultaneously come under the sanctifying influence of the Holy Spirit."

The BMW Doctrinal Statement indicates that being Spirit-filled is a privilege. Indeed it is! An unsaved person is controlled by (filled with) his old sinful nature. When he sins, he is "doing what comes naturally." One who is saved has the option of being filled with the Spirit so he or she doesn't have to follow the dictates of the old nature.

The definitive passage on the filling of the Holy Spirit is Ephesians 5:18:

Do not get drunk on wine*, which leads to debauchery. Instead, be filled with the Spirit. (NIV)

> * "Wine" is just one example of what can control us. This example is not meant to be exhaustive!

The phrase "do not get drunk on wine" is literally "do not begin to be drunk with wine." Some commentators suggest that this passage teaches that we are to totally abstain from alcohol.

The key concept of filling is *control*. Alcohol flowing through a person's veins can take over and control that person's thoughts and actions. The result of being filled with the Spirit is that He controls your thoughts and actions.

How to be filled with the Holy Spirit

- Confess known sin (1 John 1:9).

- Ask the Holy Spirit to fill you, to take control of your mind, your tongue, and your actions (Ephesians 5:18).

- Obey God's commands (do what He instructs you to do in His Word). Only obedience to God's commands allows the Holy Spirit to work within us.

How to lose the filling of the Spirit

By sinning, we can lose the filling (control) of the Holy Spirit, but not His indwelling. When we sin, the Holy Spirit obviously is not in control of our lives. Filling can be reinstated, as often as desired, by following the procedure above.

Misconceptions

Being filled with the Spirit doesn't mean a person will perform miracles. John the Baptist was the first person described as being filled with the Spirit (Luke 1:15), but he didn't perform any miracles (John 10:41).

The filling of the Holy Spirit doesn't produce weird behavior! Spiritual manifestations are not necessarily a sign of the filling of the Spirit. There are two sources of spiritual manifestations – and one of them isn't heavenly! A person can work himself or herself into a mental state where they do weird stuff – then claim it's the result of the filling of the Holy Spirit. (The "holy laughter" debacle of the so-called "Toronto Blessing" comes to mind.)

> "When the Holy Spirit's power is manifest, it does not produce mindless flops on the ground, gushing incoherent babble, ecstatic buzz, or hot flashes of emotion. All those behaviors have nothing to do with His authentic ministry. In reality, they are a mockery of His genuine work." From *Strange Fire: The Danger of Offending the Holy Spirit with Counterfeit Worship* by Dr. John MacArthur.

The Lord Jesus Christ was, of course, filled with the Spirit throughout His life (Luke 4:1). Note that this same Spirit led Christ into the wilderness to be tempted of Satan (Matthew 4:1). Thus, being filled with the Spirit doesn't mean freedom from temptation and suffering, but it does assure victory over such circumstances – if we avail ourselves of God's provision for victory (1 Corinthians 10:13).

Christ's disciples, and many members of the early church, were filled with the Spirit on at least two occasions: Pentecost (Acts 2:4) and after severe persecution (Acts 4:31). This tells us that the filling is not a once-for-all-time experience, but may be repeated. The original Greek text is in the present tense, indicating that we are to be continually being filled with the Spirit.

Some disciples are mentioned by name as being filled with the Spirit when they needed additional courage, wisdom, faith, strength, joy. Examples: Stephen (Acts 7:55), Peter (Acts 4:8), Paul (Acts 13:9). See also Acts 6:3-5; 11:24; 13:52.

Walking in the Spirit

When we allow the Holy Spirit to control our words, thoughts, deeds, and attitudes, when we live each moment in dependency on Him, sensitive to His voice, and obedient to Him, we are said to be *walking in the Spirit* (KJV), *keep*(ing) *in step with the Spirit* (NIV). It results in many practical benefits. Here's one:

> ... *walk in the Spirit and you shall not fulfill the lust of the flesh.* Galatians 5:16 (KJV)

The NIV translates this as

> ... *live by the Spirit and you will not gratify the desires of the sinful nature.*

Other characteristics of walking in the Spirit are indicated in Ephesians 5 and 6. The following quote is from the book *Strange Fire* by Dr. John MacArthur.

> "Those who are Spirit-filled are characterized by joyful singing in worship (5:19), hearts full of thanksgiving (5:20), and selflessness toward others (5:21). If they are married, their marriage honors God (5:22-23); if they have children, their parenting patiently unfolds the gospel (6:1-4); if they work for an earthly master, they work hard for the Lord's honor (6:5-8); and if they have people working for them, they treat their subordinates with benevolence and fairness (6:9). *This* is what it looks like to be a Spirit-filled Christian."

Dr. Charles Stanley said that *walking in the Spirit* ...

> "... means to live each moment in dependency on the Holy Spirit, sensitive to His voice and obedient to Him. As we go through each day, we should be aware of the presence of the Holy Spirit within us. We should be totally submitted to Him. That means we must be sensitive to the initial promptings of the Holy Spirit. When He speaks to our hearts, you and I should immediately obey." From Dr. Stanley's *Sermon Note* entitled *Walking in the Holy Spirit*.

If we want to walk in the Spirit, we are not to allow anything else to gain control of our lives.

Note that the BMW Doctrinal Statement indicates that it is our duty to walk in the Spirit. It's a command: be filled – it's what God desires and expects of us.

Other Ministries of the Holy Spirit

In addition to those discussed above, the ministry of the Holy Spirit includes at least the following:

- Giving the assurance of salvation (Romans 8:16-17; 1 John 3:24)

- Comforting us (John 14:16)

- Convicting people of sin (John 16:8-11)

- Empowering us for evangelism (Acts 1:8)

- Producing "fruit" in our lives (Galatians 5:22-23)

- Giving spiritual gifts to believers to enable them to minister to others (Ephesians 4:11, Romans 12:4-8, 1 Corinthians 12:4-12, 27-30)

- Inspiring (giving the very words to) the authors of the Bible (2 Peter 1:21, 2 Timothy 3:16)

- Instructing us in truth (John 14:26, 16:13)

- Interceding for us in prayer (Romans 8:26-27)

- Implanting in Mary's womb the specially-created cell that grew into the human body for the Lord Jesus Christ (Luke 1:35)

- Providing explicit guidance to the early church (Acts 13:2-4, 1 Corinthians 12:4-11)

- Energizing the physical creation (Genesis 1:1-2)

- Working through the Christians He indwells, the Holy Spirit restrains evil in the world (2 Thessalonians 2:6-7)

  When the Church is raptured before the Tribulation, the evil-restraining influence of Christians will be removed from the earth. The result will be an unparalleled, unprecedented, reign of evil and evil people.

  Note that during the Tribulation, the Holy Spirit will continue to convict people of sin and point them to the Savior. Those who respond and are saved will be indwelled by the Holy Spirit, just as now.

- Glorifying, and pointing people to, the Lord Jesus Christ (John 15:26)

Synopsis

The following summary of the work of the Holy Spirit is from the book, *Strange Fire: The Danger of Offending the Holy Spirit with Counterfeit Worship*, by Dr. John MacArthur.

"What is the Holy Spirit truly doing in the world today? He who was once actively involved in the creation of the material universe (Genesis 1:2) is now focused on spiritual creation (cf. 2 Corinthians 4:6). He creates spiritual life – regenerating sinners through the gospel of Jesus Christ and transforming them into children of God. He sanctifies them, equips them for service, produces fruit in their lives, and empowers them to please their Savior. He secures them for eternal glory and fits them for life in heaven. The same Source of explosive power that brought the world into existence out of nothing is today at work in the hearts and lives of the redeemed."

5. The Total Depravity of Man

*"We believe man was created in the **image and likeness of God**; in Adam's sin the race **fell**, inherited a **sinful nature**, and became alienated from God; and man is **totally depraved** and unable to remedy his **lost condition**. (Genesis 1:26- 27; Romans 3:22-23; 5:12; Ephesians 2:1-3,12)"*

The words appearing in **bold** text in the paragraph above are explained in this study note. Here's where to find those words – and more – in this note:

Depravity

"Depravity " is variously defined as
- A state of low moral standards and behavior
- Immoral conduct or practices
- The state or quality of being utterly (totally) evil

Image And Likeness Of God

And God said, Let us make man in our image, after our likeness ...   Genesis 1:26 (KJV)

What does it mean that we were created *in the image and likeness of God?* Here are some helpful notes from the *New Defender's Study Bible*:

"***in our image.*** God is, as it were, taking counsel here with Himself, not with angels, since man was to be made in the image of God, not of angels. 'Our image,' therefore, implies human likeness to the triune Godhead. Plants possess a body, and animals a body and consciousness. Man was not only to have a body (of the created 'earth') and a consciousness (of the created 'soul'), but man was also to possess a third created entity, the image of God, an eternal spirit capable of communion and fellowship with his Creator.

"***likeness.*** Man was not only created in God's spiritual image; he was also made in God's physical image. His body was specifically planned to be most suited for the divine fellowship (erect posture, upward-gazing countenance, facial expressions varying with emotional feelings, brain and tongue designed for articulate symbolic speech—none of which are shared by the animals). Furthermore, his body was designed to be like the body which God had planned from eternity that He Himself would one day assume (1 Peter 1:20).

"The 'image of God' was both 'created' (Genesis 1:27; 1 Corinthians 11:7-9) and 'made' (Genesis 1:26; Colossians 1:16-17) in man. That image was marred because of sin (Genesis

9:6; James 3:9), but is 'renewed in knowledge' through saving faith in Christ (Colossians 1:10; Ephesians 4:23; 2 Corinthians 3:18). Our 'image' will eventually be 'conformed to the image' of the Son of God when Christ returns (Romans 8:29; 1 Corinthians 15:49)."

The following two paragraphs are from the *Keyword Study Bible*.

"God is essentially Spirit (John 4:24). Therefore, man, who is similar to God, possesses an immortal spirit. We resemble God in certain respects without being equal with Him (Isaiah 40:25). Man's likeness to God is what truly distinguishes mankind from the rest of creation. Man is a person with the power to think, feel, and decide. He has the capacity for moral choices and spiritual growth or decline. In the beginning, man loved God and hated unrighteousness. The Fall reversed this. Man was still a person with the capacity for good, but his spirit was altered by sin so much that he now generally runs away from God and loves evil more than righteousness (John 3:19-20).

"After Adam's time, only those who lived uprightly before God were considered to be His offspring (Matthew 3:7-10, 13:38, John 12:36, Acts 13:10, Colossians 3:6). Man is no longer in the perfect state of innocence as at the time of creation. Therefore, he does not have the same spiritual, God-like attributes and qualities of that original state. Jesus, the Second Adam (1 Corinthians 15:45)*, came to undo Satan's works (1 John 3:8), to restore a spiritual likeness to God (2 Corinthians 3:18)."

> *   In this verse, Paul refers to Christ as *the last Adam*.
>
> *And so it is written, The first man Adam was made a living soul; the last Adam was made a quickening spirit.* (KJV)
>
> Here, Christ is called the "last Adam" because the physical bodies of both Adam and Christ were prototypes. Adam's body was the prototype of human flesh, Christ's resurrected body was the prototype of our resurrection bodies.
>
> Earlier in this same chapter, Paul wrote:
>
> *For as in Adam all die, even so in Christ shall all be made alive.* 1 Corinthians 15:22 (KJV)
>
> Note the contrast between Adam and the Lord Jesus Christ: Adam, through his original sin, brought death to the human race. We all die because we inherited Adam's sin. Christ, through His death, brought eternal life to the entire world. That life becomes the possession of all who trust the Lord Jesus Christ as their Savior from sin. For additional information, refer to *Salvation and Security*, the study note for point six of the BMW Doctrinal Statement.

Fall Of Man

As the BMW statement declares, *in Adam's sin the race fell* and we *inherited a sinful nature* with the result that we *became alienated from God*.

Adam was the federal (representative) head of the human race. Sin entered the world through Adam's disobedience, with the result that physical death was imposed on all Adam's descendents. This teaching is known as the "Doctrine of Original Sin."

> *Wherefore, as by one man sin entered into the world, and death by sin; and so death passed upon all men, for that all have sinned* Romans 5:12 (KJV)

Man's relationship to God was forever changed. Man became a sinner, in need of redemption. This is commonly referred to as "the Fall of Man" or simply "the Fall."

Adam was created innocent and sinless. As a result, he was able to not sin. Being a moral creature, he was also able to sin – and he exercised that ability, corrupting himself and all his descendents. As a result of the Fall, all people are born sinners (Romans 3:10-12, 23), unable to completely refrain from sinning. After death (or the Rapture of the Church), when we – born-again Christians – are forever with the Lord Jesus Christ, we will be free from the presence of sin and will no longer have a sinful nature (described below).

Augustine of Hippo (Africa), a fourth-century theologian, posited the following:
- Before the Fall, Adam was able not to sin
- After the Fall, all people are unable not to sin
- In heaven, we will be not able to sin

Selah (pause and reflect on that)!

In the following two paragraphs, Dr. Albert Mohler ties together creation, the Fall, and the good news of redemption.

> "The account of the Fall in Genesis 3 describes human sinfulness and Adam's headship, and, consequently, why this story has affected the creation ever since, why things are broken today, and how it happened. The world we know and observe is a Genesis 3 world – it is a fallen creation. More importantly, it is clear that if all we had were merely these first two movements (Creation and the Fall – Ed) of Scripture's redemptive historical narrative, we would be lost and forever under the righteous judgment and wrath of God.

> "But the narrative of God's revelation does not leave out the remarkable plan of redemption, which God prepared before the universe was created. Scripture presents this in terms of the person and work of Christ, the meaning of His atonement, and the richness of the Gospel."

> Excerpted from *Why Does the Universe Look So Old?* in the October, 2010, issue of *Acts and Facts*, published by the Institute for Creation Research.

The Fall of man not only brought physical death to mankind, it also resulted in God imposing a curse on the natural world. Here's more from Dr. Mohler:

> "From Genesis 3 and the entire narrative of Scripture (e.g., Romans 8), what we know in the world today as catastrophe, as natural disaster, earthquake, destruction by volcanic eruption, pain, death, violence, predation—all of these are results of the Fall."

In the Bible, the universal reign of decay and death is called "the bondage of corruption" (Romans 8:21 – KJV). In science it has come to be recognized as the Second Law of Thermodynamics. Also known as the Law of Increasing Entropy, this Law is now recognized as a universal law of science, with no known exception ever observed. It says, quite simply, that every system tends to become disordered, to run down and eventually to die. Its entropy, which is a measure of disorder, always tends to increase.

Sinful Nature

Our "natural" self, with its propensity toward sin. Also known as "the old nature," "the old man," "the old self," "the flesh," and the "indwelling principle of sin."

The sinful nature is the image of God we were created with, but badly marred. It produces everything from evil thoughts and lies to atrocities.

When Adam knowingly, willfully, committed the first sin by disobeying God and eating of the Tree of the Knowledge of Good and Evil (Genesis 2:16-17; 3:6), his God-given pure, innocent nature was forever marred, changed and corrupted.

Sin brought a constitutional change into Adam's being. He degenerated from his original identity. Unholiness became part of his nature.

How did that first sin corrupt Adam's nature? Although it's an imperfect analogy, let me suggest something that may be helpful in answering that question.

> Sin negatively affects the conscience. Each sin facilitates the next because that person's God-given conscience (Romans 2:14-15) is becoming more and more corrupt, defiled and hardened, which can eventually lead to what the Bible describes as a seared (cauterized, desensitized) conscience (1 Timothy 4:2).

> Now imagine the devastating effect of that first sin on Adam's heretofore pure and innocent nature. That sin changed him dramatically and permanently. He was now a sinner, he was no longer pure and innocent. He now knew – and had personally experienced – both good and evil, right and wrong. Disobeying God by eating of the tree had indeed given him the knowledge of good and evil.

Sinful parents produce – bring forth – sinful children. (Psalms 51:5, Romans 3:23)

> *When Adam had lived one hundred and thirty years, he became the father of a son in his own likeness, according to his image, and named him Seth.* Genesis 5:3

But there is good news! When we accept the Lord Jesus Christ as our Savior from sin, we become new creations in Christ (2 Corinthians 5:17) and we are given a new nature. God doesn't eliminate our old, sinful nature – or clean it up – He gives us an entirely new nature. Paul tells us how we acquire this new nature (which he identifies as "the new man") – it is created in us:

> *... put off concerning the former conversation (your previous manner of life) the old man, which is corrupt according to the deceitful lusts; And be renewed in the spirit of your mind; And ... put on the new man, which after God is created* in righteousness and true holiness.* Ephesians 4:22-24 (KJV)

Dr. Henry Morris wrote: "The miracle of regeneration (salvation) is a true miracle of special creation. It is comparable in quality, though not in quantity, to the creation of the universe. No natural process can accomplish or explain such a miracle."

Notice that the new nature is created perfect: *in righteousness and true holiness.* Christians have within themselves a new nature that is truly holy, without any proclivity to sin! Sin cannot originate in the new nature because that nature doesn't (and indeed cannot) sin.

What Ephesians 4:22-24 (quoted above) tells us is that Christians have a choice: by an act of our will we can choose to "put off" or "put on." In living our daily lives we can choose to heed the promptings of our corrupt old sinful nature – *the old man* – or we can obey the promptings of our new nature – *the new man* – a righteous, holy nature, a nature that produces a desire to fellowship with God, to read His Word, to please Him, to tell others about Him, and so forth.

Total Depravity

Stated succinctly, the doctrine of Total Depravity teaches that every aspect of our life is affected by sin. "Total Depravity" describes the extent of original sin.

Theologian John Calvin, after whom Calvinism is named, is probably the best-known expositor of the doctrine of Total Depravity. The next two paragraphs are excerpted from a Calvinist website located at   http://calvinistcorner.com/tulip

> "Sin has affected all parts of man. The heart, emotions, will, mind, and body are all affected by sin. We are completely sinful. We are not as sinful as we could be, but we are completely affected by sin.

> "The doctrine of Total Depravity is derived from scriptures that reveal human character: Man's heart is evil (Mark 7:21-23) and sick (Jeremiah 17:9). Man is a slave of sin (Romans 6:20). He does not seek for God (Romans 3:10-12). He cannot understand spiritual things (1 Corinthians 2:14). He is at enmity with God (Ephesians 2:15). And, is by nature a child of wrath (Ephesians 2:3). The Calvinist asks the question, 'In light of the scriptures that declare man's true nature as being utterly lost and incapable, how is it possible for anyone to choose or desire God?' The answer is, 'He cannot. Therefore God must predestine'. "

Note: Don't miss the import of the last two sentences in that last paragraph! If God didn't predestine* some to be saved, all people would be lost, condemned to spend eternity in the Lake of Fire.

> *   Foreknowledge, Predestination, and Election are described in the Supplemental Information at the end of this study note.

Lost Condition

"Lost" is the term used to describe the spiritual condition (state) of a person who has not invited the Lord Jesus Christ into his or her life to be their Savior from sin. The word "lost" (Greek *apollumi*) means "perishing" – going into eternal ruin. Without faith in Christ, a person is doomed to perish eternally, to spend eternity in the Lake of Fire.

Describing Himself, the Lord Jesus Christ said

> *For the Son of man has come to save the lost.* Matthew 18:11 (HCSB)

As the BMW Statement indicates, *man … is unable to remedy his lost condition.* Without God's intervention, we have no hope of even responding to His invitation to salvation (John 6:44). Human beings are born spiritually dead and are incapable even of cooperating in regenerating grace.

Being saved is the opposite of perishing.

> *For God so loved the world that He gave His only begotten Son that whosoever believes in Him should not perish but have everlasting life*   John 3:16 (KJV)

> *For the Lord … is not willing that any should perish, but that all should come to repentance*
> 2 Peter 3:9 (KJV)

"Perish" is such a sad word when applied to a person. There's a sense of finality to the word. Perishing – going into spiritual ruin – is spending eternity in Hell, the Lake of Fire (Revelation 20:11-15).

Salvation is described in more detail in *Salvation and Security*, the study note for point six of the BMW Doctrinal Statement.

Supplemental Information

Foreknowledge, Predestination, and Election

Overview

Before He created the world, God knew us individually and planned for our salvation (foreknowledge – 1 Peter 1:2), He predetermined that we were to be adopted into His spiritual family and become like His Son (predestination – Romans 8:29), and He chose us to be His own redeemed children (election – Ephesians 1:4).

Foreknowledge

To "foreknow" means to know before. When the Bible says God foreknew us, it means He had knowledge of us before the world was created.

For whom he did foreknow, he also did predestinate to be conformed to the image of his Son …
Romans 8:29a (KJV)

The Apostle Peter describes Christians as those who are

Elect according to the foreknowledge of God the Father, through sanctification of the Spirit, unto obedience and sprinkling of the blood of Jesus Christ … 1 Peter 1:2 (KJV)

Foreknowledge has two elements: knowledge (of course) and planning. God had knowledge of us from eternity past and He planned for our salvation from eternity past.

Think about this: Before He created the universe, God knew everything about us: the wrong things we would do, the people we would hurt, how we would mess up our lives, how we would offend Him. He knew us, "warts and all." But He still planned for our salvation! That's love and grace and mercy!

Some faith traditions (e.g., Arminianism) teach that God's foreknowledge of who would respond positively to His offer of salvation determined who He chose (elected) to be His own. This teaching is not correct. The following quote from John Murray is excellent in dealing with this issue:

"Even if it were granted that 'foreknew' means the foresight of faith, the biblical doctrine of sovereign election is not thereby eliminated or disproven. For it is certainly true that God foresees faith; He foresees all that comes to pass. The question would then simply be: whence proceeds this faith, which God foresees? And the only biblical answer is that the faith which God foresees is the faith He himself creates (cf. John 3:3-8; 6:44, 45, 65; Ephesians 2:8; Philippians 1:29; 2 Peter 1:2). Hence His eternal foresight of faith is preconditioned by His decree to generate this faith in those whom He foresees as believing." From John Murray, *The Epistle to the Romans*, Vol. I

Predestination

"Predestine" means "determine before" (and is so translated in Acts 4:28 – KJV), "decide beforehand" (NIV), or to "ordain before" (1 Corinthians 2:7 – KJV), "destine before" (NIV).

Vine's *Dictionary of New Testament Words* indicates that the word "predestine" means "to mark off first or beforehand." Thus, before the creation of the world, God sovereignly marked off some people and appointed them, predestined them, to be the heirs of salvation.

The two passages quoted below tell us that God predestined us *according to the purpose of His will.*

He predestined us for adoption as sons through Jesus Christ, according to the purpose of his will, to the praise of his glorious grace, with which he has blessed us in the Beloved. Ephesians 1:5-6 (ESV)

In him we have obtained an inheritance, having been predestined according to the purpose of him who works all things according to the counsel of his will, so that we who were the first to hope in Christ might be to the praise of his glory. Ephesians 1:11-12 (ESV)

The two paragraphs below are excerpts from the book, *Election and the Sovereignty of God*, by J. I. Packer.

"Scripture consistently teaches that predestination or election is not based upon something we do or will do. God predestinated people based on His own sovereign will to redeem for Himself a people from every tribe, tongue, and nation. God predetermined or predestinated this from before the foundation of the world (Ephesians 1:4) based solely on His sovereign will and not because of anything that He knew the people would do.

"Before God ever created the heavens and the earth, and a long time before we were ever born, God knew His elect in a personal way and chose them to be His sheep, not because they would someday follow Him but in order to guarantee that they would follow Him. His knowing them and choosing them is the reason they follow Him, not the other way around."

Election

The doctrine of election teaches that before God created the world, He chose (elected) certain people to be saved (redeemed).

> ... *He (God) hath chosen us in him (Christ) before the foundation of the world, that we should be holy and without blame before him in love* Ephesians 1:4 (KJV)

What did God choose us to be? *Holy and without blame before Him in love.* Unbelievable!

Writing for GotQuestions.org, Delores Kimball provided the following insight:

"Ephesians 1:4 says we were chosen in Him before the world was even created. We were in the mind of God to be saved by faith in Christ. That means God knit together Satan's rebellion, Adam and Eve's sin, the fall of the human race, and the death and crucifixion of Christ, all seemingly terrible events, to save us before He created us."
http://www.blogos.org/christianlifeandgrowth/in-charge-1-sovereignty-of-God.php

Numerous other scriptures refer to believers in Christ being chosen (Matthew 24:22, 31; Mark 13:20, 27; Romans 8:33, 9:11, 11:5-7, 28; Ephesians 1:11; Colossians 3:12; 1 Thessalonians 1:4; 1 Timothy 5:21; 2 Timothy 2:10; Titus 1:1; 1 Peter 1:1-2, 2:9; 2 Peter 1:10).

Many people, even professing Christians, protest that the doctrine of election is unfair. Here are some comments from *Foundations of Grace* by Dr. John MacArthur:

"To say that election is unfair is not only inaccurate, it fails to recognize the very essence of true fairness. That which is fair, and right, and just is that which God wills to do. Thus, if God wills to choose those whom He would save, it is inherently fair for Him to do so. We cannot impose our own ideas of fairness onto our understanding of God's working. Instead, we must go to the Scriptures to see how God Himself, in His perfect righteousness, decides to act.

"The Creator owes nothing to the creature, not even what He is graciously pleased to give. God does not act out of obligation and compulsion, but out of His own independent prerogative. That is what it means to be God. And because He is God, His freely determined actions are intrinsically right and perfect."

We are responsible to believe:

> *... from the beginning, God chose you to be saved through the sanctifying work of the [Holy] Spirit and through belief in the truth.* 2 Thessalonians 2:13 (NIV)

There are two sides to the coin of salvation: God's choosing (electing) us is one side; our responsibility to believe – to trust the Lord Jesus Christ as our Savior – is the other side.

> *To all who received Him, to those who believed in His name, he gave the right to become the children of God.* John 1:12 (NIV)

> *For God so loved the world that He gave His only begotten son that whosoever believes in Him should not perish but have everlasting life.* John 3:16 (KJV)

> *Everyone who calls on the name of the Lord will be saved.* Romans 10:13 (NIV)

Doesn't that sound like a person has a free will, that he or she can decide whether or not to accept the Lord Jesus Christ as Savior; that a person, by a deliberate act of his or her will, must choose to receive Christ? Yes, the Bible does teach that we can accept or reject Christ. (Ignoring Christ is the same as rejecting Him – John 3:18.)

So how do we reconcile these two seemingly contradictory teachings – that God chooses some to be saved, and that man must, by an act of his will, accept Christ as his Savior?

The short answer is "we can't." The Bible teaches that man has a free will and must choose Christ in order to be saved. The Bible also teaches that God elects and predestines some to be saved. Both facts are equally are true, even though our limited minds cannot comprehend how this could be. But God understands it – it's His plan!

With our finite minds we sometimes don't understand the ways of our infinite, omniscient God, but from what He has revealed about Himself in His word – and in our lives – we know that we can trust Him absolutely, with no reservations. Our God, the one true God, is a good God. Everything He does is good. He cannot do – or be – otherwise. When He grants mercy, He is good. When He withholds mercy, He is good. When He elects some and not others – for reasons known only to Him – He is good and just and fair.

Ultimately, we must rest in the fact that anyone who desires to be saved, to become a true child of God through faith in Christ, can do so (John 6:37). We have to rely on, rest in, the fairness of God.

God is not being unfair to those who are not chosen, because they are receiving what they deserve. We have all sinned (Romans 3:23) and are all worthy of eternal punishment (Romans 6:23). No one deserves to be saved. God's choosing to be gracious to some is not unfair to the others. No one deserves anything from God; therefore, no one can object if he does not receive anything from God.

Think of salvation as an archway. Written above the arch are the words "Whosoever will may come" (Revelation 22:17). When a person accepts Christ as Savior and walks through that arch he or she turns around and over the archway are the words "Chosen in Him before the foundation of the world" (Ephesians 1:4).

Willful Misunderstanding

Unfortunately, some people choose to misunderstand foreknowledge, predestination, and election – perhaps so they can justify a hedonistic lifestyle.

Below is a reasoned – and reasonable – answer to such people. It's from Paul E. Little's book, *Know What You Believe,* originally published in 1976.

"The popular misconception of election and predestination as the arbitrary acts of a capricious tyrant is totally foreign and unfair to Scripture. The attitude often expressed by unbelievers is that if they are elect, they'll get into heaven anyway, and if they're not, there's no use in their trying. In either case, they reason, they needn't be concerned. This is a tragic misconception. No one in hell will be able to tell God, 'I wanted to be saved, but my name was on the wrong list.'

"Election and predestination are always to salvation and its blessings – never to judgment. It is true that no one believes on the Savior unless God the Holy Spirit convicts him, but it is also true that those who do not trust Christ choose not to believe. God never refuses to save anyone who wants salvation.

"It is important to realize that all men are sinners and are under the judgment of God. 'God in sovereign freedom treats some sinners as they deserve ... but He selects others to be vessels of mercy,' receiving the 'riches of His glory' (Romans 9:22-23). This discrimination involves no injustice, for the Creator owes mercy to none and has a right to do as He pleases with His rebellious creatures (Romans. 9:14-21). The wonder is not that He withholds mercy from some, but that He should be gracious to any."

6. Salvation and Security

*"We believe the Lord Jesus Christ died for our sins according to the Scriptures as a **representative and substitutionary sacrifice** for **all people** and all who trust Him are **saved by grace through faith** on the grounds of His **shed blood, accepted in the beloved, kept** by God's power, and thus **secure in Christ forever.** (John 1:12; 6:37-40; 10:27-30; Romans 8:1,38-39; 1 Corinthians 1:4-8; Ephesians 1:6-7; 2:8-10; 1 Peter 1:5,18-19)*

*"We believe every saved person is a **new creation** with provision made for **victory over sin** through the power of the **indwelling Holy Spirit**. The sin that is present in us is not eradicated in this life. (2 Corinthians 5:17; Romans 6:13; 8:12-13; Galatians 5:16-25; Ephesians 4:22-24; Colossians 3:10; 1 Peter 1:14-16; 1 John 3:5-9)*

*"We believe it is the privilege of believers to rejoice in the **assurance of their salvation** through the testimony of God's Word, which, however, clearly forbids the use of **Christian liberty** as an occasion to the **flesh**. (Romans 13:13-14; Galatians 5:13; Titus 2:11-15; 1 Peter 2:13-20)"*

The words appearing in **bold** text in the paragraphs above are explained in this study note. Here's where to find those words – and more – in this note:

Representative and Substitutionary Sacrifice

In His death, the Lord Jesus Christ represented us, He was our substitute, He died in our place, paying the penalty that was due for our sins. For additional information, refer to the study note entitled *The Person and Work of Christ*, point three of the BMW Doctrinal Statement.

All People

Christ's sacrificial death was sufficient to cover (atone for) the sins of all people – the whole world. This is known as "unlimited atonement."

> *For there is one God, and one mediator between God and men, the man Christ Jesus; Who gave himself a ransom* for all, to be testified in due time.* 1 Timothy 2:5-6 (KJV)

> * A ransom is a payment made to secure the release of something or someone in bondage. What Paul is describing here is *redemption* – the loosing from bondage by payment of a price. That's what the Lord Jesus Christ did for us. He voluntarily laid down His life to release us from bondage to Satan, sin, and eternal condemnation!

Although Christ's death paid the penalty due for our sins, the gift of salvation is not a possession until it's personally received.

Unlimited atonement and limited atonement are further described in *The Person And Work Of Christ*, the study note for point three of the BMW Doctrinal Statement.

Saved (Salvation)

Salvation is the state (condition) of being rescued (saved, delivered) from the power and penalty of sin. It is a spiritual rebirth, frequently referred to as being "born again" (John 3:3, 1 Peter 1:3, 23).

We are saved through – on the basis of – the blood of Christ. The BMW statement expresses it thusly: "all who trust Him are saved by grace through faith on the grounds of His shed blood." The Protestant Reformers stated it succinctly: "Salvation is by grace alone through faith alone in Christ alone."

The Lord Jesus Christ is the only way to God. Jesus said,

> *I am the way, and the truth, and the life; no man comes to the Father but through me* John 14:6 (NASB)

Speaking of the Lord Jesus Christ, the Apostle Peter told the jailer in Jerusalem,

> *And there is salvation in no one else; for there is no other name under heaven that has been given among men by which we must be saved.* Acts 4:12 (NASB)

The Apostle Paul told the Christians at Galatia

> *For you are all children of God through faith in Christ Jesus* Galatians 3:26 (NLT)

A Survey of Major Biblical Doctrines – Salvation and Security

The Apostle John made it very clear:

The one who believes in the Son has eternal life, but the one who refuses to believe in the Son will not see life; instead, the wrath of God remains on him. John 3:36 (HCSB)

Other religious traditions and cults recognize – and some claim to worship – Jesus Christ, but their Jesus is not the One revealed in the Bible, he is "another Jesus" as the Apostle Paul wrote in 2 Corinthians 11:4. Only the true Jesus of the Bible died for our sins and has the power to save us.

Speaking of Himself, the Lord Jesus Christ said

… if you do not believe that I AM, you will die in your sins. John 8:24 (NKJV)

The Lord Jesus Christ is here claiming to be the great and eternal I AM. He's saying, "If you don't believe that I AM Jehovah, your Savior, your Redeemer, you will die in your sins." (Isaiah 49:26)

The person who ignores Christ, or rejects the salvation He offers, will, as the verse above says, die in his or her sins and spend eternity separated from God. William Romaine, an eighteenth-century English cleric, explains the phrase, *die in your sins.*

"Dying in sin is a clear expression, whose meaning cannot be easily mistaken. It denotes the most dreadful state of departing sinners, who have no mediator or atonement in the world of spirits to which they are going, but they leave this world with all the pollution and guilt of their crimes upon the soul; and when they appear before the tribunal of infinite justice, the horrid deformity and wickedness of them will then be manifest; they will then have no robe to cover the offensive and nauseous leprosy of their impurities; their abominable filthiness will then break out, and how can the most holy and pure God look with delight upon those loathsome lepers? He declares He cannot. He is of purer eyes than to behold the least iniquity. He cannot behold them; and therefore they must be shut out of His presence, as the lepers were shut out of the camp; and since they can never be made clean, they must be shut out forever." Excerpted from *The Self-Existence of Jesus Christ*

When you accept the Lord Jesus Christ as your Savior from sin,

- Your sins – all of them: past, present, future – are forgiven on the basis of Christ's sacrificial death in your place

- You are justified – declared righteous (in right standing with God) and not guilty of your sins

- You are adopted into God's spiritual family, becoming a true child of God

- You are rescued from a future eternity in Hell – the Lake of Fire

Salvation is available to anyone desiring it. Christ died for the sins of all people (1 Timothy 2:5-6). He promised that those who come to Him earnestly desiring salvation will not be turned away (John 6:37). No one needs to perish – God is not desirous that any should perish but that all should come to repentance (2 Peter 3:9).

God doesn't condemn anyone to Hell; a man condemns himself by his refusal to accept the free gift of salvation purchased by the death of the Lord Jesus Christ (Romans 6:23; Ephesians 2:8-9). But the gift He offers is not a possession until we receive it.

In the gospel bearing his name, the Apostle John clearly expounded the good news of salvation – and how men and women condemn themselves despite God's gracious provision for their salvation. Here's John 3:16, arguably the best-known verse in the Bible:

> *For God so loved the world, that he gave his only begotten Son, that whosoever believeth in him should not perish, but have everlasting life.* (KJV)

In this verse, note that "perish" and "everlasting life" are separated by the word "but," indicating that they are opposite results. One (perishing) is the result of failing to trust Christ as Savior, the other (everlasting life) is the result of trusting Christ. Note also that there is no middle ground. A person either accepts Christ and is granted eternal life in God's presence, or she or he perishes – goes into eternal ruin at death to spend eternity in conscious torment under the wrath of God.

God sent His Son to save, not condemn, the world (John 3:17):

> *For God sent not his Son into the world to condemn the world; but that the world through him might be saved.*

Since that's true, how do people condemn themselves? The next verse – John 3:18 – answers that question:

> *He that believeth on him is not condemned: but he that believeth not is condemned already, because he hath not believed in the name of the only begotten Son of God.*

People condemn themselves by refusing to (*believe*) in the name of the only begotten Son of God. It's done by ignoring or consciously rejecting Christ.

A man condemns himself because he prefers sin to God, thus will not believe in the name of the only begotten Son of God. Note verse 19:

> *And this is the condemnation, that light is come into the world, and men loved darkness rather than light because their deeds were evil.*

The Light that came into the world is the Lord Jesus Christ; He is the Light of the World (John 8:12). The refusal to come to the Light for salvation condemns a person to remain in spiritual darkness – now and for eternity.

God is offering each of us the gift of salvation through His Son. Have you received it? Remember, a gift is not a possession until it's received.

The proper motive for inviting Christ into your life is to save you, to rescue you, from the penalty due God for your personal sins. It is not to help you get a job, or improve your health, or resolve problems with your spouse or children, etc. Those needs and problems, serious as they may be, are temporal – they won't outlast your mortal life. But your sin debt, and the penalty it incurs, is immortal – it affects your eternal destiny. The Lord Jesus Christ died as your substitute to fully pay that debt so it could be forgiven. His death provided the only remedy for the debt of your sin. Can He solve those other problems (employment, health, relationships, finances, etc.)? Of course – and in a way that's best for you! He's omnipotent and omniscient. Nothing is too hard for Him. But your first need is to have your sins forgiven so you can spend eternity with Him. Your sin is the only thing that will keep you out of Heaven. That's the reason you need to invite Christ into your life as your Savior from sin.

At the moment of salvation – when a person first trusts the Lord Jesus Christ as their Savior from sin – he or she instantly becomes a saint, a holy one, because God imputes to him or her the righteousness of Christ Himself (2 Corinthians 5:21). ["Saint" comes from the same root word as "holy."]

By means of a procedure known as "canonization," some religious traditions designate specific deceased people, those whose lives they consider to have been especially holy, as "saints." These saints are venerated – revered, respected, held in high esteem – and prayed to. The person praying to a saint petitions the saint to intercede with God on his or her behalf, or for the benefit of another person, living or in purgatory.

Glory, honor, and praise belong to God alone; He is the only One worthy of worship. Nowhere in the Bible are we told to revere, pray to, rely on, or worship anyone but God. Directing our prayers to anyone other than God is anti-biblical and robs Him of the glory that is His alone.

Prayers to a venerated dead saint are not – and cannot be – heard. Praying to a dead saint borders on necromancy (consulting the dead), which is strictly forbidden in Scripture (Deuteronomy 18:11). The living Lord Jesus Christ is the only true, qualified intermediary between man and God (1 Timothy 2:5); not another living person (a priest)*, not a dead saint.

> * For additional information, refer to the Supplemental Information at the end of *The Church*, the study note for point seven of the BMW Doctrinal Statement.

Bottom line: God, not man, determines who is a saint. And He has told us in His written Word that everyone who is born into His spiritual family by personal faith in the Lord Jesus Christ is a saint (1 Corinthians 1:2; Acts 9:13, 32; Ephesians 4:12).

By Grace Through Faith

The Bible clearly teaches that salvation is entirely a gift of God, apart from any human works.

For by grace are ye saved through faith, and that not of yourselves, it is the gift of God, not of works lest any man should boast Ephesians 2:8-9 (KJV)

Not by works of righteousness which we have done, but according to His mercy He saved us, by the washing of regeneration* and renewing of the Holy Ghost Titus 3:5 (KJV)

> * Water baptism symbolizes – but is not – the "washing of regeneration," the regenerative cleansing performed by the Holy Spirit when we invite Christ into our lives as our Savior from sin.

Biblical Christianity teaches that Christ's bodily resurrection assures that God the Father was completely satisfied with the blood sacrifice of His Son, that the sin debt was paid in full. Christ's cry from the cross, "It is finished" (Greek *tetelestai*), literally means "paid in full."

The Bible teaches that good works are an evidence of salvation, a natural outpouring of true faith, not the basis of, or a requirement for, salvation.

> *Even so faith, if it hath not works, is dead, being alone*   James 2:17

When considering the teaching of James chapter 2, you must read verses 17 - 24 inclusive. In verse 23, we are told that righteousness (right standing before God) was imputed to Abraham because of his faith – his salvation was the result of his faith. Verse 24 tells us that a person is shown to be justified by his works. In other words, works are a proof that a person has been justified. We are not saved by works; works have no part in our salvation, but works are proof that faith is genuine.

Human works without true salvation have no eternal value.

What then is required to inherit eternal life? Perfection. The Bible says that nothing that defiles can enter Heaven (Revelation 21:27). Jesus said we must be perfect as God the Father is perfect (Matthew 5:48). No one will ever enter Heaven or dwell there who isn't perfect. Regardless of how good you are, or how many good works you do, you cannot be perfect. You are a sinner by nature and by deed (Romans 3:23). Only the blood of the sinless Son of God can wash away those sins and make you perfect in God's sight (Revelation 1:5).

If "works" (human efforts) are required to complete our salvation, as some traditions teach, the natural question is, "How many works are sufficient to 'earn' that salvation?" With a works-based salvation, can you ever have the assurance that your salvation is secure? The answer should be obvious.

(Christ's) Shed Blood

It is the blood of the Lord Jesus Christ, willingly, lovingly, shed for us on the cross of Calvary, that makes our salvation possible. It is only the blood of Christ that removes, washes away, the guilt and stain of our sin.

> *To Him who loved us and washed us from our sins in His own blood, and has made us kings and priests* to His God and Father, to Him be glory and dominion forever and ever, amen.*   Revelation 1:5b-6 (NKJV)

> *   The Lord Jesus Christ made us priests – we don't need a human intercessor to go to Him (1 Peter 2:5). This is discussed in more detail in *The Church*, the study note for point seven of the BMW Doctrinal Statement.

Leviticus 17:11 contains the profound scientific truth that "the life of the flesh is in the blood." Blood is the life source of all living things. When Christ shed His blood, he was literally giving His life for us. No other type of death could purchase our salvation.

... the law requires that nearly everything be cleansed with blood, and without the shedding of blood there is no forgiveness Hebrews 9:22 (NIV)

If Christ had not shed His blood, we would have no chance to be saved, because there would have been no forgiveness. God requires death as payment for sin (Romans 6:23). Christ's death was that payment.

The first shedding of innocent blood to cover (atone for) sin occurred in the Garden of Eden when God killed (executed) animals to provide skins to cover the nakedness of Adam and Eve – a result of their first sin (Genesis 3:21). This was the institution of the Old Testament Sacrificial System.

Sacrificing innocent animals was a reminder of mans' sinfulness before God. Offering an animal sacrifice temporarily covered the guilt of the offeror (Leviticus 1:4), but the sin remained – it was not removed. It was not until the death of the Lord Jesus Christ that the actual sins were cleansed. Animal sacrifices simply pointed forward to the future perfect sacrifice Whose blood would permanently cleanse sin.

James Emery White wrote the following regarding the Old Testament (Jewish) system of sacrificing animals:

> "The sacrifice of an animal was a common way for people of that culture to make amends for their sins. It sounds strange to us today, but there was a very important idea behind it. They saw sin as something serious, deadly and gruesome, something that could cost them their life before a holy God. So it was only through some type of atoning, sacrificial death – something equally serious, deadly and gruesome – that the sin could be addressed." Printed in the June, 2012, issue of *Decision* magazine.

Animal sacrifices had to be repeated year after year because the blood of an animal couldn't take away sin – it was an imperfect sacrifice (Hebrews 10:1-4). The sacrificial death of the Lord Jesus Christ did not have to be repeated because He is the One Perfect Sacrifice (Hebrews 10:10) – He is *the Lamb of God that taketh away the sin of the world* (John 1:29 – KJV).

With the death of the Lord Jesus Christ, animal sacrifices were no longer necessary – although the unbelieving Jews continued animal sacrifices until the second Temple was destroyed in A.D. 70 by the Roman General Titus.

God's requirement that innocent blood be shed to atone for sin indicates how seriously He views sin. Would God have sacrificed His only Son if there was any other way to provide for the forgiveness of our sins?

Who Has The Power To Forgive Sins?

Some religious traditions teach that their priests, who they claim are successors to the apostles, are authorized to forgive – absolve – sins. They base that claim on one Scripture passage:

> [21]*Jesus therefore said to them again, "Peace be with you; as the Father has sent Me, I also send you."* [22]*And when He had said this, He breathed on them, and said to them, "Receive the Holy Spirit.* [23]*If you forgive the sins of any, their sins have been forgiven them; if you retain the sins of any, they have been retained."* John 20:21-23 (NASB)

Context: The Lord Jesus Christ is meeting with the apostles after His resurrection. He is soon to return to Heaven. In this passage He's commissioning Peter and the others (and, by extension, all disciples including us) to the task of evangelizing the world.

In verse 21, Christ tells the apostles, "I'm sending you." In verse 22, He gives them the Holy Spirit, the One Who will empower them for the task, convict people of sin, and effect the salvation of those who believe. In verse 23, the Lord tells the apostles what will be the result of their evangelization: If people trust Christ as their Savior from sin, their sins will be forgiven; if they don't, their sins will be retained. The evangelists would simply confirm on earth what had already taken place in Heaven as a result of a person's faith or lack thereof.

Christians are ambassadors for our Savior (2 Corinthians 5:20). God makes His appeal to lost mankind through us. He has given us the privilege of proclaiming forgiveness of sins through faith in His name.

Being God, the Lord Jesus Christ could – and did – forgive sins (Matthew 9:2, Mark 2:5, Luke 7:47), but He never communicated that power to His disciples, and the disciples never assumed any such power to themselves or pretended to exercise it.

The apostle's preaching in the Book of Acts always stressed the forgiveness of sins through faith in Christ (example: Acts 10:43-44). To the people who trusted Christ, the apostles could declare with confidence that their sins had been forgiven in Heaven. To those who rejected Christ, the message was that their sins had been retained in Heaven.

Bottom line: Only God can forgive sins (Luke 5:21). No man, regardless of position, has the power to forgive sins. God never gave man that authority.

For additional information refer to the Supplemental Information at the end of *The Church*, the study note for point seven of the BMW Doctrinal Statement.

Accepted in the Beloved

The Greek word for accepted, *charitoo*, means "graciously honored" and "transfused with grace." This same Greek word is used in Luke 1:28 when the angel told Mary that she was "highly favored" of God and would bear the baby Jesus. That's also our standing with God – highly favored in Christ, God's beloved Son!

Kept

"Kept" means "preserved," "protected," "being guarded," "being watched over." This refers to God watching over us, guarding us, protecting us on our spiritual journey from the day of our conversion (salvation) to the day when He calls us home to be with Himself forever.

As the BMW statement indicates, we are *kept by God's power*, with the result that we are *thus secure in Christ*. If we have experienced true conversion, God will keep us safe and not allow us ultimately to fall away from Himself.

> (We) *are kept by the power of God through faith unto salvation ready to be revealed in the last time.*
> 1 Peter 1:5 (KJV)

Closely related to the doctrine of God's keeping (protecting) His saints is the doctrine known as "The Perseverance of the Saints." That's discussed immediately below.

Perseverance

"The perseverance of the saints teaches that once God has renewed the heart of a sinner through the application of the redemption wrought by Christ upon the cross, he will continue to be saved and show forth the fruits of that salvation. The sinner perseveres because of Christ, but he continually shows himself as one who has been changed by Christ. God has saved the individual and will sanctify* him until the end when he is ultimately glorified*, and in heaven. It does not mean man has a license to sin. Those who think they have a license to sin are not changed and saved by grace. They are still in sin. Those who are saved by grace and changed, desire to show forth the fruits of that salvation. God motions the heart to good work, and continues that good work to the end."
Accessed at http://www.apuritansmind.com/tulip/PerseveranceOfTheSaints.htm

> * Sanctification and glorification are described in the Supplemental Information at the end of this study note.

Bottom line: True saints persevere (continue) in the faith by God's power.

Eternal Security

The doctrine of eternal security teaches that …

"… you cannot lose your salvation. Because the Father has elected, the Son has redeemed, and the Holy Spirit has applied salvation, those thus saved are eternally secure. They are eternally secure in Christ. Some of the verses for this position are John 10:27-28 where Jesus said His sheep will never perish; John 6:47 where salvation is described as everlasting life; Romans 8:1 where it is said we have passed out of judgment; 1 Corinthians 10:13 where God promises to never let us be tempted beyond what we can handle; and Philippians 1:6 where God is the one being faithful to perfect us until the day of Jesus' return."
http://www.calvinistcorner.com/tulip.htm

The indented paragraphs below were excerpted from the book *A Survey of Bible Doctrine* by Dr. Charles C. Ryrie.

"Can a true believer ever lose his salvation by either sinning or ceasing to believe or in any other way?

"The doctrine of security, in the last analysis, depends on what God has done, so that if one can lose his salvation, then certain works of God would have to be undone or reversed. For instance,

"1. When we are saved, the Holy Spirit places us into the body of Christ (1 Corinthians 12:13). Now if a believer can lose his salvation, he would be removed from the body at that time; no such idea is even hinted in the Scriptures.

"2. Furthermore, the Holy Spirit seals the believer until the day of redemption (Ephesians 1:13; 4:30). Losing one's salvation would have to involve breaking that seal before the day of redemption.

"3. Also, it is the Father's purpose to keep us in spite of everything (John 10:28-30; 13:1) and ultimately to present us faultless in His own presence (Jude 24).

"4. But undoubtedly the most convincing Scripture reference about security is Romans 8:29-39. Notice the pileup of evidence.

- First, those who were predestined, called and justified are also said to be glorified. The past tense can be used of a future event only because it is so certain that not one will be lost. The chain from foreknowledge through predestinating, calling and justifying remains unbroken until all are glorified.

- Second, no one can charge God's elect with anything that could cause them to lose their salvation because the Judge (God) before whom such a charge would be tried is the same one who justifies (verse 33); that is, the Judge has already pronounced us righteous (to justify means to declare righteous). If anyone does bring a charge, what chance would he have of success when the accused has been declared righteous by the presiding Judge?

- Third, our Lord is continually making intercession for us, and that in itself is enough to keep us saved (verse 34, Cf. 1 John 2:1).

- Fourth, the chapter closes with the certain and sweeping promise that nothing (including ourselves 'nor any other [created thing]' verse 39) can separate us from the love of God which is in Christ Jesus our Lord. That pretty well plugs every loophole!"

Dr. Woodrow Kroll, Bible teacher on the *Back to the Bible* broadcast, commented that we didn't get ourselves into Christ, and we can't get ourselves out!

New Creation

When we accept the Lord Jesus Christ as our Savior from sin we become new creations, new creatures, in Christ:

Therefore, if any man be in Christ, he is a new creation (creature): old things are passed away; behold, all things are become new. 2 Corinthians 5:17 (KJV)

Becoming a new creature in Christ includes the creation of a new nature within us. This new nature is a true creative miracle of God! The new nature is not a rejuvenation of the old sinful nature we inherited from Adam, the federal head of mankind, it is totally new — and it is perfect:

… put off concerning the former conversation (your previous manner of life) *the old man, which is corrupt according to the deceitful lusts; And be renewed in the spirit of your mind; And … put on the new man, which after God is created in righteousness and true holiness.* Ephesians 4:22-24 (KJV)

Every true Christian has within himself or herself a totally holy, perfect, righteous new nature created by God! That's what enables us to live a life pleasing to God, through the power of the Holy Spirit.

Victory Over Sin

God has given us the ability to be victorious over the sin in our lives. Although we become new creatures in Christ at the moment of salvation, the old sinful nature is still resident within us, tempting us to sin. As the BMW Statement indicates, *the sin (nature) that is present in us is not eradicated in this life.*

God's provision for our victory over sin is indicated in Romans 6:2:

We died to sin; how can we live in it any longer? (NIV)

The Greek word translated "died" is in the aorist tense, indicating a once-for-all-time action completed at a specific time in the past. We died to sin (the sinful nature) at the moment of our salvation, when the Holy Spirit baptized us into union with Christ (Romans 6:3-4). Our death to sin is a fact, not an experience. Feelings have nothing to do with it. Whether you feel like it or not, you have died to sin!

… our old man* is crucified with (Christ), that the body of sin might be destroyed**, that henceforth we should not serve sin. For he that is dead is freed from sin. Romans 6:6-7 (KJV)

> * In Romans 6, the old man is personified as a "body" that can be put to death. The old man ("old self" in many translations) is the person you were spiritually before you trusted the Lord Jesus Christ as Savior, when you were still under sin [Romans 3:9], powerless and ungodly [Romans 5:6], a sinner [Romans 5:8], and an enemy of God [Romans 5:10].
>
> ** Greek *katargeō*, meaning "to make of none effect," "render ineffective."

Because we died to sin, we don't have to let it reign (be our master) in our lives. In fact, we're instructed to not let it reign.

Let not sin therefore reign in your mortal body, that ye should obey it in the lusts thereof. Neither yield ye your members as instruments of unrighteousness unto sin: but yield yourselves unto God, as those that are alive from the dead, and your members as instruments of righteousness unto God. For sin shall not have dominion over you: for ye are not under the law, but under grace. Romans 6:12-14 (KJV)

Note that Paul is admitting that we can continue to sin after salvation: He starts this passage with *Let not sin therefore reign* – in other words, *Don't allow sin to reign.* It's a deliberate choice.

"We have been set free from the reign and rule of sin, the kingdom of unrighteousness. Our deliverance is through our union with Christ in His death. When Christ entered the world He voluntarily entered the realm of sin, though He never sinned. When He died, He died to this realm of sin (Romans 6:10), and through our union with Him, we died to this realm also. We are to count on this fact that we are dead to sin's rule, that we can stand up to it and say no. Therefore, we are to guard our bodies so that sin does not reign in us." Excerpted from *The Pursuit of Holiness* by Jerry Bridges

The two paragraphs below are from Dr. John MacArthur's book, *The Glory of Heaven*.

"As unredeemed sinners, we were full-time slaves of sin – willing servants, in fact. As Christians who are not yet glorified, we are 'captives,' unwilling prisoners of an already-defeated enemy. Although sin can buffet and abuse us, it does not own us, and it cannot ultimately destroy us. Sin's authority and dominion are broken. It 'lies close at hand' (Romans 7:21), but it is no longer our master. Our real allegiance is now to the principle of righteousness (verse 22). It is in this sense that 'the new has come' (2 Corinthians 5:17). Even though we still fall into old patterns of sinful thinking and behavior, those things no longer define who we are. Sin is now an anomaly and an intruder, not the sum and substance of our character.

"God is changing us from the inside out. He has planted the incorruptible seed of eternal life deep in the believer's soul. We have a new desire and a new power to please God. We have a new heart and a whole new love for God. All those are factors that contribute to our ultimate growth in grace."

Why can we be victorious over sin? Because at the moment of salvation, when the Holy Spirit baptized us into union with Christ's death, burial, and resurrection, we died to the mastery of sin, breaking its power over us, rendering it ineffective. Because of this, we no longer have to be slaves to sin (the old sin nature). Our dying to sin provided the enablement to live a new life.

How can we be victorious over sin? For our death to sin to be effective in our lives, we must choose to put off the old nature and yield, offer, ourselves to God. How does this work out in practice?

- First, we must have a desire to be victorious over sin. If you enjoy a particular sin, ask God to give you a hatred for it.

- Then, when the old nature prompts you to do something you know is wrong, refuse to do it, claiming the truth that you have died to sin, that the sin nature is no longer your master, and ask God's help to make that a reality in your life at that moment.

For additional information regarding personal holiness, refer to *Separation and Unity*, the study note for point seventeen of the BMW Doctrinal Statement.

As we've seen, victory over sin is possible. Does this mean we can achieve "sinless perfection" – get to the point where we sin no more?

Sinless Perfection?

…ye know that (Christ) was manifested to take away our sins; and in him is no sin. Whosoever abideth in him sinneth not: whosoever sinneth hath not seen him, neither known him. 1 John 3:5-6 (KJV)

Does this passage teach that we can achieve "sinless perfection," as some suggest? (This "perfectionism" was a heresy in the Apostle John's day also!) Does this passage contradict John's statements in 1 John 1:8, 10 where he tells us that all Christians sin?

The following paragraphs were excerpted from *The Bible Knowledge Commentary.* (The shaded text is my editorial comment.)

"John's point is simple and straightforward. Sin is a product of ignorance and blindness toward God: *'whosoever sinneth hath not seen him, neither known him'* (verse 6b). Sin can never come out of seeing and knowing God.

"Sin can never be a part of the experience of abiding in Christ: *'Whosoever abideth in him sinneth not'* (verse 6a).

"The regenerate life is, in one sense, an essentially and fundamentally sinless life. For the believer, sin is abnormal and unnatural; his whole bent of life is away from sin*.

> * The opposite is true of the unsaved. Their natural inclination (bent) is toward sin. That's also true of the old nature within each believer, but we also have the new, sinless nature which does not have that proclivity.

"The fact remains, however, that Christians do not experience the sinless life perfectly on this earth; hence 1:8 and 1:10 remain true. The Christian still experiences a genuine struggle with the flesh and overcomes its impulses only by the help of the Holy Spirit (Galatians 5:16-26).

"Paul's thinking also conforms to this view. In his struggle with sin, he was able to conclude, *'Now if I do that I would not, it is no more I that do it, but sin that dwelleth in me'* (Romans 7:20). In this way, Paul could perceive sin as not a real part of what he was at the most inward level of his being (Romans 7:25).

"All sin is devilish (1 John 3:8); it does not stem from the believer's regenerate nature*, God's seed. ... The 'new man' is an absolutely perfect new creation**. ... Sin is not, nor ever can be, anything but satanic. It can never spring from what a Christian truly is at the level of his regenerate being."

> * Sin doesn't originate in the new nature because it cannot sin.
>
> ** *... the new man ... was created according to God in true righteousness and holiness.* Ephesians 4:24 (NKJV)

The Amplified Bible translation of 1 John 3:6 presents a more traditional meaning – that a biblical Christian does not willfully, habitually sin (i.e., with forethought), and that the person who does habitually sin really doesn't know God; he or she hasn't been born again:

No one who abides in Him [who lives and remains in communion with and in obedience to Him – deliberately, knowingly, and habitually] commits (practices) sin. No one who [habitually] sins has either seen or known him [recognized, perceived, or understood Him, or has had an experiential acquaintance with Him].

In *The New Defender's Study Bible*, Dr. Henry Morris allows for both possibilities – that the new nature is the referent, and that a believer doesn't habitually sin.

> "Two solutions can be suggested to what looks at first like an inconsistency. The believer has two natures—the old man and the new man (Colossians 3:9-10; Romans 7:16-17; 22-25). When he lapses into sin, it is not his new man, but the old man, since, as far as His new nature is concerned, '[God's] seed remaineth in him: and he cannot sin, because he is born of God' (1 John 3:9). The second possibility is that the words 'abideth' and 'sinneth' represent habitual action, not rigidly constant without exception. The verbs are in the continuing present tense, and so with later verses to the same effect (e.g., 1 John 3:7-10)."

I believe the two views above are basically positing the same thing: that the Christian who is "walking in the Spirit," "obedient to Christ," "abiding in Him" doesn't sin. When that person ceases to abide in Christ, ceases to walk in the Spirit, he or she is subject to fall into sin – but sin is not his or her habit. The person who sins habitually (purposely, with forethought) most likely doesn't have a new nature because they have never received Christ as Savior.

Indwelling Holy Spirit

At the moment of salvation, the Holy Spirit, the third Person of the Trinity, indwells us, takes up residence within us, sealing us in the family of God for eternity. This is discussed in more detail in the study note entitled *The Person and Work of the Holy Spirit*, point four of the BMW Doctrinal Statement.

Assurance of Salvation

Assurance means freedom from doubt. God wants us to have the assurance of our salvation! Instead of looking for that assurance in subjective experiences, we should find it in the objective truth of God's Word. Consider the following passage:

> *And this is the testimony, that God gave us eternal life, and this life is in his Son. Whoever has the Son has life; whoever does not have the Son of God does not have life. I write these things to you who believe in the name of the Son of God that you may know that you have eternal life.* 1 John 5:11-13 (ESV)

Did you take note of the word "know" in the passage above? Read it again! Do you believe the Lord Jesus Christ died to pay the penalty for your sins (Romans 5:8, 2 Corinthians 5:21)? Do you trust Him alone for salvation (John 14:6)? If so, then you're saved, you "have the Son" and thus, eternal life (John 1:12).

After we are saved, the Holy Spirit witnesses (testifies) to our spirit that we are children of God.

> *And this is his commandment, That we should believe on the name of his Son Jesus Christ, and love one another, as he gave us commandment. And he that keepeth his commandments dwelleth in him, and he in him. And hereby we know that he abideth in us, by the Spirit which he hath given us.* 1 John 3:23-24 (KJV)

> *The Spirit Himself bears witness with our spirit that we are children of God.* Romans 8:16 (ESV)

The Apostle John gave us a number of tests for knowing that our faith in God is true faith, not just mental assent to a tenet of faith (1 John 2:3, 5-6, 29; 3:2-3, 14, 18-19).

The Protestant Reformers coined the phrase, "It is faith alone that saves, but the faith that saves is never alone." Meaning? Obedience to Christ's words is the authentication of our faith.

In his book, *The Invitation: The Not-So-Simple Truth About Following Jesus*, Pastor Greg Sidders expressed it succinctly, "Obedience *to* Jesus is the acid test of faith *in* Jesus."

Christian Liberty

Christian liberty is being free from having to fulfill a legal code to please God, and free from the frustration of not being able to keep an external set of rules. In a positive sense, it is the freedom to function by the internal working of the Holy Spirit.

Although we have the assurance of eternal life because of our faith in the Lord Jesus Christ, and our salvation is secure, we weren't set free in Christ to do whatever we want. Christian liberty is not liberty to indulge the flesh.

You're not free to use your liberty as a springboard for the flesh. Those who think they have a license to sin are not changed and saved by grace. They are still in sin.

Flesh

In the New Testament, "flesh" refers to our fallen human nature, the part of us that is prone to sin or to rebel against God's will. It is the "old man" (Colossians 3:9), the corrupt nature of man, subject to the filthy appetites and passions. It is the indwelling principle of sin, the tendency to sin that remains even in the redeemed person.

The BMW Doctrinal Statement informs us that *God's Word … forbids the use of Christian liberty as an occasion to the flesh.* In other words, our liberty in Christ is not to be used to justify sinful acts.

What About Those Who Have Never Heard The Gospel? Can They Be Saved?

Our Spiritual Condition

Every person's native spiritual condition can be described by a four-letter word: LOST. We are by nature sinners, doomed to perish, to spend eternity apart from God (Romans 3:10-12, 23; 6:23; John 3:18)*. The guilt of Adam's sin (Genesis 3:2-3, 6) was passed to all his descendents (Romans 5:12) – there are no exceptions.

> * For additional information, refer to *Eternal Life / Everlasting Punishment* on page 146.

Every person is totally depraved*; every aspect of our lives is affected by sin. We are sinners from birth (Psalm 51:5). We are all dead in trespasses and sins (Ephesians 2:1). Spiritually, the aborigine in a loin cloth is no different from the man in a three-piece suit in downtown Manhattan.

> * Total Depravity is discussed in *The Total Depravity of Man*, the study note for point five of the BMW Doctrinal Statement.

Mankind is innately religious, it's part of his nature from birth. Because God created us in His image, we possess an eternal spirit capable of communion and fellowship with Him. Thus, we have an innate sense that there must be Someone greater than ourselves (a priori argument – ontological), and, for various reasons, we have a desire to worship that One. If man doesn't have a knowledge of the one true God, or rejects that knowledge, he will invent – and worship – a god from his imagination (Romans 1:21-23).

Man knows he is a sinner; that's why he tries to appease God. Without a knowledge of God's true provision for our forgiveness, man turns to self-effort and self-punishment – trying to earn forgiveness.

God's Provision

God desires that all men be saved and come to a knowledge of the truth, but He will not force His salvation on anyone. We have the freedom to accept or reject that salvation.

> *The Lord is not slow to fulfill his promise as some count slowness, but is patient toward you, not wishing that any should perish, but that all should reach repentance.* (2 Peter 3:9 – ESV)

> (God) *desires all people to be saved and to come to the knowledge of the truth.* (1 Timothy 2:4 – ESV)

Sin is universal; God's provision for the forgiveness of sins likewise must be universal – and it is. Christ died for the sins of the whole world; His atonement is unlimited (1 Timothy 2:5-6).

The substitutionary death of the Lord Jesus Christ is the only provision God made for the forgiveness of our sins. It is the same for every person in every age. In principle and in God's foreknowledge and eternal plan, the Lord Jesus Christ, the Lamb of God, had been slain before the foundation of the world (1 Peter 1:18-20, Revelation 13:8). Our personal acceptance of Christ as our Savior from sin is the only way of salvation (Acts 4:12, John 1:12, 14:6). Thus, before a person can be saved, God must ultimately make him or her aware that He has provided a sacrifice for their sins. God has always given people enough revelation to exercise faith.

How It Happens

Because He is omniscient and omnipotent, God is able to communicate with each individual in a way he or she can understand. The infinite God has unlimited ways to make Himself known to man, and He knows how to tailor His message to each individual. To each person He gives a clear, understandable revelation of basic spiritual truth which, if acted upon positively, leads to the revelation of additional truth, and ultimately to the opportunity to make a decision regarding salvation.

What has God revealed to us and how has He revealed it?

- Through nature, God has revealed His existence and invisible attributes, His eternal power and Godhead (Godhood – His nature). Observing nature should tell us that the Person Who created this world must be infinitely more powerful, more knowledgeable, more ancient, than us. Romans 1:20 indicates that because God has made himself known to all men, all are without excuse. No one can claim ignorance of God's existence and power.

General revelation (revelation through nature) is not sufficient to produce salvation, but it either leads to the desire for more spiritual truth or produces condemnation as a result of rejecting the revelation.

- God created us with a conscience. We are moral, reasoning beings, created in God's image. We all innately know right from wrong, good from evil, based on the moral Law of God written in our hearts (Romans 2:15). At least initially, we know when we are doing wrong because our conscience convicts us. We can, of course, suppress our conscience, harden our heart, and become morally dull.

  The existence of a moral code must mean that there is a Lawgiver, Someone Who established the standards of right and wrong. When we transgress – overstep – those standards, we sin against the Lawgiver and stand guilty before Him. That realization should cause us to seek a means to obtain forgiveness.

- The Apostle John describes the Lord Jesus Christ as "The One Who is the True Light, Who gives light to everyone" (John 1:9a – NLT). The implication is that every person has enough God-given spiritual light to be responsible to Him.

If a person (of any ethnicity, in any age) comes to fear the one true God and desires to know Him more perfectly, God will, by some means, reveal Himself to them in sufficient detail for her or him to make a reasoned decision regarding salvation.

Cornelius (Acts 10) wanted to know God more perfectly – God sent Peter and other believers (verse 45) to present the Gospel. When an Ethiopian eunuch (Acts 8:25-39) didn't understand the Old Testament passage he was reading, God interrupted a revival to send Philip to the desert to explain the passage to the Ethiopian. After the Ethiopian believed and was baptized, God supernaturally snatched Philip away to continue his ministry.

Synopsis

If God went to such great lengths to reveal Himself to us, and loved us enough to send His only Son to pay the full penalty for the sins of every person (John 3:16) – and He did – then surely He will somehow make salvation available to all people.

God has provided ample evidence of His existence (in nature) and His moral law (in our hearts). People know enough for God to hold them accountable for responding to that evidence. If a person responds positively and desires further spiritual light, God will send it to him by some means. If, on the other hand, a person ultimately rejects the spiritual light they are given, their sin of unbelief dooms them.

Can people be saved without ever reading a Bible or hearing a missionary? The answer is, "yes." We have to rest on God's absolute fairness and justice. No one will be able to stand before Him at the judgment and truthfully say, "You never gave me a chance to be saved."

Infant Salvation

All salvation is based on the sovereign grace of God apart from anything we can do, achieve, or merit. This is true for all people, from infants to adults. We are all sinners by inheritance; sinners from conception (Psalm 51:5), guilty before God, morally corrupt, worthy of death. Regardless of their age or mental capacity, sinners are saved only by – on the basis of – the sacrificial work of the Lord Jesus Christ (John 14:6).

Children sin, but they are incapable of understanding the moral essence of their sin. They may have a basic (simple) understanding of what their parents told them to do or not to do, but they have no real understanding of good and evil, of sin and rebellion and righteousness, of their sinful condition or God's remedy for that condition. They are incapable of exercising a true repentance toward God and a saving faith. Thus, they are not accountable to God.

Because each child is different, there is no specific "age of accountability" when he or she becomes accountable to God, but there is a "condition of accountability."

In his sermon, *The Salvation of Babies Who Die*, Dr. John MacArthur explains it thusly:

> "All children who die before they reach the condition of accountability by which they convincingly understand their sin and corruption and embrace the gospel by faith are graciously saved eternally by God through the work of Jesus Christ, being elect by sovereign choice, innocent of willful sin, rebellion and unbelief by which works they would be justly condemned to eternal punishment."

Adults are justified by saving faith, infants are justified apart from faith because without the ability to understand sin and salvation, they cannot exercise that faith. Thus, people who die before they are able to comprehend the issues of sin and salvation go immediately to Heaven.

How About You?

Reader, have you accepted God's offer of salvation? You can do that right now, right where you are. You can pray a simple prayer like the one below or use your own words. God knows your heart.

> God, I know I am a sinner. I'm sorry for my sin. Forgive me. I want to turn from my sin. I now receive the Lord Jesus Christ as my Savior. I confess Him as my Lord. From now on I want to follow Him. Thank you for saving me. I pray this in the name of Jesus. Amen

Supplemental Information

Salvation, Justification, Sanctification, Glorification

Salvation – being spiritually born into God's family, becoming a true child of God – occurs immediately as a result of having personally invited the Lord Jesus Christ into your life as your Savior from sin. At that moment, you permanently possess eternal salvation.

Salvation results in God instantly *justifying* and *positionally sanctifying* the new Christian. From that point, God expects us to grow spiritually, to progress in our Christian life, becoming more like His Son – a process known as *practical sanctification*. Ultimately, we will be *glorified* – made perfect as our Savior is perfect – to spend eternity in Heaven with Him, free from sin.

The chart below presents the essential elements of justification, sanctification, and glorification.

What	When	Description	Requires	References
Justification (being declared righteous and not guilty of sin)	Past	We *have been saved* from the *penalty* of sin. This occurs at the moment of salvation. It is a once-for-all-time event.	Christ's death and resurrection.	Romans 3:28, 5:1; Galatians 3:24
Sanctification (progressively becoming more Christlike in this life)	Present	We *are in the process of being saved* from the *power* (control) of sin. This is an ongoing process, not an event.	Christ's ascension and present advocacy.	John 17:17; Ephesians 5:25-26; 1 Thessalonians 5:23; Hebrews 10:10; Romans 8:29
Glorification (being made perfect)	Future	At our death or at Christ's return, *we will be saved* from the *presence* of sin. There is no sin in Heaven! Glorification is an event.	Our demise or Christ's second coming.	Romans 8:30; 1 Corinthians 13:10-13; 1 John 3:2; Revelation 21:27

Positional sanctification, our being set apart for God at the moment of salvation, is a result of the Savior's death on our behalf:

> ... *we are sanctified through (by means of) the offering of the body of Jesus Christ once for all*
> Hebrews 10:10 (KJV)

Practical sanctification (also known as *consecration*) is the dynamic process of turning from the secular and sinful and becoming more Christlike. The words *sanctification* and *holiness* have the same Greek root (*hagiasmos*), meaning "set apart," "separate."

Here's an excellent description of practical sanctification:

> "Sanctification begins with regeneration (salvation), the implanting of spiritual life in a believer. From that starting point, sanctification is God's progressively separating a believer from sin to Himself and transforming his total life experience toward holiness and purity. The process of sanctification for a believer never ends while he is on this earth in his mortal body. It is consummated in glorification when that believer through death and resurrection or through the Rapture stands in the presence of God 'conformed to the likeness of His Son' (Romans 8:29). A believer's identification with Jesus Christ by faith is both the ground and goal of sanctification." *Bible Knowledge Commentary*

Note that practical sanctification is something we must participate in. We must cooperate with the Holy Spirit as He works in us to conform us to the image of Christ (Romans 8:29).

Glorification means that when we are finally at home in Heaven with the Lord Jesus Christ, we will be perfect – absolutely sinless. Some people refer to this as *ultimate sanctification*.

7. The Church

*"We believe the **Church**, which began with the baptizing work of the Holy Spirit on the day of **Pentecost**, is the **body and bride of Christ**. It is the spiritual organism made up of all **born-again** persons of the present age. (Acts 2:1-36; 1 Corinthians 12:13-14; 2 Corinthians 11:2; Ephesians 1:22-23; 5:25-27)*

*"We believe the establishment and continuance of **local churches** is clearly taught and defined in the New Testament Scriptures. (Acts 14:27; 20:17, 28-32; 1 Timothy 3:1-13; Titus 1:5-11)"*

The words appearing in **bold** text in the paragraphs above are explained in this study note. Here's where to find those words – and more – in this note:

Church

The Greek word for "church" is "ecclesia" (ECK-lay-SEE-ah). It means "called out by God" or "separated unto God." Some commentators define the word as "an assembly of called-out people."

The Bible uses the word "church" in two different ways. It can mean the *true Church* or the *local church*.

True Church

The true Church is not a denomination. It does not meet in a building. Its membership roll is known only to God. The members of the true Church have never assembled together, and will not assemble together until the Lord Jesus Christ comes to rapture those who have trusted Him as their Savior from sin. The true Church exists without limitations of geography, theology, or human distinctions.

Thus, the true Church consists of all who have trusted Christ as Savior during the Church Age. If that's true of you, you're a member of the true Church. Note that the true Church consists *only* of those who are believers in Jesus Christ:

And the Lord added to the church daily those who were being saved Acts 2:41b   (NKJV)

The true Church is sometimes referred to as the *universal* Church or the *invisible* Church, but some commentators object to the latter, pointing out that the Church is composed of real, visible people!

Note that the Roman Catholic Church sometimes refers to itself as "the true Church." "Catholic" means "universal."

Local Church

The local church is the visible church. It is the institutional church that meets in a home, a church building – wherever, as the Lord Jesus Christ said, *two or three are gathered together in My name* (Matthew 18:20*). The local church is very important to God. He tells us, through Paul, not to forsake the assembling of ourselves together (Hebrews 10:25). That's a command!

> * This verse applies to both formal church services and to an informal gathering of two or three believers.

Not all members of a local church are members of the true Church. There are many unsaved people who attend and may even be members of local churches. The converse is also true: there are members of the true Church who do not attend a local church.

Christ Himself established the Church (Matthew 16:18). The Church is the "apple of God's eye," as witnessed by His designating her as the Body and Bride of the Lord Jesus Christ, and the fact that Christ died for her.

A study of Church history reveals how God has protected His Church since its founding. Truly, as the Lord Jesus Christ said, *the gates of Hell shall not prevail against it* (Matthew 16:17-18).

For its first 300 years (+ or -), Satan tried to destroy the Church with severe persecution. That only served to make the Church grow larger! In the fourth century, through the Roman Emperor Constantine, Satan found a tool that accomplished his purposes: indulgence. The church was given the protection of the state and was even funded by the state. In exchange for his protection, Constantine, who never renounced his priesthood in a pagan religion, asked certain favors of the church. This led to bringing pagan rites into the church, diluting doctrine, etc. Eventually, the Bible was taken from the common people and a "priesthood" was instituted*. The Church lost its evangelistic zeal. The Church entered the spiritual dark ages, and didn't emerge until the Protestant Reformation in the sixteenth century.

> * A description of the priesthood is included in the Supplemental Information at the end of this study note.

The purposes of the Church include at least the following:

- Glorifying God (Ephesians 3:21)

- Preaching and teaching God's Word

- Equipping the saints for service (Ephesians 4:12)

- Evangelism – spreading the Gospel – locally and worldwide (Acts 1:8)

- Corporate worship of our Creator and Savior

- Mutual edification and encouragement of the saints

- Supporting other believers in prayer

- Christian fellowship

- Religious education and training

- Assisting the needy

God knew His children would be persecuted (experience everything from criticism to martyrdom) and would need the fellowship and support of others in an assembly of believers.

Pentecost

Pentecost, meaning "50 days," was a Jewish feast* observed 50 days after the Feast of Firstfruits.

> *   The seven Jewish feasts are described in the Supplemental Information at the end of this study note.

The Church, thus the Church Age, began on the day of Pentecost (Acts 2) when the Holy Spirit descended on and spiritually baptized the first group of Christians assembled after Christ's ascension. Pentecost is thus the birthday of the church.

Body and Bride of Christ

The Church is the mystical (spiritual) Body of Christ (Ephesians 1:22-23). We, as members of the true Church, are the Body of Christ on earth. The Lord Jesus Christ Himself is the Head of the Body (Ephesians 4:15).

The Apostle Paul uses the figure of the human body to depict the unity of believers during the Church Age. The Body of Christ is formed by the baptizing work of the Holy Spirit (1 Corinthians 12:13). This baptism unites believers to one another and to Christ (Romans 6:3-4). In 1 Corinthians 12, Paul compares individual Christians and their diverse spiritual gifts to the diverse parts of the body (eye, hand, etc.) and concludes with this:

Now you are the body of Christ, and members individually   1 Corinthians 12:27 (NKJV)

The church is also the Bride of Christ. Currently the Church belongs to Christ in the sense of betrothal (1 Corinthians 11:2). We are watching and waiting for the appearance of the Bridegroom at the Rapture of the Church when Christ comes to claim His bride and take her to the Father's house.

The Marriage of the Lamb will occur in Heaven while the seven-year Tribulation is taking place on earth.

Many marriages include a wedding meal. And so it will be when the Church (the Bride) and Christ (her Groom) are finally together. After the Church returns to earth with Christ following the Tribulation, a great feast, the Marriage Supper of the Lamb, will take place on earth (Revelation 19:7-9). The guests will be the redeemed (saved people) of all ages – except the Church Age, of course! – and the heavenly host.

In fairness, it should be stated that expositors have debated whether the Wedding Supper will be in heaven or on earth. Comparing the wedding described in Revelation 19 to the pattern of earthly weddings in the first century, many commentators have concluded that the Wedding Supper is indeed an earthly feast that will occur at the beginning of the Millennium.

The expression, "The Bride of Christ," is not found in the King James translation of the Bible. So what is the basis for referring to the (true, invisible) Church as "The Bride of Christ"?

- In John 3:29, John the baptizer referred to Christ as the Bridegroom, and himself as the friend of the Bridegroom. John's ministry was to point people to the Savior, to prepare for the arrival of Christ (John 1:23).

- Writing to the church at Corinth, the Apostle Paul said he had "espoused" (engaged, promised) the believers there to one husband, who he identified as the Lord Jesus Christ (2 Corinthians 11:2).

- In Ephesians 5:27-32, Paul speaks of Christ presenting the Church to Himself (verse 27). In verse 31 Paul quotes Genesis 2:24 regarding the establishment of marriage. In verse 32 (of Ephesians 5), Paul says he is *speak(ing) concerning Christ and His Church*.

- Revelation 19:7-9 describes the Marriage of the Lamb (Christ) and identifies His bride as being "arrayed in white linen" which is the "righteousness (righteous acts) of the saints." The Bride must be the church-age saints who were raptured. They received their white linen at the Bema Seat Judgment (2 Corinthians 5:10).

In the Old Testament, Jehovah is described as the husband of the earthly nation Israel (Isaiah 54:5). In the future, Israel will be restored as God's earthly wife (Hosea 2:14 - 23). The Church will be claimed as Christ's Bride.

From Ephesians 5 we learn that

- Christ loved the Church and died for her (verse 25)

- The Church is to submit to Christ (verse 24)

- Christ has cleansed (washed) the Church by means of His Word (verse 26)

- In the future, the Church will be presented to Christ (by Christ) as a radiant (glorious) Church, without blemish (verse 27)

- Christ nourishes and cherishes His Church (verse 29)

Born Again

Speaking to Nicodemus, a Pharisee who came at night to ask about salvation, Jesus said

> *Verily, verily, I say unto thee, Except a man be born again, he cannot see* (enter) *the kingdom of God.*
> John 3:3 (KJV)

When a person invites the Lord Jesus Christ into his or her life as their Savior from sin, they become a spiritual child of God, they change their spiritual parentage from Satan (John 8:44) to God (Galatians 3:26) – they are literally "born again" spiritually.

Being born into God's family is also referred to as the *new birth, regeneration, salvation.* Here are two of God's promises regarding salvation:

> *To all who received Him* (Christ), *to those who believed in His name, He gave the right* (legal authority) *to become children of God*   John 1:12 NIV

> *He who believes in the Son has everlasting life, and he who does not believe the Son shall not see life, but the wrath of God abides on him.*   John 3:36 NKJV

In the verses above, the word "believe" means more than just a mental assent. Many people believe that there was a man named Jesus, that he was a good man who sincerely thought himself to be the Son of God, and that he died on a Roman cross. But that's not the meaning of "believe" (Greek *pisteuo*) in the verses just quoted.

Pisteuo means *to adhere to, cling to, trust completely, have faith in, rely on fully.* Thus, the words *believe on the Lord Jesus Christ and you will be saved* (Acts 16:31) mean to have an absolute personal reliance upon the Lord Jesus Christ as your Savior from sin. It's to realize that He is the only way to God (John 14:6) and your only hope of salvation (Acts 4:12), then to trust Him completely for that salvation.

It's one thing to say you believe there was a person named Jesus in history, it's quite another to base your entire eternal destiny on Him. But that's what you must do to be saved. The death of the Lord Jesus Christ is the only provision God has made for our salvation.

It's vitally important that we lean our eternal destiny on the real Jesus Christ*. The Apostle Paul warned the people in Corinth against teachers who preach "another Jesus" (2 Corinthians 11:4). In the Olivet Discourse (the most detailed end-times discourse delivered by Christ), Jesus Himself warned against false christs (Matthew 24:24) – and there have been, and continue to be, many. To be saved from sin, your faith must be in the Jesus of the Bible. There is no salvation in worshipping a false Christ. Only the Jesus of the Bible has the power to save.

> *   More information regarding the real Jesus is available in *The Person And Work Of Christ,* the study note for point three of the BMW Doctrinal Statement.

Church Age

The Church Age is the time period when the members of the true Church are on earth.

As noted earlier, the Church Age began at Pentecost; it will end when the Church is raptured (snatched away) before the Tribulation period* (1 Thessalonians 4:13-18).

> * The Tribulation, Rapture, and other end-time events are described in *The Second Advent Of Christ* and *The Eternal State*, the study notes for points thirteen and fourteen of the BMW Doctrinal Statement.

Even though the saints will be raptured before the seven-year Tribulation period, the organized Church will continue.

The harlot of Revelation 17 is the organized Church of the Tribulation period. She represents the apostate, liberal, non-Gospel-preaching churches, some of which are in existence today.

Biblical Christianity will also exist during the Tribulation. The activities of 144,000 Jewish evangelists during the first half of the Tribulation will produce a tremendous harvest of souls (Revelation 7). The true Church may have to meet underground because of persecution, much as she does now in some countries. Great numbers of Christians will be martyred during the Tribulation.

All churches probably will be shut down in the second half of the Tribulation, when the Antichrist (the "Beast") destroys the harlot (Revelation 17:16). Politics will trump religion.

Uniqueness of the Church-Age Saints

The saints of the Church Age have a privileged position! Consider these distinctives:

- We will be the only group resurrected or raptured before the Tribulation

- We will be the first group of saints to receive rewards in Heaven

- We will return with Christ at the end of the Tribulation

- We are the Body of Christ

- We will participate as the Bride of Christ in the Marriage of the Lamb

Much additional material regarding the Church is available in *Separation and Unity*, the study note for point seventeen of the BMW Doctrinal Statement.

1. Priesthood

Old Testament Priesthood

God initiated the Aaronic priesthood in Israel (Exodus 28:1). These men represented God to the people and the people to Him. Sinful people could not come directly into God's presence. In fact, only the High Priest could enter God's presence in the Temple's Holy of Holies (Exodus 26:33-34), and that once a year, after stringent preparation.

The veil of the Temple separated man from God's presence in the Holy of Holies. When Christ's flesh was torn on the cross, the veil of the Temple was supernaturally torn from top to bottom, signifying that the way into God's presence was open to all who would trust the once-for-all-time sacrificial death of the Lord Jesus Christ as their sin bearer.

The death of the Lord Jesus Christ annulled the Aaronic (Old Testament) priesthood (Hebrews 7-10, Romans 10:4).

After The Death Of Christ

There is no indication in the New Testament that the first-century church had priests.

Because in and through Christ, born-again Christians have the imputed righteousness of God (2 Corinthians 5:21), we have immediate, direct access to God, we are welcome in His presence. Because the Lord Jesus Christ alone is the way to God (John 14:6), we don't need a human intermediary (e.g., a priest).

Related Scriptures

1 Peter 2:5-9 Born-again Christians – the family of God – constitute a royal priesthood; each of us is a believer-priest with the same privileges and direct access to God.

As a family of believer-priests, we are to

- Confess our sins to one another (James 5:16). Man cannot grant forgiveness, but we confess to one another so we can "bear one another's burdens."

- Instruct one another (Romans 15:14).

- Admonish one another (Colossians 3:16).

- Encourage and edify one another (1 Thessalonians 5:11).

- Exhort one another (Hebrews 3:13).

- Settle disputes with one another (1 Corinthians 6:1-8).

- Serve one another (Galatians 5:13).

Hebrews 10:19-22 We have access to the Holy of Holies (God's presence) through the blood of the Lord Jesus Christ.

1 John 1:9 We are to confess our sin to God. He alone grants forgiveness, not man.

1 Timothy 2:5 The Lord Jesus Christ is the only Mediator between God and man.

Hebrews 4:14-16 Christ is our High Priest; we can come before the throne of God with confidence.

Revelation 1:6; 5:10 As believer-priests, we have the right to enter the presence of God directly.

2. Jewish Feasts

Seven Jewish Feasts were ordained in the Old Testament. Here are the New Testament meanings of those feasts:

Feast of Passover testifies of the shedding of blood of the Lamb of God. (1 Corinthians 5:7)

Feast of Unleavened Bread speaks of the Lord's Supper, which would be instituted by Him on the night of Passover and would serve to remind His followers again and again to walk in communion with Him. (1 Corinthians 5:8)

Feast of Firstfruits foreshadows the coming resurrection and restoration. (1 Corinthians 15:23)

Feast of Pentecost was fulfilled in the descent of the Holy Spirit on the first group of Christian believers after Christ's ascension. (Acts 2:36)

Feast of Trumpets promises that someday the "the Lord shall descend from Heaven with the trump of God" when "the trumpet shall sound, and the dead shall be raised incorruptible." (1 Thessalonians 4:16, 1 Corinthians 15:52)

Day of Atonement testifies of the certain judgments to come – on Israel, on believers and on the lost.

Feast of Tabernacles speaks of the coming eternal rest in the holy city. (Revelation 21:3)

8. Ordinances

*"We believe the Lord Jesus Christ established two **ordinances** for the **Church** in this present age. These are **believer's water baptism**, practiced by **immersion**, and the **Lord's Supper**, observed as a memorial of His death. (Acts 8:12, 35-39; 10:47-48; 1 Corinthians 1:14; 11:23-34)"*

The words appearing in **bold** text in the paragraph above are explained in this study note. Here's where to find those words – and more – in this note:

Baptismal regeneration?   Page 104
Believers water baptism / immersion   Page 103
Church   Page 103
Lord's Supper   Page 105
Ordinance   Page 103

Ordinance

In the current context, the word "ordinance" refers to a practice (rite) ordained by the Lord Jesus Christ. (The word "ordinance" is derived from "ordain.")

Church

The Greek word for "church" is "ecclesia" (ECK-lay-SEE-ah). It means "called out by God" or "separated unto God." Some commentators define the word as "an assembly of called-out people."

The Bible uses the word "Church" in two different ways. It can mean the *true Church* or the *local church*. For an explanation of the differences, refer to *The Church*, the study note for point seven of the BMW Doctrinal Statement.

Believer's Water Baptism / Immersion

Baptizo, the Greek word from which we get "baptize," means "immerse." It describes the method – immersion in water – used by the early church to publicly identify new believers in Christ. The one baptized was telling the world that he was now a follower of Christ. And so it is today. Christian baptism is a means of identifying with Christ, it's an expression of salvation.

The act of water baptism by immersion graphically depicts the death, burial and resurrection of the Savior. Note that this act is referred to as *believer's* water baptism. Baptism is for those who have invited the Lord Jesus Christ into their lives as their Savior from sin. Indeed, He commanded that believers be baptized (Matthew 28:18-20) – not to be saved, but because they have been.

Because baptism is only for those who have knowingly, by a deliberate act of their will, accepted the Lord Jesus Christ as Savior, it isn't for infants.

Water baptism is not efficacious or required for salvation – we are saved by grace through faith (Ephesians 2:8-9), not by a human "work" (effort) such as water baptism.

Not by works of righteousness which we have done, but according to His mercy he saved us, by the washing of regeneration*, and renewing of the Holy Ghost Titus 3:5 (KJV)

> * Being regenerated (saved) is indeed a washing (cleansing) – it washes away our sins! The "washing of regeneration" is symbolized by – but is not – water baptism. In regeneration, the Holy Spirit renews us from spiritual death to spiritual life.

Baptism is for living believers. There is no true biblical support for "baptism for the dead" as practiced by some religious traditions. Yes, there is one verse – and only one: 1 Corinthians 15:29 – that references baptism for the dead (most likely practiced by a pagan cult known to Paul), but it cannot mean that a dead unbeliever could be saved by someone being baptized in his place. Baptism doesn't save anyone, dead or alive. The Bible teaches that there is no possibility for salvation after death. After death comes judgment, not another opportunity to be saved. Here's the way the Apostle Paul expressed it:

> *… it is appointed unto men once to die, but after this the judgment* Hebrews 9:27 (KJV)

Water baptism is to be distinguished from the baptism of the Holy Spirit. The latter, which occurs at the moment of salvation, is a work of the Holy Spirit by which He unites us with the spiritual family of God (1 Corinthians 12:13). This is further discussed in *The Person And Work Of The Holy Spirit*, the study note for point four of the BMW Doctrinal Statement.

Baptismal Regeneration?

> *Then Peter said to them, "Repent, and let every one of you be baptized in the name of Jesus Christ for the remission of sins; and you shall receive the gift of the Holy Spirit".* Acts 2:38 (NKJV)

Based on the verse above and other New Testament passages, some religious traditions teach that water baptism is required for salvation, that it is the means by which our sins are forgiven. This teaching is known as Baptismal Regeneration.

The teaching is incorrect for several reasons, the chief being that it contradicts dozens of passages that clearly teach that salvation is by faith alone. That fact by itself is sufficient to reject this teaching.

Here are some additional considerations – many more could be cited!

- In light of the context of Acts 2:38 and other similar verses, the Greek preposition *eis*, translated "for" in some Bible versions, is better translated "because of" or "on the basis of." Thus, the phrase "for the remission (forgiveness) of sins" is better translated "because of the remission of sins" or "on the basis of the remission of sins." We are baptized physically because our sins are forgiven, not to secure forgiveness.

- In Acts 2:41, forgiveness of sins (salvation – "receiving the Word") preceded baptism in the Apostle Peter's evangelistic crusade.

- Cornelius and his family believed, received the Holy Spirit, then were baptized (Acts 10:44-48). Baptism is an indication of belonging to Christ, not a condition for it.

A Survey of Major Biblical Doctrines – Ordinances

- In 1 Corinthians 1:17, the Apostle Paul distinguishes between salvation and baptism, saying "Christ did not send me to baptize but to preach the gospel."

- Romans 1:16 states that it is the Gospel of Christ that is "the power of God unto salvation." No mention of baptism.

- In 1 Peter 3:20-21, the Lord Jesus Christ is our ark of safety and salvation from judgment because we were spiritually baptized into Him at the moment of salvation (1 Corinthians 12:13). That the baptism in this passage is not water baptism is clear from the phrase "not as a removal of dirt from the body" (ESV).

- The baptism spoken of in Galatians 3:27 is spiritual, not physical. We know from other verses that our "put(ting) on Christ" is the result of the spiritual baptism that occurs at the moment of salvation. Note that the method of salvation is presented in the preceding verse:

  ... for in Christ Jesus you are all sons of God, through faith (Galatians 3:26 – ESV).

Lord's Supper

The Lord's Supper is so-named because it was instituted by the Lord Jesus Christ the night He and His disciples ate their last meal together – the night He was betrayed (1 Corinthians 11:23-25).

The elements used in celebrating the Lord's Supper (the bread and the cup) represent the flesh and blood of the Lord Jesus Christ. They do not become His actual flesh and blood, as erroneously taught by some religious traditions. This incorrect doctrine is known as "transubstantiation."

Each time we celebrate the Lord's Supper, we *proclaim the Lord's death until He comes* (1 Corinthians 11:26 – NASB). The Savior requested that we *do this in remembrance of* (Him) (1 Corinthians 11:24); this supper is a special time for reflecting on His sacrifice for us. It is thus a solemn time, not to be entered into lightly.

The Lord's Supper is for all who have professed saving faith in the Lord Jesus Christ. We are instructed to examine our hearts before participating in this supper, to be sure we are saved and to confess known sin. This is a serious matter. Physical illness, even death, may result from participating in an "unworthy" manner (1 Corinthians 11:27-30).

9.   Missions

*"We believe that Christ commissioned individuals in the **church** to make **disciples** from among all **nations**, to **baptize** them in the name of the Father, the Son, and the Holy Spirit, and to teach them to observe all things whatsoever He has commanded. (Matthew 28:18-20; Acts 1:8; 2 Corinthians 5:19-20)"*

The words appearing in **bold** text in the paragraph above are explained in this study note. Here's where to find those words – and more – in this note:

Missions

"Missions" refers to efforts to evangelize, take the Gospel – the "evangel," the good news of Christ – to unsaved people with the goal of seeing them come to a saving knowledge of the Lord Jesus Christ. A "missionary" is anyone who works toward that goal. Evangelization is the root purpose of missionary activity.

The Lord Jesus Christ admonished us to engage in missionary (evangelistic) activity:

> *Go ye therefore, and teach all nations, baptizing them in the name of the Father, and of the Son, and of the Holy Ghost: Teaching them to observe all things whatsoever I have commanded you: and, lo, I am with you alway, even unto the end of the world. Amen.*   Matthew 28:19-20 (KJV)

The above passage, commonly known as the "great commission," could be renamed the "great assumption." The first phrase of the passage can be translated "as you go," or "when you have gone." The Lord Jesus Christ expects His disciples to engage in evangelism.

Evangelism can be praying for the unsaved, becoming a foreign or home missionary, financially supporting missionaries and missionary organizations, personal witnessing, internet witnessing, leaving/distributing gospel tracts, and many other endeavors – all with the intent of seeing people come to Christ for salvation.

The Apostle Paul told us we are ambassadors, representatives, for Christ (2 Corinthians 5:20). This is at the same time an awesome privilege and a weighty responsibility. Christ's ambassadors should be dedicated to evangelism – telling others about the One they represent.

It has been reported that in the twentieth century, 75% of all missionaries came from the United States. In the aftermath of World War II, Americans reportedly started 1,800 missions agencies and sent out more than 350,000 missionaries. Unfortunately, that missionary zeal is no longer present.

"The American missionary force has decreased substantially over the past fifty years. Albert Mohler believes the reason is that inclusivism* and pluralism* have seeped their way into the church: 'At base, the issue is a failure of theological nerve – a devastating loss of biblical and doctrinal conviction …' If salvation can be found apart from Christ, then why have a sense of urgency concerning the lost?"   Excerpted from *The Doctrine Debate: Why Doctrine Matters Now More Than Ever* by Sean McDowell. *Christian Research Journal*, Volume 31, Number 1

> *   Inclusivism, Exclusivism, Mysticism, Pluralism, Universalism, Paganism, Pantheism, and Polytheism are described in the Supplemental Information at the end of this study note.

Inclusivist teaching is incorrect. On their own, people do not seek God (Romans 3:10-12). In fact, they take the knowledge of God available through general revelation* and pervert it to their own liking (Romans 1:21-23). The condition of those without God is not one of seeking salvation, but one of rebellion, darkness, and idolatry.

> *   General revelation can be defined as "the revelation of God to all people, at all times, and in all places, that reveals that God exists and that He is intelligent, powerful and transcendent."
>
> General revelation is discussed in more detail in *The Holy Scriptures*, the study note for point one of the BMW Doctrinal Statement.

The Bible prescribes only one means of salvation: faith in the Lord Jesus Christ (John 3:16, 14:6; Acts 4:12). Rather than hope that some people are being saved by believing what can be known about God through general revelation, God calls us to go into all the world and proclaim the Gospel.

Pluralism is obviously incorrect because of its failure to recognize the possibility of heresy. Any religious tradition that denies the essential doctrines of the Christian faith* is a heresy. Paul (1 Corinthians 11:9), and Peter (2 Peter 2:1) both addressed the subject of heresies in the church.

> *   Essential doctrines are listed in *Separation and Unity*, the study note for point seventeen of the BMW Doctrinal Statement.

Church

The Greek word for "church" is "ecclesia" (ECK-lay-SEE-ah). It means "called out by God" or "separated unto God." Some commentators define the word as "an assembly of called-out people."

The Bible uses the word "church" in two different ways. It can mean the *true Church* or the *local church*. For an explanation of the differences, refer to *The Church*, the study note for point seven of the BMW Doctrinal Statement.

Disciple

"Disciple" means "follower" and, implicitly, "learner." Every true Christian should be a disciple of the One who saved them. We should study God's Word, learn the truth (John 17:17) then go out and put that truth into practice, serving the Lord.

A true disciple is not just a hearer of the Word, but a doer as well (James 1:22, 2:17). The true disciple abides (continues) in and obeys the Word (John 8:31).

Nations

The Greek word for "nations" is *ethnos* – from which we get our words "ethnic," "ethnicity," etc. Thus, in Scripture, "nations" is an ethnic term; it points to the historic division of Noah's descendants, driven by language and ultimately manifested in "ethnic" people groups, of which Genesis 10 (the "Table of Nations") indicates about 70. We are to take the gospel to all people groups.

Baptize

Believer's water baptism is a means of identifying with the Lord Jesus Christ. This subject is discussed in detail in *Ordinances*, the study note for point eight of the BMW Doctrinal Statement.

Supplemental Information

Inclusivism and Exclusivism

'Inclusivism' is the view that people actually appropriate God's gift of salvation only on the basis of Jesus Christ's atoning work, but that the sinner need not explicitly believe the gospel in order to receive this salvation. Inclusivism teaches that Christianity is the only true religion (including the belief that Christ is the only Savior of men), but that this salvation could be made available through means other than explicit faith in Christ. The inclusivist believes that adherents of other religions and even atheists can be saved by responding to God's revelation in creation ('general revelation') or through the elements of truth contained within their non-Christian religion.

'Exclusivism' or 'restrictivism' is the traditional evangelical Christian view dealing with the salvation of non-Christians. This is the view that a sinner can be saved only by a conscious explicit faith in the gospel of Jesus Christ. Exclusivists argue that a positive response to general revelation is simply insufficient to ensure salvation from a biblical perspective. Exclusivists appeal to multiple scriptures to support their view, including John 3:16-18, 14:6 and Romans 10:13-15.

The information in the paragraphs above was adapted from various sources on http://www.gotquestions.org

Mysticism

"Mysticism" is from the Greek *muo*, meaning "concealed." Christianity is mystical in the sense that it espouses an internal, heart religion and promises a communion with the supernatural. But many forms of mysticism reject the written Word of God, claiming that divine revelation must come from within. Mysticism substitutes meditation for prayer. In this meditation, God becomes a subjective experience rather than an objective reality as taught in the Bible.

From a sermon by Dr. John MacArthur:

"Mysticism is beliefs and ideas which are the product of personal intuition. Further, assumed to transcend ordinary understanding. That's mysticism. It is a system of beliefs and ideas which are the product of my own personal intuition which I assume transcends ordinary understanding.
To put it simply, it is sheer speculation believed to be reality. Mystical belief systems are collections of ideas that have arisen out of emotion, out of self-authenticated ideas unrelated to objective fact or evidence." http://www.biblebb.com/files/MAC/61-3.htm

Paganism

From a Christian viewpoint, paganism is any religious ceremony, act, teaching, or practice that is not distinctly Christian.

Paganism is a corruption of an earlier, pure religion. Paganism began to develop when sin corrupted the worship of the true God (Romans 1:18-23). Paganism includes Pantheism, Polytheism, and Universalism.

Pantheism

"Pantheism is the view that God is everything and everyone, and that everyone and everything is God. Pantheism is similar to polytheism, but goes beyond polytheism to teach that everything is God. A tree is God, a rock is God, an animal is God, the sky is God, the sun is God, you are God, etc. Pantheism is the supposition behind many cults and false religions (e.g., Hinduism and Buddhism to an extent, the various unity and unification cults, and 'mother nature' worshippers)." Ravi Zacharias

Panthiests believe that everything is God or is a part of God, making Him equal to His creation and unable to act upon it.

Genesis 1:1, the first verse in the Bible, refutes pantheism because it tells us that God is transcendent to that which He created.

Pluralism

Pluralism is the teaching that all religious traditions must be given equal weight and considered valid. In pluralism, no religious tradition has the right to pronounce itself right or true and the other competing traditions false, or even inferior. Under pluralism there is no longer any religious heresy.

Polytheism

"Polytheism is the belief that there are many gods. Polytheism has perhaps been the dominant theistic view in human history. The best-known example of polytheism in ancient times is Greek/Roman mythology (Zeus, Apollo, Aphrodite, Poseidon, etc.). The clearest modern example of polytheism is Hinduism, which has over 300 million gods." Ravi Zacharias

Genesis 1:1, refutes polytheism because it tells us that one God created everything.

Universalism

Universalism (a.k.a., universal salvation) is the belief that everyone will be saved. Universalism directly contradicts what the Bible teaches.

10. The Ministry and Spiritual Gifts

"We believe the Lord Jesus Christ gives the Church **evangelists** *and* **pastor-teachers**. *These gifted* **men** *are to equip the saints for the work of the* **ministry**. *(Ephesians 4:7-14)*

"We believe the Holy Spirit bestows **spiritual gifts** *upon believers for Christian service and the edification of the Church. (Romans 12:3-8; 1 Corinthians 12:4-11; 1 Peter 4:10-11)*

"We believe the **church age** *was initiated through the ministry of the* **apostles** *and* **prophets** *accompanied by* **sign gifts** *to confirm their message. These sign gifts gradually ceased by the time of the completion of the New Testament. (1 Corinthians 12:28-31; 13:8-10; 14:1-28; 2 Corinthians 12:12; Ephesians 2:19-22; Hebrews 2:3-4)*

"We believe God hears and answers prayer in accord with His own will for **healing** *of the sick and afflicted. (John 14:13-14; 15:7; 1 John 5:14-15)"*

The words appearing in **bold** text in the paragraphs above are explained in this study note. Here's where to find those words - and more – in this note:

Apostles   Page 117
Church age   Page 117
Evangelists   Page 115
Healing   Page 118
Men   Page 115
Ministry   Page 113
Pastor-teachers   Page 115
Prophets   Page 117
Sign gifts   Page 118
Spiritual gifts   Page 113

Ministry

"Ministry" is from the Greek words *diakoneo*, meaning "to serve," or *douleuo*, meaning "to serve as a slave." In the New Testament, ministry is seen as service to God and to other people in His name.

Every Christian should be in the ministry of helping other believers.

Spiritual Gifts

Spiritual gifts (Greek *charismata*, from *charis* = grace) are gifts of grace from the Holy Spirit. Because they are from the indwelling Holy Spirit, only Christians are the possessors of spiritual gifts.

The Holy Spirit gave the early church two types of spiritual gifts:

- Miraculous gifts of divine revelation and healing, given temporarily in the apostolic era for the purpose of confirming the authenticity of the apostles' message (2 Corinthians 12:12; Hebrews 2:3-4). These gifts are also known as "sign" or "revelatory" gifts.

- Ministering gifts, given to equip believers for edifying one another.

When the New Testament was complete, Scripture became the sole test of the authenticity of a man's message. Confirming gifts and gifts of a miraculous nature were no longer necessary to validate a man and his message (1 Corinthians 13:8-12). Thus, gifts of this type ceased by the end of the apostolic era.

The comments below are from two nineteenth-century theologians.

"The extraordinary gifts of the Spirit, such as the gift of tongues, or miracles, or prophecy, &c., are called extraordinary because they are such as are not given in the ordinary course of God's providence. They are not bestowed in the way of God's ordinary providential dealing with His children, but only on extraordinary occasions, as they were bestowed on the Prophets and Apostles to enable them to reveal the mind and will of God before the canon of Scripture was complete, and so on the primitive church, in order to the founding and establishing of it in the world. But since the canon of Scripture has been completed, and the Christian church founded and established, these extraordinary gifts have ceased." From the book, *Charity and Its Fruits,* by Jonathan Edwards

"The supernatural or extraordinary gifts were temporary, and intended to disappear when the Church should be founded and the inspired canon of Scripture closed; for they were an external proof of an internal inspiration." From the book, *The Doctrine of the Holy Spirit,* by George Smeaton

Scripture teaches that every believer has been given at least one spiritual gift, and we are responsible to use it (or them).

As every man hath received the gift, even so minister the same one to another, as good stewards of the manifold grace of God. 1 Peter 4:10 (KJV)

The reason for our receiving spiritual gifts is to edify (build up), minister to, other members of the true Church, the Body of Christ (Ephesians 4:11-12).

There are four primary lists of spiritual gifts in the New Testament; this one is from Romans 12:6-8:

- Prophesying (*forthtelling* [preaching], not *foretelling* – foretelling *per se* has been extinct since the end of the Apostolic period when the Bible was completed)

- Serving

- Teaching (the only gift included in all three lists of gifts)

- Encouraging

- Giving (contributing to the needs of others)

- Leadership

- Showing mercy

The other three lists – 1 Corinthians 12:8-10, 27-30 and Ephesians 4:8-16 – include gifts that are not in operation today. These include the office of an apostle, the office of a prophet, healing, speaking in tongues (known languages that are unknown to the speaker), interpreting of tongues, and working of miracles. The only gifts that are operational today are the non-revelatory equipping gifts given for edification.

When considering spiritual gifts we need to be aware that Satan can counterfeit miraculous gifts so convincingly that even believers can be deceived (Matthew 24:24).

Evangelists

The word "evangel" is from two Greek words: *eu* = good + *angelion* = message. Thus, the evangel, the gospel (same word), is the good news about Christ and the redemption He purchased for us.

An evangelist is one who proclaims the gospel.

Pastor-Teachers

The Latin word *pastor* means "shepherd." In the context of the BMW Doctrinal Statement, a pastor is one who shepherds, cares for, watches over, protects (spiritually) those in his congregation (his "flock").

In John 10:11, the Lord Jesus Christ described Himself as the Good Shepherd Who gives His life for the sheep (those who have trusted Christ as their Savior from sin). Church pastors are under-shepherds to Christ, Who is the Chief Shepherd (1 Peter 5:4).

Many people consider "pastor-teacher" to be a single spiritual gift. Note that there is also a separate gift of "teaching."

Men

The BMW Statement describes evangelists and pastor-teachers as "gifted *men*."

In God's economy (mode of operation), men and women are equal but have different roles in the home and in the Church. Paul clearly taught this in passages such as 1 Timothy 2:12:

> *And I do not permit a woman to teach or to have authority over a man, but to be in silence.* (NKJV)

The practical application of this verse is that women can teach other women and children, but cannot teach men – and a woman is not to have a position of authority over a man in the church.

Does this mean God values men more than women as some people claim? Are women second-class citizens in God's economy? Of course not! Under Christianity, women and men are of equal value – God is not a respecter of gender!

There is neither Jew nor Greek, there is neither slave nor free, there is neither male nor female; for you are all one in Christ Jesus Galatians 3:28 (NKJV)

In Genesis 1:27, we're told that man and woman were created equally in the image of God. (In this verse, the word "man" is used in a generic sense to include men and women.)

Referring to the story of the Samaritan woman who had had five husbands and was living with a sixth man (John 4:1-42), Ravi Zacharias wrote, "Which religion in the world today would have chosen this woman as their first evangelist?" Dr. Zacharias' comment is based on verses 28-30 which tell us that after talking to Jesus, the woman left the well where she was drawing water, went back to her city, and invited the people to return with her to the well to hear Jesus' teaching, exclaiming, "Come, see a man who told me all that I ever did. Can this be the Christ?" Verse 39 records that "many Samaritans from that town believed in him (Jesus) because of the woman's testimony, 'He told me all that I ever did' ".

Here's another quote from Dr. Zacharias' book, *Why Jesus? Rediscovering His Truth In An Age of Mass Marketed Spirituality*:

"(After the resurrection) to whom did Jesus first reveal himself? In that society, the most important people would have been the high priest and his entourage. … It is an incredible thing in that culture that he revealed himself first to the women, whose testimony at a court in that day would not even have been taken as reliable. … To those who think Christianity has done a disservice to women, it is critical that they understand from whom the gospel first came.

"In one of his final letters to his son in the faith, Timothy, Paul reminded Timothy that the Scriptures that were able to make him wise to salvation were taught to Timothy by his mother and his grandmother. That hardly smacks of chauvinism."

Dr. Tim LaHaye wrote the following in *Jesus, Why The World Is Still Fascinated By Him*:

"Jesus treated the women He encountered with respect, dignity, esteem and care; and most importantly, as men's equal. Based on this precept, the Apostle Paul wrote something in his letter to the Ephesian church that forever changed the relationship between husbands and wives and elevated the status of women to a level previously unknown in history.

Husbands, love your wives, just as Christ also loved the church and gave Himself for her (Ephesians 5:25)

"For the first time, men were told that their wives were worth dying for. This was positively unheard of. Women were used to being threatened, beaten, secluded, and controlled. Now their husbands were being asked, through the teachings of Christ, to treat their wives as equals."

Church Age

The time period from the first Feast of Pentecost after Christ's resurrection until the Church – the body of believers – is raptured before the seven-year Tribulation period. Stated differently, the Church Age is the time period when the members of the true Church are on earth.

The Church Age began with the Holy Spirit descending on and spiritually baptizing the first group of Christians assembled after Christ's ascension (Acts 2).

Apostles

"The apostles were prime officers in the Christian church, being extraordinary ministers appointed for a time only. They were furnished by their great Lord with extraordinary gifts and the immediate assistance of the (Holy) Spirit, that they might be fitted for publishing and spreading the gospel and for governing the church in its infant state." *Matthew Henry Commentary*

Because one of the requirements for being an apostle was that the person must have personally witnessed the resurrected Savior (Acts 1:21-22), there can be no true apostles today – or for the last 1900 years. The apostolic age ended when the last Apostle – John – died.

The role of an apostle (a "sent one") was to proclaim God's revelation, to teach the new truth the church would need to grow and thrive. The apostles and prophets completed this mission by giving us the Word of God.

From his book, *Strange Fire: The Danger of Offending the Holy Spirit with Counterfeit Worship*, here's additional insight from Dr. John MacArthur:

> "(The apostles) were those on whom (Christ) had bestowed His own authority. To be an apostle of the Lord Jesus was to have been personally appointed by Him. Ephesians 2:19-20 equates the apostles with the church's foundation. It means nothing if it doesn't decisively limit apostleship to the earliest stages of church history. When the apostles gave instruction regarding the future of the church and how the church ought to be organized, they did not suggest new apostles should be appointed. Nowhere in the pastoral epistles does Paul say anything about the perpetuation of apostleship. The unilateral consensus of the early church was that the apostolic period ended and was not expected to continue.

> "No one alive today can possibly meet the biblical criteria for apostleship. And even in the first century, when all agree the miraculous gifts were fully operational, only a very select group of spiritual leaders were regarded as apostles. In subsequent centuries, no church father claimed to be an apostle; rather, Christian leaders from the second century on saw the apostolic period as unique and unrepeatable."

Prophets

"Prophet" literally means "speaker." Thus, a prophet of God is a person who speaks by divine inspiration to reveal the will of God.

When the canon of Scripture was complete (circa A.D. 96), the need for prophets ceased. Everything God wants us to know about Himself and His will is revealed in the Bible. There are no genuine prophets of God today.

Sign Gifts

Temporary gifts given to the early Church to enable the gospel to be preached to all nations and in all known languages. Sign gifts include the office of an apostle, the office of a prophet, healing, speaking in tongues (known languages that are unknown to the speaker), interpreting of tongues, and working of miracles.

The purpose of sign gifts was to confirm the message of the apostles and prophets. Sign gifts have ceased because they are unnecessary – we now have the Bible, the completed revelation of God, and have no need of apostles and prophets (1 Corinthians 13:8-12).

Healing

No one possesses the gift of healing (the ability to produce miraculous healings) today, but, as the Doctrinal Statement indicates, "God hears and answers prayer in accord with His own will for the sick, suffering, and afflicted."

God doesn't promise physical healing in this life. Isaiah 53:5 (*with His stripes we are healed* – KJV) refers to our spiritual healing, not physical healing. Read Isaiah 53 verses 4 and 5 together.

A lack of healing does not necessarily indicate a lack of faith on the part of the afflicted, as some Word of Faith* proponents teach. It isn't always God's will to heal a believer, but it is always His will to do what's best for the believer – and we can rest in that fact.

> * The Word-of-Faith Movement is described in the Supplemental Information for *Unity and Separation*, point seventeen of the BMW Doctrinal Statement.

Even the most godly face sickness, disabilities, and eventually, death. The Apostle Paul three times asked God to remove a "thorn in the flesh" (most likely, a chronic illness) but God told him, "My grace is sufficient for you" (2 Corinthians 12:9).

Ultimate physical healing occurs when the Christian goes home to be forever with the Lord. In Heaven there will be no more pain ... *no more death* (Revelation 21:4).

11. Dispensationalism

*"We believe the Scriptures interpreted in their **natural, literal sense** reveal divinely determined **dispensations**, which define man's responsibility in successive ages. A dispensation is not a way of salvation, but a divinely-ordered stewardship by which God directs man according to His purpose. (John 1:17; 1 Corinthians 9:17; 2 Corinthians 3:9-18; Galatians 3:13-25; Ephesians 1:10; 3:2-10; Colossians 1:24-25; Hebrews 7:19; Revelation 20:2-6)*

*"We believe **salvation** is always by grace through faith regardless of the dispensation in which the believer may have lived. God's purpose of salvation by grace through faith alone has always been based upon the substitutionary **atonement** of our Lord Jesus Christ upon the cross. (Ephesians 2:8-10; Hebrews 11:6; 1 Peter 1:10-12)"*

The words appearing in **bold** text in the paragraphs above are explained in this study note. Here's where to find those words – and more – in this note:

Natural, Literal Sense

"This is sometimes called the *grammatical-historical* interpretation since the meaning of each word is determined by the grammatical and historical considerations. The principle might also be called *normal* interpretation since the literal meaning of words is the normal approach to their understanding in all languages. It might also be designated *plain* interpretation so that no one receives the mistaken notion that the literal principle rules out figures of speech. Symbols, figures of speech, and types are all interpreted plainly in this method and they are in no way contrary to literal interpretation. After all, the very existence of any meaning for a figure of speech depends on the reality of the literal meaning of the terms involved. Figures often make the meaning plainer, but it is the literal, normal or plain meaning that they convey to the reader." From the book, *Dispensationalism,* by Dr. Charles C. Ryrie

"When the plain sense of Scripture makes common sense, seek no other sense; therefore, take every word at its primary, ordinary, usual meaning unless the facts of the immediate context, studied in light of related passages and axiomatic and fundamental truths, indicate clearly otherwise." *The Golden Rule of Interpretation* formulated by Dr. David L Cooper

"If one takes God at His Word, accepting the meaning of words and sentences as determined by grammar and context, *one reads* (not interpreting) God's Word literally. Taking God literally means, of course, that the parables are taken as parables, poetry as poetry, visions as visions, metaphors as metaphors, figurative language as figurative language, commandments as commandments, and history as history. The foundational belief of the literalist is that the Bible is God's revelation, a revealing of Himself, so God wants to speak clearly, and be clearly understood, by those who accept Him with the trusting faith and the desire to learn of a loving child." *After Eden: Understanding Creation, the Curse, and the Cross* by Dr. Henry M. Morris III

"In determining what the God-taught writer is asserting in each passage, we must pay the most careful attention to its claims and character as a human production. In inspiration, God utilized the culture and conventions of his penman's milieu, a milieu that God controls in His sovereign providence; it is misinterpretation to imagine otherwise. So history must be treated as history, poetry as poetry, hyperbole and metaphor as hyperbole and metaphor, generalization and approximation as what they are, and so forth. Differences in literary conventions in Bible times and in ours must be observed ... Non-chronological narration and imprecise citation were conventional and acceptable and violated no expectations in those days ... Scripture is inerrant, not in the sense of being absolutely precise by modern standards, but in the sense of making good its claims and achieving that measure of focused truth at which its authors aimed." From *The Chicago Statement on Biblical Inerrancy.*

Dispensationalism

Dispensationalism is one way of classifying the different methods (economies, modes) God has been using to relate to mankind through the ages. Dispensationalism sees God as dealing with mankind differently at various stages of history. For example, God's governance was different with Adam than with Abraham, etc.

God has a plan for the ages and He's working it out according to His will and His timetable. That plan has been in place since eternity past and is invariant. God doesn't make up His game plan as He goes along. Dispensationalism is simply one way of viewing the outworking of God's plan for the ages.

Dispensationalism teaches the following:

- God is sovereign – in absolute control. He does things His way, according to His will and timetable.

- God has a plan for the ages, a plan put in place before the world was created.

- God reveals and administers (dispenses) His plan in stages over time. Those stages are called *dispensations*.

- God deals with man differently in each stage (dispensation) but not in regard to salvation.

- A literal reading of the Bible.

- Prophecy is future – many prophetic passages will be fulfilled in the future. Dispensationalists are futurists. (Prophecy is history written in advance.)

- Israel and the Church are separate entities.

- The Church began at Pentecost and will end with the pretribulational Rapture of the Church.

- The present Church Age is an historical parenthesis during which God has temporarily suspended his primary purpose with Israel.

Classical Dispensationalism defines seven dispensations. The chart at the end of this study note describes each of these dispensations in some detail. We are living in the sixth dispensation, identified as the Grace-Church dispensation, also known as the "Church Age."

Each dispensation cycles through these four events:

- God reveals His will to man – a different revelation in each dispensation

- Man is tested relative to obeying God's will

- Man fails to obey

- God administers judgment – differently in each dispensation

A dispensation has a beginning and an ending. Dispensations progress over time. That leads some people to consider dispensations to be time periods. Strictly speaking, a dispensation is not a period of time – but, as Dr. Charles Ryrie states, "dispensations and ages are connected ideas."

Salvation

Salvation is the state (condition) of being rescued (saved, delivered) from the power and penalty of sin. It is a spiritual rebirth, frequently referred to as being "born again."

We are saved only through – on the basis of – the blood of Christ.

This subject is discussed in more detail in *Salvation and Security*, the study note for point six of the BMW Doctrinal Statement.

Atonement

Literally, a covering. In the New Testament, "atonement" refers to Christ's covering our sins by the shedding of His own blood as our substitute. He has *washed us from our sins in His own blood* (Revelation 1:5b).

The third point of the BMW Doctrinal Statement, *The Person and Work of Christ*, indicates that Christ's sacrificial death was "sufficient for the sins of the whole world." This is known as "unlimited atonement." There are others – principally, proponents of Reformed Theology – who believe in "limited atonement"; that is, that the Lord Jesus Christ died only for those He chose to be His own, those who He elected to be saved.

Both positions, limited atonement and unlimited atonement, have scriptural support, but regardless of which position we subscribe to, we can rest in the fact that Christ's death was sufficient to cover the sins of all who desire to trust Him as their Savior!

The Seven Dispensations

Dispensation	Event / Person		Revealed Will / Test	Man's Failure	God's Judgment
	From	To			
Innocence	Creation of Adam	Expulsion from the Garden	Don't eat of the Tree of the Knowledge of Good and Evil	Disobedience – ate of fruit	Ground cursed; man subject to physical death
Conscience	Fall of Adam and Eve	Flood	Do what you know is right	Great wickedness on the Earth	Universal Flood
Civil Government	Noah	Tower of Babel	Self government; scatter and multiply	Did not scatter; built a tower to heaven	Confusion of languages
Promise	Abraham	Moses	Keep the Covenant; stay in Canaan	Went to Egypt	Bondage in Egypt (400+ years)
Law – Israel	Moses	Christ	Obey the Law	Went after other gods in the wilderness and in the Promised Land	Worldwide dispersion
Grace – Church	Cross	Rapture	Believe on the Lord Jesus Christ; keep doctrine pure	Unbelief; impure doctrine	Apostasy; false doctrine; tribulation on Earth
Millennial Kingdom	Glorious Appearing of Christ	Beginning of eternal state	Obey and worship Lord Jesus Christ	Satan gathers nations together against God	Great White Throne Judgment; Hell

A Survey of Major Biblical Doctrines – Dispensationalism

12. The Personality of Satan

"We believe Satan is a created being, the author of sin, the tempter in the fall, the declared enemy of God and man, and the god of this age. He shall be eternally punished in the lake of fire. (Job 1:6-7; Isaiah 14:12-17; Matthew 4:2-11; 25:41; Revelation 20:10)"

Here's an index to the words explained in this study note:

Satan

Satan is an immaterial, invisible, immortal, supernatural being. He was created as Lucifer, the highest-ranking, most-beautiful, most-powerful angel, covering (guarding) the throne of God. He evidently was of incomparable beauty and wisdom. Because of his pride, he chose to exercise his free will and rebel against God, his Creator (Ezekiel 28:13-17). Thus Satan became the author, the originator, of sin – the first sinner. The first sin was pride (1 Timothy 3:6).

Scripture says that when Satan rebelled, one-third of the angels rebelled with him (Revelation 12:3-4). These are the "bad" or "fallen" angels, also referred to as "demons." They do Satan's bidding – he is their leader.

After Satan's rebellion, God cast him down to the earth where he possessed and used the body of a serpent (at that time an attractive creature) and tested Adam and Eve in the Garden of Eden (Genesis 3:1-5). After Eve, then Adam, succumbed to the temptation, God cursed the serpent to henceforth crawl on its belly, eat its food off the ground, and be covered with the dust of the earth (Genesis 3:14).

Because Satan is a created being, he is not omnipotent, omniscient, omnipresent, eternal, immutable, etc., as is God. But Satan is much more intelligent and powerful than we are. He cannot read our minds, but he doesn't have to. By our words and deeds we reveal to him our true selves. He knows each of us very well, and thus knows where we are vulnerable to attack.

Fortunately for us, God limits Satan's power. The story of Job is ample testimony to that (Job 1:6 - 2:7). We shouldn't fear Satan because the One Who is in us, the One we serve, is "greater than he that is in the world (Satan)" (1 John 4:4). But we need to be aware of Satan's schemes ("wiles") to defeat us, and we need to put on the whole armor of God for the spiritual battles we face (Ephesians 6:10-18).

Satan will be very active during the seven-year Tribulation period. The full fury of Satan will be unleashed on mankind – and especially on the Jews – during this time. Satan will be indwelling and directing the Antichrist and the False Prophet, empowering them to perform miracles. For more detailed information, refer to *The Second Advent of Christ*, the study note for point thirteen of the BMW Doctrinal Statement.

During the Millennium, when Christ is physically reigning for 1000 years on a restored earth, Satan will be bound (locked) in the bottomless pit (Revelation 20:2-3). The fallen angels (Satan's hosts) will also be bound in Hades (Hebrew *Sheol*) during this time. At the end of the Millennium, all will be released for a short time. They will attempt to convince humans to rebel against God, will be supernaturally defeated, and will then be cast into the Lake of Fire for eternity (Revelation 20:7-10).

Because Satan and the other angels are created beings, they, like us, have an eternal destiny. Matthew 25:41 indicates that Hell, the Lake of Fire, was prepared for the devil and his fallen angels.

Here are some of Satan's activities, past and present, as recorded in the Word:

- He was in the Garden of Eden (Genesis 3) and successfully tempted our forbears to sin, thus bringing sin and death upon all people (Romans 5:12)

- He tried to pollute the bloodline of Adam in an attempt to thwart God's plan of redemption through the promised Messiah (Genesis 6)

- He was at the Tower of Babel convincing man to establish a universal, idolatrous religion (Genesis 11)

- He was instrumental in the temptation of Job (Job 1-2)

- He attempted to destroy the Hebrew race when they were in Egypt by convincing Pharaoh to order the death of all Hebrew male babies (Exodus 1:15-17, 22)

- He attempted to get the baby Jesus (the Messiah) killed by Herod (Matthew 2:16)

- He made several subsequent attempts to kill Jesus (John 7:30, 8:59, 10:39)

- He tried to destroy the Church through persecution and false teaching (Revelation 2:8-11; 1 John 4)

- He was very active before the flood of Noah's day (Genesis 6), in New Testament times (e.g., the Maniac of Gadara – Mark 5:1-17), and will be again in the end times preceding the return of the Lord Jesus Christ (Satan knows his time is short)

"Satan" means "adversary" (Revelation 12:10 – KJV). He is described as a "roaring lion, seeking whom he may devour" (1 Peter 5:8 – KJV). Other names used for our arch enemy are:

- "Lucifer" [shining one, day star] (Isaiah 14:12).

- "The devil" [slanderer, accuser] (Matthew 4:1).

    Satan accuses believers before God, but to no avail. The Lord Jesus Christ is our intercessor (Romans 8:33-34)!

- "The serpent" (Genesis 3:1).

- "The great dragon" (Revelation 12:3).

- "An angel of light"   (2 Corinthians 11:14).

- "The prince [Greek *archon*, 'ruler'] of this world"   (John 12:31).

- "The prince of the power of the air"   (Ephesians 2:2).

    The air is ... "That sphere in which the inhabitants of the world live and which, through the rebellious and godless condition of humanity, constitutes the seat of (Satan's) authority." Vine's *Expository Dictionary of New Testament Words*

- "The god of this world [age]" who "blinds the minds of them which believe not" (2 Corinthians 4:4 – KJV).

    Satan is the god of every age. Have you noticed how many intellectuals seem unable to understand and accept the simple, easy-to-understand gospel? Their minds are blinded by Satan.

- "The wicked [evil] one"   (1 John 5:18 – KJV).

    In the succeeding verse (1 John 5:19), the Holy Spirit tells us that "the whole world lieth in wickedness." The NIV translates this as "the whole world is under the control of the evil one." That was true in John's day and in ours. This old world, and every unredeemed (unsaved) person in it, is lying in Satan's lap!

- "The ruler of the darkness of this world"   (Ephesians 6:12 – KJV).

    We live in a very dark world, spiritually. Some men and women choose to live their lives in the darkness of sin (John 3:19-20).

In Scripture, Satan is also identified as a liar (John 8:44), a deceiver (Revelation 12:9), a murderer (John 8:44), a tempter (Matthew 4:3), an enemy of God and His work (Matthew 13:8).

Angels

"Angel" is derived from the Greek word *angelion*, meaning "message." Thus, an angel is a messenger.

Angels are very powerful spirit beings. It is believed that "innumerable" angels (Hebrews 12:22) were created on the first day of creation. Because angels do not procreate (Matthew 22:30), their number is unchangeable.

In Job, the oldest book of the Old Testament, angels are referred to as "sons of God" because they have no human parentage (Job 1:6).

There are good angels and bad (fallen) angels (demons). There is Scriptural support for "guardian angels" – angelic beings assigned to minister to and protect individual Christians (Matthew 18:10; Hebrews 1:14). During His temptation in the wilderness, the Lord Jesus Christ was ministered to by angels (Matthew 4:11).

Because we are indwelled by the Holy Spirit, Christians cannot be possessed by demons. But demons can afflict us. They can tempt us to sin, tempt us to doubt God's Word, try to prevent our learning God's Word and applying it to our lives, cause us to be persecuted by other people, etc. Demons are also behind false religions – they want to keep people from learning the truth about their standing with God and the provision God has made for salvation from sin.

As a result of their evil activities, some demons were confined to Tartarus* immediately before the Flood (Genesis 6:1-4, 2 Peter 2:4); some were bound in the River Euphrates, to be released during the Tribulation (sixth trumpet judgment – Revelation 9:14); others were bound in the bottomless pit, also to be released during the Tribulation (fifth trumpet judgment – Revelation 9:1-11). This latter group of fallen angels is led by Abaddon** – another fallen angel, or possibly Satan himself – to torment men five months before being herded back to the bottomless pit to await judgment. Even though many are currently captive, there are still vast hordes of demons loose in our world today, doing Satan's bidding.

* Tartarus is thought to be the lowest compartment of Hades. Tartarus is also referred to as the "bottomless pit" (Greek *abussos*, meaning "without a base" or "without a bottom"). If, as some believe, Tartarus is indeed at the center of the current physical earth, it is a chamber with no top, bottom, or sides – every surface is a ceiling, hence, it is "bottomless." Some Bible versions translate *abussos* as "abyss."

** *Abaddon* is a Hebrew word. The Greek equivalent is *Apollyon*. The words mean "Destroyer."

Angels are not to be worshiped – and they are not to be prayed to. As created beings, they are not divine.

Angels are *ministering spirits sent out to serve for the sake of those who are to inherit salvation* (Hebrews 1:14 – ESV).

Note that angels are *spirits* – spirit beings – with no physical bodies. They can, however take on human form when required. We are told that some people have entertained (hosted) angels unaware (Hebrews 13:2), but Scriptural accounts of these incidents are rare.

Angels are organized into a divinely ordained chain of command:

"The orders of angels are not fully enumerated or explained by the Bible. But the angelic host includes at least one archangel, the seraphim, and the cherubim. The archangel, Michael, is named in Daniel 10:13, 21; Jude 9, and Revelation 12:7. He seems to be the highest of all angelic creatures. Only one other holy angel, Gabriel, is explicitly named (Daniel 8:16; 9:21; Luke 1:19, 26). Some think he is therefore similar in rank to Michael, but Scripture doesn't actually designate Gabriel as an archangel.

"The seraphim are mentioned only in the heavenly vision recounted in Isaiah 6:2-6, where the prophet describes them as glorious and imposing figures who stand before God's throne and praise Him constantly, guarding the holiness of His throne.

"The cherubim, far from the chubby-faced childlike figures often pictured in popular art, seem to represent the power and majesty of the angelic host. They were positioned as guards by the entrance of Eden (Genesis 3:24). They were also the symbolic guardians of the ark of the covenant (Exodus 37:7). And they formed a living chariot of fire on which the Lord would ride (2 Samuel 22:11; Psalm 18:10; see also Ezekiel 10:1-22). They are always described as fearsome and awe-inspiring creatures.

"Other angelic beings are called thrones, dominions, principalities, and powers (Colossians 1:16). Similar terms are applied even to the fallen angels (Ephesians 6:12; Colossians 2:15)."

The above four paragraphs were accessed at http://www.ligonier.org/learn/articles/angels-messengers-and-ministers-god/

The Occult

"Occult" means "hidden, secret." In the spiritual realm, occultism is the seeking for secret (hidden) knowledge and/or power, usually from the powers of darkness – demonic or Satanic sources. This seeking frequently takes the form of rituals or occultic procedures.

"Divination," meaning "to foresee" or "to be inspired by a god," is another word that is frequently associated with the occult. Divination is the attempt to gain insight into a question or situation by way of an occult process or ritual. Those who do not have the guidance of God through His Word or by His Spirit may seek various magical devices to help them "divine" which way to go. Compared to God's truth, divination is false, deceitful, and worthless.

Many people get into the occult by means of divination (horoscopes, Ouija boards, tarot cards, palm reading, etc.).

Satan is ultimately behind all occultic activities. He and his demons are set on the destruction of our souls by any means whatever. Satan is described as *a roaring lion, seeking whom he may devour* (1 Peter 5:8 – KJV). He sometimes *masquerades as an angel of light,* as do his demons (2 Corinthians 11:14-15 – NIV).

There are numerous references to occult practices in the Old Testament, all of them denouncing the practices, and warning of dire consequences. As an example, read Deuteronomy 18:9-12. In that passage, God calls people who practice occultism "abominable" (detestable). He also told the Israelites that He was driving the heathen out of the promised land because of the heathens' abominations (verse 12).

Here are a few additional examples from the Old Testament:

- Being a spiritual medium in Israel was punishable by death (Leviticus 20:27)

- One of the reasons King Saul died was because he consulted a medium for guidance instead of God (1 Chronicles 10:13-14)

- Queen Jezebel practiced witchcraft and brought catastrophe on herself and all Israel (2 Kings 9:22)

- The presence of a medium or spiritist among God's people was considered a defilement (Leviticus 19:31)

The New Testament also includes many accounts of occultic activity. Here are three:

- The Apostle Paul rebuked Elymas (the name means "sorcerer"), a false prophet, calling him a "son of the devil." God struck Elymas with a temporary blindness (Acts 13:6-10).

- Acts 16:16-18 describe a slave girl who was demon-possessed and claimed to be able to predict the future. The Apostle Paul exorcised the demon, much to the displeasure of her owners who were making money from the girl's activities.

- The "maniac of Gadara" was possessed of "legion" (possibly 2,000) demons. The Lord Jesus Christ cast the demons out of the man into a herd of pigs feeding nearby. The pigs ran into the water and were drown. (Mark 5:1-20)

Although occultism has been present in various forms for millennia, the New Testament indicates that an increased interest in the occult will accompany the end of the age:

Now the Holy Spirit tells us clearly that in the last times some will turn away from the true faith; they will follow deceptive spirits and teachings that come from demons. 1 Timothy 4:1 (NLT)

We have seen this prediction fulfilled with the explosion of the New Age* movement.

> * The New Age movement is briefly described in the Supplemental Information at the end of this study note.

All practitioners of occultism face eternity in Hell, the Lake of Fire. Writing through the Apostle John, the Holy Spirit warned:

... those who practice magic arts ... will be consigned to the fiery lake of burning sulfur. This is the second death. Revelation 21:8 (NIV)

Here are some practical guidelines for avoiding occultic practices. As Christians, we are not to

- Attempt to communicate with the dead (necromancy)

- Attempt to determine or foretell the future* apart from God's Word

> * Do you really want to know the future? Would you want to know it even if your personal future were to include the death of a child, or a fatal accident, or a horrible, debilitating illness? Think about it. It's an act of God's mercy that He doesn't show us the future.
>
> The only sure source of information about the future is God's Word, the Bible. The yet-future prophecies therein will be fulfilled as precisely as the hundreds of Bible prophecies that have already been fulfilled.

- Seek guidance or power from any supernatural source other than God and His Word

- Participate in any activity that purposely leaves our minds open to demonic influence

So you can recognize them for what they are, here's a partial list of occultic activities:

- Astrology
- Kabbalah
- Ouija boards
- Satanism
- Spiritism
- Transcendental Meditation
- Reiki

- Horoscopes
- Magic
- Parapsychology (ESP, telepathy, etc.)
- Séances
- Tarot card reading
- Witchcraft (Wicca, sorcery) of all types

And here's a partial list of occultic practitioners:

- Channelers
- Clairvoyants
- Fortune Tellers
- Reiki Masters

- Mediums
- Palm Readers
- Psychics

Occultism in any form is sin. It is not harmless entertainment or an alternate source of wisdom.

Christians are not to experiment with or dabble in occultic practices – not even once. If you have been involved with those practices, confess it to God, ask for His forgiveness, and request His help in renouncing those activities, then destroy everything you have that is associated with the occult – books, music, games, jewelry, crystals, and other paraphernalia. That's what the people did in ancient Ephesus (Acts 19:19).

Occultism is one aspect of the spiritual warfare that Satan launches against Christians (Ephesians 6:10-18). That's the reason why the Apostle Paul admonished us to *put on the full armor of God, that you may be able to stand firm against the schemes of the devil* (verse 11 – NASB).

Christians are not to fear the spirits involved in the occult, neither are we to seek wisdom from them. Our wisdom comes from God (James 1:5).

Ghosts

Ghosts (spirit beings) are not the disembodied spirits of deceased people, they are demons in disguise. When people die, their souls go immediately to Hades or Paradise, they do not remain on earth or return to earth because they cannot. This is described in detail in *The Eternal State*, the study note for point fourteen of the BMW Doctrinal Statement.

The Apostle Paul told us that Satan and his demons can masquerade as "angels of light" (2 Corinthians 11:14-15). They will do all they can to deceive people, to lead them away from God. This is the likely explanation of "ghostly" activity today.

New Age Movement

"The New Age movement is a loosely related array of ideas and philosophies that have much in common with both Hinduism and ancient Gnosticism. New Age religions are *pantheistic* (believing in the divinity of both Creator and creation), *mystical* (viewing truth as something one finds within oneself), and *syncretistic* (blending and merging religious ideas from any number of sources). There is also a large dose of occult superstition in most New Age thought." (Emphasis in original.) From the book, *The Glory of Heaven*, by Dr. John MacArthur

13. The Second Advent of Christ

*"We believe in the **personal**, **imminent**, **pretribulational** and **premillennial** coming of the Lord Jesus Christ for His redeemed ones. We believe that at the end of the seven-year **tribulation** He will return to earth with the saints in power and glory to reign for a **thousand years**. (Zechariah 14:4-11;1 Thessalonians 1:10; 4:13-18; 5:9; Titus 2:13; Revelation 3:10; 19:11-16; 20:1-6)"*

The words appearing in **bold** text in the paragraph above are explained in this study note. Here's where to find those words – and more – in this note:

The Advents of Christ

The first advent (coming) of the Lord Jesus Christ was His incarnation – His coming to earth as a humble baby. It is described in *The Person And Work Of Christ*, the study note for point three of the BMW Doctrinal Statement.

The second advent of Christ will be His coming to earth in power and great glory as conquering King of kings and Lord of lords. The second advent is mentioned eight times more frequently in the Old and New Testaments than is Christ's first advent. All first-advent prophecies were fulfilled precisely – the same will be true of the second-advent prophecies!

The second advent of Christ will occur in two phases:

- Phase one: He will come to rapture* the Church** from earth to Heaven before the seven-year Tribulation period. This first phase is frequently referred to as the "Blessed Hope" of the Church. The Rapture will end the current Church Age which began on the Day of Pentecost.

> * "Rapture" is from the Latin word *rapio*, meaning "to seize, snatch, carry away." The Greek equivalent is *harpazo*, translated "caught up" in 1 Thessalonians 4:17.
>
> ** The Church consists of all people who, during the Church Age, personally receive the Lord Jesus Christ as their Savior from sin.

- Phase two: He will come at the close of the seven-year Tribulation period to destroy the armies of Antichrist at the Battle of Armageddon. This second phase is commonly known as the "Glorious Appearing" of Christ.

Both phases of Christ's second advent are mentioned in Titus 2:13:

> *Looking for that* blessed hope, *and the* glorious appearing *of the great God and our Saviour Jesus Christ* (KJV)

The first phase is for Christians; the second phase is for the world of unbelievers. As described later in this study note, the two phases of His one second coming occur in different places, at different times (they will be at least seven years apart), for different people, and for different purposes.

Personal

The Lord Jesus Christ Himself will return in person to effect both phases of His second advent – He will not send an emissary or representative.

Imminent

Describing the second advent as "imminent" indicates that Christ could come at any moment, without warning. There is nothing that needs to be fulfilled before this event. It could be while you are reading this page!

Last Days

The terms "last days," "latter days," and "last hour" usually refer to the time period from just before the Rapture to the glorious appearing of Christ at the end of the seven-year Tribulation period (Titus 2:13) which precedes the Millennium. Some commentators loosely define the last days as the entire time period between the two advents of Christ.

When the Holy Spirit wrote the book of Revelation (through the Apostle John), He quoted Christ as telling John, *Surely I come quickly* (Revelation 22:20). The people in New Testament times therefore thought they were living in the last days. The New Testament writers consistently described the then-present age as the "last days." They were expecting the return of the Lord Jesus Christ during their lifetime.

> "Every generation of believers, including the present generation, have [sic] lived in times that cry out the sense of impending and overhanging destiny. The last of these last days is always imminent and impending. Since no man knows God's time schedule, the time of fulfillment is always 'at hand.' These events are near, in that they are the next events on God's prophetic calendar. There is a nearness, a next-ness, or at-hand-ness of the time." Excerpted from *Breaking the Apocalypse Code* by Mark Hitchcock and Thomas Ice

> "In eschatology and apocalyptic, the future is always viewed as imminent without the necessity of intervening time." *The Expositor's Bible Commentary*

Are we living in the "last of the last days"? Many people believe we are. Remember that the Rapture of the Church is a "signless" event – meaning there is nothing yet to be fulfilled before it occurs. It is thus imminent, it can occur any time.

Below are a few reasons why many believe the Rapture may be very close.

- We now have a global economy with worldwide banking, facilitating the establishment of the one-world government of the Antichrist.

- It's only recently that we've developed the technology needed to facilitate the fulfillment of some prophecies. Two examples:

  ❖ The technology that allows the instant global communication required in Revelation 11:9

  ❖ The implanting of computer chips in people. Those chips could serve as the mark of the Beast, described in Revelation 13:16

- The rise to power of Islam in certain countries has set the stage for fulfillment of Ezekiel 38 - 39, where it is prophesied that Russia and her Islamic allies attack Israel and are supernaturally defeated by God.

- The European Union could be part or all of the revived Roman Empire represented by the ten toes of the statue in Nebuchadnezzar's vision (Daniel 2:31-45). Modern Europe emerged from the rubble of the Roman Empire.

Caution! Although we may see what we consider "signs of the times," we should not engage in "newspaper exegesis" – using the headlines to determine the meaning of Bible prophecy. Christ warned us against trying to set dates relative to His return, telling us that no man knows the day or the hour of that event, not even the Son in His humanity (Mark 13:32; Matthew 24:42, 44, 50).

Speaking of time periods, we are told that certain sins will intensify in the period identified as the last days:

But know this, that in the last days* perilous** times will come: For men will be lovers of themselves, lovers of money, boasters, proud, blasphemers, disobedient to parents, unthankful, unholy, unloving, unforgiving, slanderers, without self-control, brutal, despisers of good, traitors, headstrong, haughty, lovers of pleasure rather than lovers of God, having a form of godliness but denying its power. And from such people turn away! 2 Timothy 3:1 (NKJV)

> *   In this verse, "days" is an inexact term, indicating an indefinite period of time. Note that in most other passages where it's used, the word "day" (Hebrew *yom*, Greek *hemera*), is also used in an exact sense to refer to one solar day, a period of 24 hours, one rotation of the Earth (Genesis 1:5; Mark 4:35).
>
> **   "Perilous" could also be translated "fierce" or "furious." The world will become increasingly violent and dangerous as the end approaches.

> During the Tribulation period, evil will be virtually unchecked. When Christians are removed from the earth at the Rapture of the Church (1 Thessalonians 4:13-17) there will be very little to restrain evil.

Should these things cause us to fear? No, just the opposite! We should have a sense of excitement, knowing that Christ could come today! It should also motivate us to evangelism and holy living:

> *Beloved, now are we the sons of God, and it doth not yet appear what we shall be: but we know that, when he shall appear, we shall be like him; for we shall see him as he is. And every man that hath this hope in him purifieth himself, even as he is pure.* 1 John 3:2-3 (KJV)

Christ's return is also:
- A blessed hope (1 Thessalonians 2:19)
- A comforting hope (1 Thessalonians 4:13-18)
- A hope of glory (Colossians 1:27)
- An anchoring hope (Hebrews 6:19)

Pretribulational

The rapture of the Church will occur before the start of the seven-year period of Tribulation, thus this phase is pre-tribulational. The Tribulation period is described below and depicted in the *Bible Prophecy Timeline* at the end of this study note.

When He returns to rapture His Church, the Lord Jesus Christ will come secretly (only His saints will see and hear Him). His coming will be in the air (His feet will not touch the earth) to call living and dead saints of the Church Age to Heaven.

The definitive passage on the Rapture is 1 Thessalonians 4:13-17. Here are verses 16 and 17 of that passage:

> *For the Lord himself shall descend from heaven with a shout, with the voice of the archangel, and with the trump of God: and the dead in Christ shall rise first: Then we which are alive and remain shall be caught up together with them in the clouds, to meet the Lord in the air: and so shall we ever be with the Lord.* (KJV)

Notice the order given above: Those who have died "in Christ" (saved people) will be resurrected out of their graves and rise to meet the Lord first. Then the living saints will ascend to meet the Lord in the air. At this point, there will be no saved people on earth.

Premillennial

The Glorious Appearing of Christ will terminate the Battle of Armageddon at the end of the Tribulation. The Glorious Appearing occurs before the Millennium, thus it is pre-millennial. The Millennium is described below.

In contrast to the secret Rapture, the Glorious Appearing will be public. Every eye shall see Him (Matthew 24:30). Christ will return to earth from Heaven, followed by the armies of Heaven which include the saints raptured seven years earlier (Revelation 19:11-18).

Tribulation

A future seven-year period of unprecedented judgment on the earth and its inhabitants. During this time, a future leader – known as the Antichrist* because he will be the antithesis of Christ – will rule the entire world, dominating both the political and economic world scenes.

> * The Antichrist is further described on page 140.

The Antichrist will sign a seven-year covenant of peace and protection with Israel. (The signing of this covenant is the actual start of the Tribulation period.) During the first 3½ years, the Jews will be allowed to rebuild the Jerusalem Temple* – destroyed by the Roman general Titus in 70 A.D. – and resume worship rituals. At mid-Tribulation, the Antichrist will break the covenant (Daniel 9:27) and desecrate the Temple by sacrificing unclean animals on the altar and by erecting a statue of himself to be worshiped. This is described as "the abomination that makes desolate" ("the abomination of desolation" in some translations). It is also possible that the Antichrist himself may take a seat in the Temple (Matthew 24:15, 2 Thessalonians 2:3-4, Revelation 13:14-15).

> * This will be the third Jewish Temple. Additional information is available in the Supplemental Information at the end of this study note.

The Tribulation combines the wrath of God, the fury of Satan, and the unbridled evil nature of man. When the Church is raptured before the Tribulation, the evil-restraining influence of Christians will be removed from the earth (2 Thessalonians 2:6-7). The result will be an unparalleled, unprecedented, reign of evil and evil people. The Lord Jesus Christ predicted that due to its severity, the Tribulation would be shortened for the sake of the elect, those He has chosen for salvation (Matthew 24:22).

During the Tribulation, there will be a one-world government led by the Antichrist, and an apostate, ecumenical, one-world church that will persecute those who trust Christ as Savior. The Antichrist* will tolerate the church until mid-Tribulation when he will destroy her and give the False Prophet* authority over the world religious system.

> * The unholy Trinity will consist of these members:
>
> - Satan – the antithesis of God the Father
>
> - Antichrist – the antithesis of the Lord Jesus Christ, God the Son
>
> - False Prophet – the antithesis of God the Holy Spirit
>
> Note that the Antichrist and the False Prophet are men – human beings.

Satan will empower the False Prophet to perform miracles and lead people to worship the Antichrist. Toward the end of the Tribulation, the False Prophet will require people to receive a mark on their forehead or on their hand to show their allegiance to the Antichrist. No one will be able to buy or sell without this mark (Revelation 13:11-17). Receiving this mark – the "Mark of the Beast*" – will doom the recipient to eternal punishment in the Lake of Fire (Revelation 14:9-11).

> * Two men are identified as "beasts" in the book of Revelation: The "beast out of the sea" – the Antichrist (Revelation 13:1-10) – and the "beast out of the earth" – the False Prophet (Revelation 13:11-18). God calls them "beasts" to indicate how He views them.

During the Tribulation there will be seven Seal Judgments, followed by seven Trumpet Judgments, then seven Bowl (Vial) Judgments

- The Seal Judgments are so named because they correspond to the Lamb of God, the Lord Jesus Christ, opening the seven seals on the title deed to the earth. The first four Seal Judgments are four horsemen – known as the "Four Horsemen of the Apocalypse" – representing militarism, war, famine, and death. They result in the deaths of one-fourth of the world's population. The next three seals represent Christian martyrdom, physical disturbances on the earth, and silence.

- In the ancient world, trumpets were used to signal major events. The seven Trumpet Judgments are indeed major events! In these judgments, God pours out His wrath on plants, the seas, the fresh water, all creation, and mankind. Each judgment is more severe than its predecessor, but men stubbornly refuse to repent of their wickedness. When the Trumpet Judgments have concluded, at least half of the world's population will have died.

- The Bowl Judgments are the most severe. Because of man's sin, the bowls of God's wrath have been filling for millennia. Now they are full and are ready to be poured out onto the earth. Each of seven angels pours out a bowl of God's wrath upon the earth. God judges the land, seas, fresh water, skies, government, the holy land, and the entire earth. And the people will still stubbornly reject God!

During the first half of the Tribulation, God will commission 144,000 newly saved Jewish Christians to spread the gospel worldwide (Matthew 24:14; Revelation 7:3-8). This will produce a great harvest of people won to Christ (Revelation 7:9-10, 13-14). Many of these new saints will be martyred by the Antichrist.

Also during the first half of the Tribulation, God will send two divinely protected witnesses to Jerusalem to speak on His behalf and declare divine truth. They will prophesy for 1,260 days* and have the ability to perform miracles to authenticate their message (Revelation 11:3-13). After the two witnesses have finished their mission, God will allow the Antichrist to kill them. Their bodies will lie in the streets of Jerusalem without burial. People will be so happy to see the witnesses die that they will send gifts to each other in celebration. After three days, God will resurrect the witnesses and call them to Heaven with the words, "Come up here."

> * Prophecy dates are based on twelve 30-day months per year.

In mid-Tribulation, the Antichrist is killed by one of his political enemies (Revelation 17:8). Satan then indwells the dead body of the Antichrist and brings it back to life*, duplicating the resurrection of the Lord Jesus Christ (Revelation 13:3).

> *   The Antichrist (the "beast out of the sea" – Revelation 13:1) is described as having seven heads and ten horns, representing his political empire and power. Some commentators suggest that one of the beast's heads, and not necessarily the beast himself, will receive a fatal wound.

Also in mid-Tribulation there is war in the atmospheric heavens (Revelation 12:7-13). The archangel Michael and his angels defeat Satan and his evil angels and cast them down to earth, permanently. Satan then turns his full fury and wrath on the Jews.

While the Tribulation is transpiring on earth, the raptured saints in Heaven will stand before the judgment seat of Christ (the Bema Seat – 1 Corinthians 3:13-15, 2 Corinthians 5:10) to receive or lose eternal rewards, based on their service to the Lord while they were on earth. This judgment will not affect their salvation; it's eternally secure because of the work of the Savior on their behalf. The Bema Seat Judgment is so named because the Greek word translated "judgment seat" in 2 Corinthians 5:10 is *bema*. It means "steps" or "steps leading up to a platform." The picture is that of a judge sitting on a raised platform with steps leading up to it.

After the Bema Seat Judgment, the Bride of Christ (the Church) and her Bridegroom (the Lord Jesus Christ) will be wed in Heaven (Revelation 19:6-8). A Marriage Feast will take place on earth at the start of the Millennium.

At the end of the Tribulation period, the Antichrist and the world rulers who are loyal to him will marshal their armies at the Mountain of Megiddo (literal meaning of *Armageddon*) and in the surrounding plain (the Valley of Jezreel) for a final assault on the Jews and Jerusalem. The ultimate purpose is to annihilate God's people, the Jews.

The Battle of Armageddon, as it is popularly known, is actually one battle of a war, a military campaign, that the Bible describes as "the battle of that great day of God Almighty" (Revelation 16:14 – KJV). The following synopsis of the Campaign of Armageddon is excerpted from Dr. Arnold Fruchtenbaum's book *The Footsteps of the Messiah*, pages 308 - 357:

- The allies of Antichrist assemble in the Valley of Jezreel (frequently mislabeled as the Valley of Armageddon). Psalm 2:1-6; Joel 3:9-11; Revelation 16:12-16

- Antichrist's enemies destroy the revived city of Babylon which is Antichrist's headquarters and the center of world politics and business. The Antichrist is not in Babylon when this occurs – he's marshaling forces in Jezreel. Isaiah 13-14; Jeremiah 50-51; Zechariah 5:5-11; Revelation 17-18

- Antichrist's armies move south and conquer Jerusalem. Half the population is taken into slavery, half is left in the city. Micah 4:11 - 5:1; Zechariah 12-14

- Antichrist's armies move south and east, to attack the Jews at Bozrah* in Edom (southern Jordan). The Campaign of Armageddon enters the last three days. Jeremiah 49:13-14; Micah 2:12

- Israel confesses her national sin (two days) and Jewish leaders lead the nation to the recognition of Christ's Messiahship. All remaining Jews (the remnant) are spiritually saved! Psalm 79:1-13; 80:1-19; Isaiah 64:1-12; Hosea 6:1-3; Joel 2:28-32; Zechariah 12:10 - 13:1; 13:7-9; Romans 11:25-27

- The Lord Jesus Christ returns to earth (Glorious Appearing) to fight the armies of Antichrist at Bozrah. Isaiah 34:1-7; 63:1-3; Micah 2:12-13; Habakkuk 3:3

- The battle continues west and north toward Jerusalem – from Bozrah to the Valley of Jehoshaphat (part of the Kidron Valley) – where it ends. Christ kills the Antichrist; his body is trampled by his own troops. As a result of this final battle, the blood of slain armies and their animals is four feet deep in the Valley. Jeremiah 49:20-22; Joel 3:12-13; Zechariah 14:12-15; Revelation 19:11-21

- Christ makes a victory ascent up the Mount of Olives – the location from which He ascended after His resurrection (Acts 1:9). The victory ascent will be accompanied by lightning, thunder, voices, the most severe global earthquake ever to afflict the earth, hailstones weighing 120 pounds, and other physical disturbances. Joel 3:14-17; Zechariah 14:3-5; Matthew 24:29-31; Revelation 16:17-21

Following the Campaign of Armageddon, Satan and his fallen angels (demons) will be bound in the bottomless pit for the 1000-year Millennium (Revelation 20:1-3).

At the end of the Tribulation, there will be three groups of people left alive on earth: (1) Gentile Christians who escaped martyrdom, (2) unsaved Gentiles, and (3) Jews who accepted their Messiah and thus were saved. (Unbelieving Jews will not survive to the end of the Tribulation.)

The Lord Jesus Christ will judge the living Gentiles at the Judgment of the Nations (Matthew 25:31-46, where "nations" should be translated "Gentiles") during a 75-day period between the Tribulation and the Millennium. The unsaved Gentiles will be sent to Hades, to ultimately stand before God at the Great White Throne Judgment and be cast into the Lake of Fire. Jewish and Gentile Christians will continue alive into the Millennium.

The Old Testament saints and the slain Tribulation saints will be resurrected during the 75-day period (Revelation 20:4-6).

The Tribulation period is also known as the "Seventieth Week* of Daniel" (Daniel 9:24-27), "The Time of Jacob's Trouble" (Jeremiah 30:7), "the day of the Lord" (1 Thessalonians 5:2), and "the last day" (2 Timothy 3:1).

The end of the Tribulation period also marks the end of "The Times of the Gentiles" (Luke 21:24) which began with Nebuchadnezzar's destruction of the Jewish Temple in 586 B.C. The Times of the Gentiles is that period when the Gentiles have dominance over the city of Jerusalem. There have been short periods when the Jews had control of the city since 586 B.C., but permanent control of Jerusalem by the Jews will occur only after the Tribulation.

Millennium / Thousand Years

A future 1000-year period (Latin *mille* = 1,000 + *annum* = year) following the Tribulation. This 1000-year period is also known as the Millennial Kingdom and the Messianic Age.

The physical earth will be severely damaged by events of the Tribulation. During the 75-day interval between the Tribulation and the Millennium, God will renovate His creation in preparation for the Millennial Kingdom.

During the Millennium, the Lord Jesus Christ will physically reign on a restored earth, occupying the throne of David. The saints who return with Christ at the Glorious Appearing and those who were resurrected during the 75-day interval will rule and reign with Him during this time. It will be a time of true peace because Christ will rule with an iron fist. The physical environment will be ideal. The desert will blossom and become productive; all creatures will live in harmony (Isaiah 11:6-7). Conditions will be conducive to long life. Only those unsaved people who refuse to accept the Lord Jesus Christ as Savior will die during the Millennium.

Israel will be the head over all nations. God will continue fulfilling His promises to that nation.

The Marriage of the Lamb took place in Heaven during the Tribulation. The seven-day Marriage Feast will occur on earth and will initiate the Millennial period. Only the Church-Age saints (the Bride of Christ) were present at the marriage. At the Feast, the resurrected Old Testament saints and the saints from the Tribulation will be present as guests, "friends of the bridegroom" (Revelation 19:9).

Another Jewish Temple ("Ezekiel's Temple," the fourth Temple) will be constructed at the beginning of the Millennium. This Temple will be the center of worship in the Millennial Kingdom. The Jews will once again offer animal sacrifices (Ezekiel 40 - 48). These sacrifices relate exclusively to purification of the priests and objects used for Temple service. The sacrifices do not depict or represent Christ's atoning sacrifice, as did the sacrifices of the Old Testament period. The sacrifices teach that mankind can only approach God through holiness and that humanity is not holy. Only through the death of Christ can sin be permanently dealt with because the blood of bulls and goats could never take away sin (Hebrews 10:4).

In the article *The Problem Of Animal Sacrifices In Ezekiel 40 - 48*, author Jerry Hullinger wrote the following:

> " … animal sacrifices during the millennium will serve primarily to remove ceremonial uncleanness and prevent defilement from polluting the Temple envisioned by Ezekiel. This will be necessary because the glorious presence of Yahweh will once again be dwelling on earth in the midst of a sinful and unclean people." Published in *Bibliotheca Sacra*, Volume 152, Number 607

Jewish and Gentile Christians who escape martyrdom during the Tribulation will continue into the Millennial Kingdom. They will produce physical offspring. Like those in prior ages, these children will have to make a personal choice to accept or reject the offer of salvation through the Lord Jesus Christ. Those who reject Christ (or ignore Him – John 3:18) will ultimately be consigned to the Lake of Fire forever.

Satan and his fallen angels (demons) who have been bound during the Millennium will be released at the end of the 1000 years to once again deceive unsaved mankind into rebelling against God and attacking Israel and Jerusalem. God will destroy these massive armies by sending fire from heaven (Revelation 20:7-9). Satan and his demon hordes will be sent to the Lake of Fire for eternity.

The Great White Throne Judgment (Revelation 20:11-15) of the unsaved of all ages occurs after the Millennium. Everyone who appears before Christ at this judgment will be sentenced to eternal conscious torment in the Lake of Fire. Refer to *The Eternal State*, the study note for point fourteen of the BMW Doctrinal Statement.

The Antichrist

The word "Antichrist" (with an uppercase "A") is not found in the King James Version (KJV) of the Bible, but it is in the New KJV, the Holman Christian Standard Bible (HCSB), and others. It is a personal name (Greek *Antichristos*) and thus should be capitalized.

The Lord Jesus Christ referred to the Antichrist as the *abomination of desolation* (Matthew 24:15). Paul called him *the man of sin ... the son of perdition* (2 Thessalonians 2:3) and *the wicked one* (2 Thessalonians 2:8). John identified him as *the beast* (Revelation 11:7, 13:1-4) that came up out of the sea, thus associating him with the fourth beast described in Daniel's prophecy (Daniel 7:7).

The Antichrist will be the epitome, the embodiment, of all that is evil. He is against Christ and all that is Christian – thus his name: Antichrist. Some commentators believe he will most likely be a Gentile of Roman origin, the same nationality as the people who destroyed Jerusalem and the Temple in 70 A.D. (Daniel 9:26-27).

According to 1 John 2:18, there will be many antichrists (lowercase "a") – those who oppose Christ – who precede the one Antichrist (uppercase "A"). The *NIV Study Bible* indicates that the antichrists are characterized by the following traits:

- They deny the incarnation of Christ (1 John 4:2, 2 John 7) and that Jesus is the divine Christ (1 John 2:22)

- They deny the Father (1 John 2:22)

- They do not have the Father (1 John 2:23)

- They are liars (1 John 2:22) and deceivers (2 John 7)

- They are many (1 John 2:18)

- They left the church [in John's day] because they had nothing in common with believers – they were, in fact, unbelievers, never saved by the blood of Christ (1 John 2:19)

How About You – Are You Ready?

The Lord Jesus Christ is coming to earth again – that's His promise (John 14:3). His return is imminent; it could be today. Are you ready?

In this study note, we've looked in some detail at the seven-year Tribulation period, the horrific, devastating time period yet to come. No one who truly understands what the Tribulation will entail would choose to be on earth during that time.

Reader, if you are alive when the Lord Jesus Christ comes to rapture the Church, will you be left behind? The only way to avoid that is to invite Christ into your life to be your Savior from sin. You can do that right now, right where you are. You can pray a simple prayer like the one below or use your own words. God knows your heart.

> God, I know I am a sinner. I'm sorry for my sin. Forgive me. I want to turn from my sin. I now receive the Lord Jesus Christ as my Savior. I confess Him as my Lord. From now on I want to follow Him. Thank you for saving me. I pray this in the name of Jesus. Amen

Perhaps you're reading this after Christ has returned for His saints and you have been left behind. You still have the opportunity to trust Christ as Savior and be assured that you will spend eternity in His presence. Right now, pray the prayer in the paragraph above or use your own words.

Supplemental Information

Jewish Temples

The Hebrew word for "Temple" literally means "big building" or "palace." The Greek word for "temple" means "a sacred place." A temple is a building set apart for the worship of a deity.

The historical Jewish Temples provided a permanent home for the Ark of the Covenant and for the worship of the Lord.

Here's a list of the Temples, past and future:

- The first Temple was Solomon's Temple (built by Solomon). It was completed in 960 B.C., and destroyed (burned) by Nebuchadnezzar in 586 B.C.

- The second, somewhat smaller, Temple was built approximately 70 years later by Zerubbabel and Joshua. It was desecrated by Antiochus (IV) Epiphenes, a Greco-Syrian ruler, in 167 B.C. by sacrificing a sow on the altar and setting up a statue of Zeus in the Temple. Soon thereafter, a fight to reclaim Jewish autonomy was initiated by Mattathias, an elderly Jewish priest, and his five sons. It ended in 164 B.C. when Judah (Judas) Maccabee (Maccabaeus), third son of Mattathias, and his band of Hassidaeans* recaptured the Temple. They then cleansed it, purified it, and rededicated it to God.

    * The Hassidaeans were a group of Jewish patriots and religious freedom fighters. The Hassidaean party of the early days of the Hasmonean revolt (second century B.C.) developed into the group known as the Pharisees. Hashmon, for whom the

Hasmoneans were named, was an ancestor of the Maccabees.

The Menorah – the seven-branched candelabrum symbolizing the divine presence – was rekindled on the 25th day of the Jewish month of Kislev (Chislev) in mid-December, three years to the day after the first pagan sacrifices were offered in the Temple. The Jewish holiday of Chanukah (Hanukah), the Festival of Lights, celebrates this event.

Herod had the second temple remodeled and enlarged, finishing circa 40 A.D. "Herod's Temple" was destroyed when Titus sacked Jerusalem in 70 A.D.

- A new Temple (the "third Temple") will be built on the Temple Mount* before or during the Tribulation, certainly before the midpoint in the Tribulation. The Jews will resume blood sacrifices in this Temple. Reportedly, all the furnishings for the third Temple have already been produced.

  * The current site of the Dome of the Rock, an Islamic Shrine, houses the Foundation Stone (the holiest spot in Judaism). The Dome edifice is also known as The Mosque of Omar. It was completed by the Arabs in 691 A.D. Some believe the Foundation Stone was the location of the Holy of Holies in the first Temple, and that the Temple Mount is Mount Moriah where Abraham was told to offer his son Isaac as a sacrifice to God.

This third Temple will be desecrated by the Antichrist at the middle of the Tribulation. The False Prophet, acting on behalf of the Antichrist, will set up an image of the Antichrist in the Holy of Holies, defiling it, thus fulfilling the prophecy of "abomination of desolation" (the abomination that makes desolate). For this reason, the third temple is sometimes referred to as "Antichrist's Temple."

This Temple probably will be destroyed by the final earthquake associated with Christ's Glorious Appearing (Revelation 19:11-21; Titus 2:13), or by the final military invasion of Jerusalem.

- A fourth Temple will be constructed at the beginning of the Millennium. The Jews will again offer animal sacrifices during the Millennium.

Animal sacrifices in the fourth Temple will also be temporary, covering the defilement of the objects used in the Temple rituals.

In contrast, Christ's sacrifice was perfect because it was permanent, once-for-all-time, and covered not only the guilt, but the actual sin itself – in fact, all sins of all people in all ages!

Because it's described in the Old Testament book of Ezekiel, the fourth Temple is sometimes referred to as "Ezekiel's Temple." It will be the focus of the entire world during Christ's thousand-year reign from Jerusalem. Israel and the Temple will serve as the center for priestly rituals and offerings that will provide guidance in the worship of Jesus, the Messiah.

Two Other Temples

The Bible also speaks of another Temple, but it's not an earthly Temple, as were the other four. The Apostle John speaks of a heavenly Temple from which God oversees the judgments of the Tribulation and sends forth His angels at His command (Revelation 7:15; 11:19; 14:15, 17; 15:5-6,8; 16:1,17). The heavenly Temple, in some senses, serves as a model for the various earthly dwellings of God (Tabernacle, physical Temples, and spiritual Temple – the Church).

The body of a true Christian is also a temple – it's the dwellingplace of the Holy Spirit of God. At the moment of salvation, God the Holy Spirit baptizes us into the body of Christ (the true Church – 1 Corinthians 12:13) and indwells, takes up permanent residence within, the new Christian (1 Corinthians 6:19-20). Because of this, the believer is eternally sealed into God's family, forever secure, the Holy Spirit Himself being the Seal guaranteeing our eternal inheritance (Ephesians 1:13-14, 4:30).

Bible Prophecy Timeline

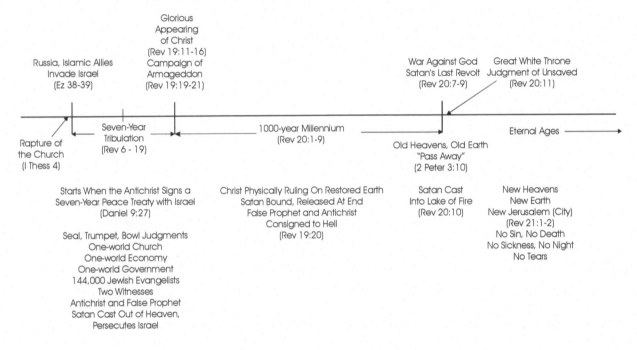

Glorious
Appearing
of Christ
(Rev 19:11-16)
Campaign of
Armageddon
(Rev 19:19-21)

Russia, Islamic Allies
Invade Israel
(Ez 38-39)

War Against God
Satan's Last Revolt
(Rev 20:7-9)

Great White Throne
Judgment of Unsaved
(Rev 20:11)

Seven-Year
Tribulation
(Rev 6 - 19)

1000-year Millennium
(Rev 20:1-9)

Eternal Ages

Rapture of
the Church
(I Thess 4)

Old Heavens, Old Earth
"Pass Away"
(2 Peter 3:10)

Starts When the Antichrist Signs a
Seven-Year Peace Treaty with Israel
(Daniel 9:27)

Seal, Trumpet, Bowl Judgments
One-world Church
One-world Economy
One-world Government
144,000 Jewish Evangelists
Two Witnesses
Antichrist and False Prophet
Satan Cast Out of Heaven,
Persecutes Israel

Christ Physically Ruling On Restored Earth
Satan Bound, Released At End
False Prophet and Antichrist
Consigned to Hell
(Rev 19:20)

Satan Cast
Into Lake of Fire
(Rev 20:10)

New Heavens
New Earth
New Jerusalem (City)
(Rev 21:1-2)
No Sin, No Death
No Sickness, No Night
No Tears

14. The Eternal State (of Mankind)

*"We believe in the **bodily resurrection** of all men, the **saved** to **eternal life** and the unsaved to **judgment** and **everlasting punishment**. (Matthew 25:46; John 5:28-29; 11:25-26; Revelation 20:5,6,12-13)*

*"We believe the souls of the redeemed are, at death, **absent from the body** and **present with the Lord**, where in conscious bliss they await the **first resurrection** when spirit, soul, and body are reunited and **glorified** to be forever with the Lord. (Luke 23:43; 2 Corinthians 5:8; Philippians 1:23; 3:21; 1 Thessalonians 4:16-17; Revelation 20:4-6)*

*"We believe the souls of unbelievers are, at death, absent from the body and in conscious misery until the **second resurrection**, when with soul and body reunited they shall appear at the **Great White Throne Judgment** and shall be cast into the **lake of fire**, not to be **annihilated**, but to suffer everlasting conscious punishment. (Matthew 25:41-46; Mark 9:43-48; Luke 16:19-26; 2 Thessalonians 1:7-9; Jude 6-7; Revelation 20:11-15)"*

The words appearing in **bold** text in the paragraphs above are explained in this study note. Here's where to find those words – and more – in this note:

Absent from the body   Page 148
Annihilation   Page 154
Bodily resurrection   Page 145
Book of Life   Page 150
Dominion Mandate   Page 156
Eternal life / everlasting punishment   Page 146
First resurrection / second resurrection   Page 149
Glorified   Page 150
Great White Throne Judgment   Page 150
Heaven   Page 154
Judgment   Page 147
Lake of Fire   Page 152
Present with the Lord   Page 149
Saved / salvation   Page 146
What will Christians do in Heaven for eternity?   Page 155

God created man as a tri-unity: body, soul, and spirit. Man's physical body was created to live forever, but when Adam and Eve sinned (Genesis 3:6), God pronounced a curse on all nature – the entire cosmos (Genesis 3:17-19). As a result, corruption (decay) and physical death became a part of the human condition (Romans 5:12). Man's body would no longer live forever; it came from dust, it would return to dust.

Although man's physical body dies, his soul and spirit survive physical death. This fourteenth point of the BMW Doctrinal Statement describes what the Bible teaches regarding the destiny of man's soul at death and his eternal (final, never-ending) state.

Bodily Resurrection

Bodily resurrection refers to physically bringing a dead body back to life. Resurrection is the opposite of physical death.

Everyone who has ever died will live again. Their physical body will be brought back to life and changed into a form that will live forever, consciously aware of their existence.

The resurrection bodies of the unsaved (unregenerate, those who didn't accept Christ while they were physically alive on earth) will experience unimaginable torment forever, yet without perishing.

In his book, *The Glory of Heaven,* Dr. John MacArthur provides the following regarding the resurrection bodies of the saved:

> "The creation of a new heaven and earth demands that we have bodies – a physical earth calls for its inhabitants to have physical bodies. … The best picture of what we'll be like in heaven is the resurrection body of Jesus Christ. … Our resurrection bodies *are* our earthly bodies, glorified. The bodies we receive in the resurrection will have the same qualities as the glorified resurrection body of Christ. … They will be real, physical, genuinely human bodies – the very same bodies we have while on this earth – yet wholly perfected and glorified. … We will be ourselves, only perfect.

> "Human graveyards are seed plots for the resurrection of the dead. But the resurrection body is new, changed in virtually every way imaginable. It was sown in death and decay; it is raised to be *imperishable*. It was buried as a thing of defilement, ingloriously placed under the earth; but it is raised as something *glorious*. When entombed it is dead, utterly inanimate and impotent; but it is raised to be *powerful*. It is planted as a lifeless material thing, yet raised as something full of life and *spiritual*." (Italics in original)

Dr. Charles Stanley provides further insight:

> "What kind of body will we have in the resurrection? A body that will not wear out or grow old. One that will not be subject to sickness, but will be healthy and strong for all eternity. And most of all, it will be a body that cannot be corrupted by sin, so we will be able to magnify and glorify the living God the way we were created to do!" *From the Pastor's Heart* newsletter, April, 2007

Saved / Salvation

Salvation is the state (condition) of being rescued (saved, delivered) from the power and penalty of sin. It is a spiritual rebirth, frequently referred to as being "born again."

We are saved only through – on the basis of – the blood of Christ.

This subject is discussed in more detail in *Salvation and Security*, the study note for point six of the BMW Doctrinal Statement.

Eternal Life / Everlasting Punishment

Eternal Life refers to never-ending, conscious, blissful life lived in the favorable presence of God.

Everlasting Punishment refers to never-ending life lived in conscious physical torment, apart from the favorable presence of God.

The punishment of the wicked in Hell will occur in the very presence of the angels and the Savior they rejected (Revelation 14:9-11 – quoted below), but they will not benefit from an awareness of His presence (2 Thessalonians 1:8-9 – quoted below). They will endure the unlimited and unceasing fury of God because of their sin. The angels will be the executioners of God's sentence on the unsaved.

> *A third angel followed them and said in a loud voice: "If anyone worships the beast and its image and receives its mark on their forehead or on their hand, they, too, will drink the wine of God's fury, which has been poured full strength into the cup of his wrath. They will be tormented with burning sulfur in the presence of the holy angels and of the Lamb. And the smoke of their torment will rise for ever and ever. There will be no rest day or night for those who worship the beast and its image, or for anyone who receives the mark of its name." Revelation 14:9-11* (NIV)

> *In flaming fire taking vengeance on them that know not God, and that obey not the gospel of our Lord Jesus Christ: Who shall be punished with everlasting destruction from the presence of the Lord, and from the glory of his power* 2 Thessalonians 1:8-9 (KJV)

Judgment

Everyone who has ever lived will stand before the Lord Jesus Christ for judgment; the saved to receive rewards for faithful service (2 Corinthians 5:10), the lost (unsaved) to be sentenced to the Lake of Fire for their ultimate rejection of Jesus Christ, God's only provision for man's salvation (John 14:6).

The saints (saved people) who lived during the Church Age* will be judged at the Bema Seat Judgment. This judgment is so named because the Greek word translated "judgment seat" in 2 Corinthians 5:10 is *bema*. It means "steps" or "steps leading up to a platform." The picture is one of a judge sitting on a raised platform with steps leading up to it.

> *   The terms *Church Age* and *Tribulation* are discussed in conjunction with point thirteen of the BMW Doctrinal Statement, *The Second Advent of Christ*. Refer also to the *Bible Prophecy Timeline* at the end of that study note.

The Bema Seat Judgment will take place in Heaven while the Tribulation is occurring on earth. Saints who lived in periods other than the Church Age will be judged after their resurrection at the end of the Tribulation.

At the Bema Seat Judgment, Christians will receive rewards for what they did for their Savior during their lifetime. There will also be loss of potential rewards (1 Corinthians 3:13-15). Note that this is a judgment of the Christians' works, not their salvation. The payment for their sins was paid on Calvary by the Lord Jesus Christ. Their salvation is eternally secure.

The unsaved dead of all ages will be judged at the Great White Throne Judgment (described below).

God's judgment will be absolutely fair because it will be according to truth. God is keeping records of each person's life. When those records are presented, no unsaved person will be able to claim that he wasn't given the opportunity for salvation.

Before the death of the Lord Jesus Christ, the souls/spirits (let's shorten that to "souls") of all the deceased went to *Hades* (Greek – the Hebrew name is *Sheol*) at the time of physical death.

Luke 16:19-31 describes Hades as having three compartments or levels:

- A place of bliss ("Abraham's Bosom" or "Paradise" – verse 23)

- A place of torment (this is Hades proper – verse 23 – commonly [and incorrectly] known today as Hell*)

> *   Unfortunately, the KJV translates *Sheol, Hades, Tartarus* and *Gehenna* as "Hell." The English word *Hell* comes from a Teutonic root meaning "to cover" or "to hide."

- An impassable chasm ("great gulf" – verse 26) between them. The souls of the righteous dead went to Paradise, the unrighteous dead to the place of torment

Those in the place of torment and those in Paradise were conscious, could see each other, and could verbally communicate with each other across the chasm.

Note that Luke 16:19-31 is not a parable, as some teach, it is the account of an actual experience; it is the factual record of two men who lived and died. In this detailed account, we are given the name of one of the men (Lazarus, the beggar), we are told that the other man (the "rich man") had five unsaved brothers, we know the conditions each man in Hades was experiencing (comfort *vs.* torment of fire), and we are allowed to "listen in" on some of the conversation between the rich man and Abraham.

When the Lord Jesus Christ died, His soul descended to Paradise (Matthew 12:40, Acts 2:27). There He announced that the atonement had been made, and proclaimed to those in the place of torment that His death guarantees the judgment of the unsaved (Ephesians 4:8-10*). Then, at His resurrection, Christ took the souls of the righteous dead to Heaven with Him – He emptied the Paradise compartment of Hades. It no longer exists. Paradise is now in Heaven. Now, when a Christian dies his soul goes directly to Heaven (2 Corinthians 5:8) to remain there until the first resurrection when bodies and souls will be reunited. In the eternal future, Paradise will be in the New Jerusalem because that's the future home of the redeemed (Revelation 21:2).

> *   Some expositors interpret Ephesians 4:8-10 as teaching that at death, the Lord Jesus Christ went directly to Heaven, not to the Paradise side of Hades. They interpret the phrase, *He ... first descended into the lower parts of the earth* (verse 9) to refer to Christ's incarnation, His coming to earth as a baby.

The souls of all the unsaved dead of all ages will remain in the place of torment until the second resurrection when their bodies and souls will be reunited to stand before Christ at the Great White Throne Judgment. At that point, Hades will be empty. When the physical earth is completely changed and purified at the end of the Millennium (2 Peter 3:10-13), Hades will be destroyed because it is in the center of the present earth (Matthew 12:40, Ezekiel 26:20; 32:18, 24).

Note that some religious traditions teach "soul sleep" – the belief that after a person dies, his or her soul "sleeps" (is unconscious) until the resurrection and final judgment. Although it is found in some of the non-canonical writings of the early church, the concept of "soul sleep" is not biblical. When the Bible describes a person "sleeping" in relation to death (Luke 8:52; 1 Corinthians 15:6), it does not mean literal sleep. Sleeping is just a way to describe death because a dead body appears to be asleep. At death, the body is indeed unconscious and unresponsive until the resurrection, but the soul is very much alive.

As noted above, at the moment of physical death, the conscious soul of the believer goes to be with the Lord in Paradise (2 Corinthians 5:6-8); the soul of the unbeliever goes to the place of conscious continual torment in Hades, to await the Great White Throne Judgment.

Hades is a place of torment for the soul only. The Lake of Fire will be a place of torment for both body and soul.

Present With The Lord

Since the death and resurrection of the Lord Jesus Christ, when a believer dies, his or her conscious soul goes directly into the presence of the Lord, to remain with Him forever (2 Corinthians 5:8).

First Resurrection / Second Resurrection

The Bible speaks of two future bodily resurrections, appropriately named the *first resurrection* and the *second resurrection*.

The first resurrection is for those who, during their lifetime, received the Lord Jesus Christ as their Savior from sin; the second resurrection is for those who didn't.

The first resurrection is also described as the *resurrection to life* (John 5:29). This bodily resurrection will occur in stages: the Church Age saints at the Rapture* of the Church (1 Thessalonians 4:16-17), the Old Testament saints and Tribulation saints (those martyred during the Tribulation period) at the end of the Tribulation (Daniel 12:12, Revelation 20:4). The resurrected saints will reign with Christ during the Millennium* (Revelation 20:4-6).

> * The terms *Rapture* and *Millennium* are discussed in conjunction with point thirteen of the BMW Doctrinal Statement, *The Second Advent of Christ*.

Currently, the souls and spirits of all deceased saints of all ages are in Heaven with the Lord Jesus Christ (2 Corinthians 5:8). Their dead bodies are in the earth or sea, awaiting the first resurrection when body, soul and spirit will be reunited at the Rapture (Church Age saints) or when Christ returns after the Tribulation (Old Testament saints and Tribulation saints).

Since their physical deaths, the souls and spirits of the unsaved of all ages have been tormented in Hades. Their bodies will be resurrected at the end of the Millennium (Revelation 20:11-15).

This is the second resurrection. It is referred to as the *resurrection to death* (John 5:29) since every person who participates in this resurrection is already condemned to eternal death in the Lake of Fire. Their condemnation was sealed at the moment of physical death.

All opportunity for salvation ends at death. The Bible doesn't teach postmortem salvation – just the opposite:

> *And as it is appointed unto men once to die, but after this the judgment* Hebrews 9:27 (KJV)

Note that this verse negates the teaching of reincarnation, also known as the transmigration of the soul, the teaching that a person can experience multiple birth/death cycles.

Glorified

In simplest terms, *glorification* means being made perfect, conformed to the image of the Lord Jesus Christ (Romans 8:29-30). We will be perfect in Heaven because we will be free from the presence (influence and control) of sin.

At the time of salvation, we were saved from the penalty of sin (that's *justification*), we are currently in the process of being saved from the power of sin (that's *sanctification*), and in Heaven we will be saved from the presence of sin (that's *glorification*). This is described more fully in the Supplemental Information at the end of *Salvation and Security*, the study note for point six of the BMW Doctrinal Statement.

Great White Throne Judgment

The Great White Throne Judgment (GWTJ) gets its name from the first few words of Revelation 20:11 – *And I saw a great white throne …*

Everyone who stands before the Lord Jesus Christ at the GWTJ is already condemned because they didn't accept Christ as their personal Savior from sin (John 3:17-19) before they died. They will spend eternity in the Lake of Fire. What is to be determined at this judgment is the degree of their punishment.

Sentencing at the GWTJ will be based on the content of these books:

- The Book of Life – also known as The Lamb's Book of Life

- The Book of Deeds (referred to in the Bible simply as "books")

The Book of Life

There are many passages that refer to the Book of Life. Revelation 13:8 indicates that names were written in the Book *from the foundation of the world.*

There is some discussion among commentators regarding the scope of names written in the Book of Life. Some believe the Book includes the names of all who are conceived. These commentators indicate that a person's name remains in the Book unless and until he or she irrevocably rejects the Lord Jesus Christ as Savior. Final rejection of the Savior erases their name from the Book. Other commentators believe the only names written in this Book are those whom God elected to salvation before the foundation of the world (Ephesians 1:4).

In the final analysis, since all who are saved are eternally secure (can never lose their salvation), their names will never be removed from the Book.

Scripture explicitly states that if a person's name is not found in the Book at the time of judgment, he or she will not inherit eternal life:

> *And if anyone's name was not found written in the book of life, he was thrown into the lake of fire.*
> Revelation 20:15 (NASB)

The message is clear: the names of those who have received Christ as Savior are indelibly written in the Book of Life. They will not face an eternity in the Lake of Fire. Those whose names were never in the Book – or were erased from the Book – will spend eternity in the Lake of Fire.

Note that some commentators consider the Book of Life and the Lamb's Book of Life to be distinct. However, since at the time of judgment the name of every saved person – and only those names – will appear in this Book(s), it seems inconsequential whether there is one Book or two – the result is the same.

The Book of Deeds

The title, *Book of Deeds*, is not found in the Bible. The title was chosen for our purposes because it is descriptive of the content of these volumes.

That God is keeping a record of all our deeds is apparent from the passage below. The reference is to the Great White Throne Judgment of the unsaved of all ages.

> *And I saw the dead, the great and the small, standing before the throne, and books were opened; and another book was opened, which is the book of life; and the dead were judged from the things which were written in the books, according to their deeds. And the sea gave up the dead which were in it, and death and Hades gave up the dead which were in them; and they were judged, every one of them according to their deeds.* Revelation 20:12-13 (NASB)

The fact that the unsaved stand before the Great White Throne indicates that ultimately they will be sentenced to the Lake of Fire to be eternally punished. The degree (intensity, not duration) of that punishment will be determined by their deeds, as recorded in the Book of Deeds.

Make no mistake: although the intensity of punishment will be determined by a person's deeds, everyone who rejects the salvation offered by Christ will be sentenced to unending torment that will be indescribably excruciating. The white-hot fury of God's righteous wrath against sin – all sin – will be poured out eternally on all those who died without trusting Christ as Savior.

Another Book

One other book will be opened at the Great White Throne Judgment: God's book, the Bible. The deeds of the unsaved will be measured against God's standard, as recorded in His Word. The Lord Jesus Christ said

> *… all who reject Me and my message will be judged on the day of judgment by the truth I have spoken.*
> John 12:48 (NLT)

The Lake of Fire is the eternal abode of all the unrighteous – both men and angels. The punishment in the Lake of Fire includes both body and soul. The Greek word *Gehenna*, translated *Hell* in the New Testament, is the proper name for this place of everlasting torment; "Lake of Fire" is the descriptive name. The source of torment is somehow associated with fire and brimstone.

Mark 9:43-48 describes the Lake of Fire as a place …

> … *Where the worm dieth not, and the fire is not quenched* (KJV)

The undying worm indicates never-ending disintegration, and the unquenchable fire indicates eternal suffering.

The Lake of Fire is also described as *outer darkness, weeping and gnashing of teeth* (Matthew 8:12), *a furnace of fire* (Matthew 13:42), *everlasting fire* (Matthew 25:41), *everlasting punishment* (Matthew 25:46), a place where people are *tormented day and night forever and ever* (Revelation 20:11).

Someone has chillingly described the Lake of Fire thusly:

> "Total blackness. Absolute loneliness. Conscious suffering. Excruciating pain. Unending torment. Total weariness. Indescribable terror. Horror that never stops. No rest. No sleep. No comfort. No consolation. No relief. No hope. Unable to die. The constant screaming of millions of people in agony.

> "That's the Lake of Fire. Yes, it's a real place. The Lake of Fire is where the full wrath of the holy God is poured out on evil. That's why the Lake of Fire is so horrible. Nothing on earth can be compared to the Lake of Fire. The most heinous death anyone has ever died is nothing compared to the Lake of Fire.

> "There are no visitors in the Lake of Fire. Everyone is a permanent resident. There is no reprieve, no pardon, no parole from the Lake of Fire. The sentence is for eternity – time without end. A billion years is like the first second of eternity.

> "If you really understood what the Lake of Fire is like you would do anything, **ANYTHING**, to avoid it. You would pay any price, do anything you were asked to do."

(Editor's note: All God asks you to do to avoid the Lake of Fire is to repent of – turn from – your sins and invite the Lord Jesus Christ into your life as your Savior. Refer to *How About You?* on page 156.)

Some people believe that God "sends people to Hell." The truth is that God sent His Son to save us, not condemn us (John 3:17).

Salvation is available to anyone desiring it. Christ died for the sins of all people (1 Timothy 2:5-6). He promised that those who come to Him earnestly desiring salvation will not be turned away (John 6:37). No one needs to perish – God is not desirous that any should perish but that all should come to repentance (2 Peter 3:9).

God doesn't condemn anyone to Hell; a man condemns himself by his refusal to accept the free gift of salvation purchased by the death of the Lord Jesus Christ (Romans 6:23; Ephesians 2:8-9). But the gift He offers is not a possession until we receive it.

J. I. Packer explains it thusly:

> "Scripture sees Hell as self-chosen. Hell appears as God's gesture of respect for human choice. All receive what they actually choose, either to be with God forever, worshiping Him, or without God forever, worshiping themselves." From *Concise Theology: A Guide To Historic Christian Beliefs.*

The Lake of Fire was originally created for Satan and the angels who rebelled with him (Matthew 25:41).

At the end of the seven-year Tribulation period, the False Prophet and the Antichrist (both are men) will be cast alive into the Lake of Fire (Revelation 19:20). At the end of the Millennium, Satan too will be cast into the Lake of Fire.

The Lake of Fire is also known as the *Second Death* (Revelation 20:14). Those who die without trusting the Lord Jesus Christ as Savior will experience the Second Death. The Second Death is a physical death – as is the First Death – but it is of eternal duration, it will continue forever. The person in the Lake of Fire will be in the process of dying forever.

Hades and the Lake of Fire are not a "purge-atory" – that is, a place for peoples' sins to be purged and forgiven so they can go to Heaven. The concept of purgatory, as taught by some religious traditions, is not biblical. There is no opportunity for forgiveness or salvation after death (Hebrews 9:27). The decision you make while you are alive is final.

The doctrine of purgatory teaches that man can and must pay for his own sins. If this teaching is correct – and it isn't – then Christ's death was not sufficient to fully pay the penalty due God for our sins.

In reality, there is nothing we can do to pay for even one of our sins. Just one sin against our holy God is sufficient to condemn us to the Lake of Fire for eternity (James 2:10). Only the death of the sinless Son of God could satisfy God's righteous demands for justice.

When a person accepts the Lord Jesus Christ as their Savior, their sins – all of them: past, present, future – are immediately forgiven, never to be held against them. This is the doctrine of *justification**. Justification is a one-time event, not a continuing process. Because God fully justifies the believer at the moment of salvation, there is no need for a purgatory. Christ has already paid in full for our sins, there is nothing left to be "purged."

* Justification, sanctification, and glorification are described in the Supplemental Information at the end of *Salvation and Security*, the study note for point six of the BMW Doctrinal Statement.

Some religious traditions teach that we should pray for those who have died. This is not a biblical concept. Prayers for the dead have no bearing on the deceased person. No change in a person's spiritual condition can be made following his or her death. Once life is over, there are no more choices to be made.

Death is final. After death, no amount of praying will avail a person of the salvation he or she rejected in life. The time to pray for a person is while he or she is alive, while there is still the possibility of salvation.

Annihilation

The Bible doesn't teach annihilation – the belief that physical death is the end of a person's existence, or that a person suffers for his sin only for a limited time and then ceases to exist. In contrast to annihilation, the Bible teaches the immortality of the soul of both the saved and unsaved.

Heaven

The Bible teaches that there are three heavens :

- The first heaven is the atmospheric heaven – the sky, the troposphere, the breathable atmosphere surrounding our earth.

- The second heaven is the planetary heaven – "outer space," the location of the stars, planets, moon, etc.

- The third heaven is a dimension outside our universe, it is the location of God's throne, it's where God dwelled before time began, and where He dwells now.

The Apostle Paul was caught up to the third heaven (2 Corinthians 12:2). The elect, those people whom God has chosen as His own (Ephesians 1:4), will dwell with Him in the third heaven for eternity. It is the Heaven of heavens.

Although the third heaven is God's dwelling place, He is not contained there. Our infinite God cannot be contained!

The third heaven is eternal; the first and second heavens are temporary, they will completely pass away (2 Peter 3:10). Thus, the first and second heavens cannot be where people will spend eternity, as some religious traditions teach. An individual's eternal destiny is either Heaven or the Lake of Fire (Hell) – there is no middle ground, there are no other options. There is one eternal Heaven and one eternal Hell.

What will Heaven be like? Here's a description from Dr. John MacArthur's book, *The Glory of Heaven*:

> "Heaven is a realm of unsurpassed joy, unfading glory, undiminished bliss, unlimited delights, and unending pleasures. Nothing about eternal glory can possibly be boring or humdrum. It will be a perfect existence. We will have unbroken fellowship with all heaven's inhabitants. Life there will be devoid of any sorrows, cares, tears, fears, or pain."

In his book, *Evangelical Theology,* nineteenth-century theologian A. A. Hodge provided this description of Heaven:

"Heaven, as the eternal home of the divine Man and of all of the redeemed members of the human race, must necessarily be thoroughly human in its structure, conditions, and activities. Its joys and its occupations must all be rational, moral, emotional, voluntary, and active. There must be the exercise of all faculties, the gratification of all tastes, the development of all talent capacities, the realization of all ideals. The reason, the intellectual curiosity, the imagination, the aesthetic instincts, the holy affections, the social affinities, the inexhaustible resources of strength and power native to the human soul, must all find in heaven exercise and satisfaction."

Will there be marriage in Heaven? Here are relevant comments from Dr. John MacArthur, from *The Glory of Heaven*:

"Jesus Himself expressly taught that marriage is an earthly union only. ... There will be no marrying or giving in marriage. Marriage as an institution will pass away. ... All the reasons for marriage will be gone. Here on earth man needs a helper, woman needs a protector, and God has designed both to produce children. In heaven glorified men will no longer require wives as helpers because they will be perfect. Women will no longer need husbands as protectors because they will be perfect. The population of heaven will be a fixed number. Thus marriage as an institution will be utterly unnecessary. ... You will enjoy an eternal companionship in heaven that is more perfect than any earthly partnership."

Will we know each other in Heaven? Dr. MacArthur says ...

"The answer is yes. We will forever be who we are now – only without any of our faults or infirmities. ... All the redeemed will maintain their identify forever, but in a perfected form."

What Will Christians Do In Heaven For Eternity?

Here are some thoughts from Dr. Henry Morris.

"Surely the Lord does not intend for us to sit around just singing and playing harps through all eternity. He gave the first man work to do in his immediate home at the beginning of Eden, even before there was any sin. The Bible does say that *His servants shall serve Him* (Revelation 22:3). That's us, not the angels!

"I like to believe that God's primeval Mandate* to have dominion over the earth may be enlarged eventually to cover the whole creation.

> *   The Dominion Mandate is described in the Supplemental Information at the end of this study note.

"Now, although the Bible does not say it specifically, it seems reasonable that we shall be able to learn much more about the universe in the ages to come than we can ever do in this life. The universe and its intricate complexities are infinite, and the time to study them will be endless. We shall never lack for challenging, enjoyable, and useful work to do in these ages to come.

"This is not to suggest that everyone will always be out exploring the cosmos. God will no doubt assign many different forms of service to His redeemed and glorified servants –

depending probably on their God-given talents and also on their faithfulness in this present life. ... Our future work probably will be somewhat in relation to our former work.

"For a time, no doubt, even in the holy city we shall have tears to shed, especially for unsaved friends and loved ones who have been imprisoned forever in the lake of fire, but then *God shall wipe away all tears* (Revelation 21:4) and the glories of life in the New Jerusalem and the new earth will be so magnificent that *the former shall not be remembered, nor come into mind* (Isaiah 65:17)."

The five paragraphs above were excerpted from the book, *For Time and Forever*, by Henry M. Morris.

Did you get tired just reading about what we may be doing for eternity? Where will we get the energy to do all that? Remember that we will have new resurrected bodies that never need rest, never get old, never get sick.

In Philippians 3:21 we are told that our old earthly body will be transformed and be conformed to Christ's glorious body. Comparing our physical body to our resurrection body, Paul wrote:

> *The body that is sown* [buried] *is perishable, it is raised imperishable, it is sown in dishonor, it is raised in glory; it is sown in weakness, it is raised in power; it is sown a natural body, it is raised a spiritual body.*
> 1 Corinthians 15:42-44 (NIV)

How About You?

In this study note, we've discussed the terrifying prospects of spending eternity in the Lake of Fire, away from God, forever in conscious torment.

Reader, how about you? Are you absolutely sure that you've trusted the Lord Jesus Christ as your Savior from sin? That's the only way to be saved, rescued from eternity in the Lake of Fire. Trusting Christ for salvation is the most important decision of your life because it affects your eternal destiny.

If you're not sure you're saved, you can settle that right now. You can pray a simple prayer like the one below or use your own words. God knows your heart.

God, I know I am a sinner. I'm sorry for my sin. Forgive me. I want to turn from my sin. I now receive the Lord Jesus Christ as my Savior. I confess Him as my Lord. From now on I want to follow Him. Thank you for saving me. I pray this in the name of Jesus. Amen

Supplemental Information

The Dominion Mandate

In Genesis 1:28, God gave Adam and Eve (and us, by extension) dominion over His creation:

> *And God blessed them, and God said unto them, Be fruitful, and multiply, and replenish the earth, and subdue it: and have dominion over the fish of the sea, and over the fowl of the air, and over every living thing that moveth upon the earth.*

This was God's first command to His newly created man and woman.

According to the verse above, we are to "subdue" the earth and "have dominion over every living thing that moveth upon the earth." This means to intensely study the earth (processes and systems) and use that knowledge for the benefit of the earth's inhabitants. Science and technology. Learn and implement what you learn. Research and Development. Theory and application. Study and practice.

The first man, Adam, was given dominion over the earth and its creatures (Genesis 1:26-28), but sin intervened and God cursed the universe (Genesis 3:17-18). It remains for the Son of Man, the Lord Jesus Christ, the Last Adam (1 Corinthians 15:45) to regain mans' lost dominion. (We contrasted the first Adam and the Last Adam in *The Total Depravity of Man*, the study note for point five of the BMW Doctrinal Statement.)

The Psalmist describes man's dominion over nature as follows:

> *You have given him dominion over the works of your hands; you have put all things under his feet, all sheep and oxen, and also the beasts of the field, the birds of the heavens, and the fish of the sea, whatever passes along the paths of the seas.* Psalm 8:6-8 (ESV)

The Dominion Mandate has never been revoked. It was renewed after the flood (Genesis 9:1-9).

Dr. Henry Morris III wrote this sweeping description of the Dominion Mandate:

> "Th(e) Dominion Mandate implies authorization for the following human enterprises:
>
> • Discovery of truth – science, research, exploration
>
> • Application of truth – agriculture, engineering, medicine, technology, etc.
>
> • Implementation of truth – commerce, transportation, government, etc.
>
> • Interpretation of truth – fine arts, literature, theology
>
> • Transmission of truth – education, communication, homemaking
>
> Excerpted from the May 10, 2015, reading in *Days of Praise*, published by the Institute for Creation Research

15. Creation

*"We believe the triune God, by a **free act** and for His own **glory**, **without the use of existing materials** or **secondary causes**, brought into being - **immediately and instantaneously** in six **literal days** by the **word of His mouth** - the whole visible and invisible universe. (Genesis 1:1-27; Exodus 20:8-11; Nehemiah 9:6; Psalm 104:25-26; Isaiah 40:21-31; John 1:1-5; Colossians 1:16-17)"*

The words appearing in **bold** text in the paragraph above are explained in this study note. Here's where to find those words – and more – in this note:

Free Act

God's creating the universe (cosmos) was a free act; He was not coerced by outside influences. He created because He wanted to. He created for His own glory. God is sovereign, no one constrains Him to do anything.

(God's) Glory

In both Old and New Testaments, *glory* means

- Excellence and praiseworthiness set forth in display

  The heavens are telling of the glory of God; And the expanse [of heaven] is declaring the work of His hands. Psalm 19:1 (Amplified Bible)

- Honor and adoration expressed in response to this display

God's glory is the beauty of Who He is, emanating from His character, from all that He is. It is the public display of the infinite beauty and worth of God, the radiance of His holiness, the radiance of His manifold, infinitely worthy and valuable perfections. God's glory is manifested in nature and can be expressed in people.

In his book, *Basic Theology*, Dr. Charles Ryrie wrote

"God's purpose was to create a world in which His glory could be manifest in all its fullness. The glory of God is the overarching goal of creation. In fact, it is the overarching goal of everything He does. The universe was created to display God's glory (Psalm 19:1), and the wrath of God is revealed against those who fail to glorify God (Romans 1:23). Our sin causes us to fall short of God's glory (Romans 3:23), and in the new heaven and new earth, the glory of God is what will provide light (Revelation 21:23). The glory of God is manifest when His attributes are on perfect display, and the story of redemption is part of that.

"The ultimate exhibition of God's glory was at the cross where His wrath, justice, and mercy met. The righteous judgment of all sin was executed at the cross, and God's grace was on display in pouring His wrath for sin on His Son, Jesus, instead of on us. God's love and grace are on display in those whom He has saved (John 3:16; Ephesians 2:8-9). In the end, God will be glorified as His chosen people worship Him for all eternity with the angels, and the wicked will also glorify God as His justice and righteousness will finally be vindicated by the eternal punishment of all unrepentant sinners (Philippians 2:11)."

Without The Use Of Existing Materials

Before He created the universe, only the Triune God existed. There was nothing from which to create something else. God created this universe *ex nihilo*. (*Ex nihilo* is a Latin term meaning "out of nothing.") God created freely; He was not constrained by the limitations of pre-existing material.

Only God can create *ex nihilo*. Man can make one thing from another, invent something new, but must use existing materials to do so.

Before day one of creation, before there was time as we know it, only God existed, and had always existed. Our finite, time-constrained minds cannot fully grasp that.

Secondary Causes

A "cause" is something or someone who is capable of making things happen. The triune God is the Primary Cause, the First Cause, the Uncaused Cause. He is the one absolute Cause that initiated everything. He alone created the universe solely by His omnipotence and omniscience. No secondary causes were involved in creation. God is the sole Source of all creation.

Immediately and Instantaneously

God's timetable for the creation was that He spoke the fully formed universe into existence in six literal (24 hour) days. Every created thing appeared instantaneously when God spoke it into existence.

From Dr. John D. Morris,

"When Adam was created, he no doubt looked like a mature adult, fully able to walk, talk, and care for the garden. When God created fruit trees, they were already bearing fruit. In each case, what He created was functionally complete right from the start. Stars, created on Day Four, had to be seen on Day Six in order to be useful in telling time; therefore, their light had to be visible on earth. God's evaluation that the completed creation was "very good" (Genesis 1:31) necessitated that it be functionally complete, operating in harmony, with each part fulfilling the purpose for which it was created.

"The world today is not as it was at creation. God's creative powers are at rest now and He is maintaining the creation using the present laws of nature. The original created world, perfect and non-decaying at first, was subsequently cursed and made subject to decay and death (Genesis 3:17; Romans 8:20). Furthermore, even *that* world was destroyed by the Flood of Noah's day, so that the world we observe is a relic of destructive processes, not creative processes. Any effort to apply present processes and process rates to creation will not succeed." Adapted from the article *Creation with the Appearance of Age*, accessed at https://www.icr.org/article/5717/

As implied in Dr. Morris's article, the present is not the key to the past. During the six days of creation, God suspended the physical processes we are familiar with today. The same is true of the great worldwide flood of Noah's day. God suspended the rates of all today's processes during that period.

By its very essence, true creation involved processes no longer in operation.

In the article, *Why Does The Universe Look So Old?* (ICR Acts & Facts, October 2010), Dr. Albert Mohler wrote:

"Why does the universe look so old? First, the most natural understanding from Scripture on the age of the universe is this: The universe looks old because the Creator made it whole.

"When He made Adam, Adam was not a fetus; Adam was a man. He had the appearance of a man, which by our understanding would have required time for Adam to get old. But not by the sovereign creative power of God. He put Adam in the garden. The garden was not merely seeds; it was a fertile, fecund, mature garden. The Genesis account clearly claims that God creates and makes things whole."

As we saw earlier in this study note, God declared His finished creation to be "very good" (Genesis 1:31). Dr. Henry Morris III provides some insight into what that means:

"Because God is omniscient, everything in the universe works as designed. Because God is omnipotent, everything has all it needs to operate, live, reproduce, and populate under the orders of and in agreement with the Creator's design. Each component was designed to function without flaw. Every part works as ordered, and all living things function under the limits and in the places for their lives. Nothing was misplaced. Nothing was left to chance.

"For the holy, omniscient, omnipotent, loving Creator to conclude that everything that He had created was 'very good,' there could be nothing in that completed creation that did not function as designed. Nothing existed in conscious rebellion against the immutable nature of the Creator—there was no sin." From the article *Genesis and the Character of God* accessed at http://www.icr.org/article/6755/

Literal Days

The days of creation were solar days ("morning and evening"), 24-hour days just as we experience today.

Some people try to stretch the six days of creation to cover the long ages required for evolution. This is problematic for several reasons. Here are two of those reasons:

- The Hebrew word for "day" (*yom*) is used consistently in the Old Testament to mean a 24-hour day. If the days were thousands or millions of years, God would have said so. God says what He means. God is truth (John 3:33, 14:6) therefore He cannot and will not deceive us.

- If each of the days in Genesis 1 is a long period of time, then millions of living creatures died prior to Adam's first sin in the Garden of Eden (Genesis 3:6). But Romans 5:12 states that death came upon creation only as a result of Adam's sin.

Evolution

Here are some quotes from the book *5 Reasons to Believe in Recent Creation* by Dr. Henry M. Morris III, published by the Institute For Creation Research (ICR).

"Let there be no doubt. The Bible contains no reference, no inference, no metaphorical allegory – indeed, no hint of evolutionary development from simple to more complex life forms by blind, random chance." (page 7)

"Evolution is a story invented by man in order to exclude God from his life." (page 8)

"The only reason to translate 'day' as 'age' is to accommodate the required eons of evolution."
(page 10)

"Without the death of countless billions of life forms over eons of unrecorded time, evolution could not occur." (page 13)

"The theory of evolution is a means to an end. The sole and stated purpose of a naturalistic or mechanistic cosmogony is to provide an atheistic explanation for the existence of all things."
(page 21)

"There is no such thing as a 'simple' cell. If it is alive, it is *not* simple." (page 28, emphasis in original)

"The only reason not to believe in an omniscient Creator is that one *refuses* to believe."
(page 28, emphasis in original)

By The Word Of His Mouth

God spoke and the universe came into being, fully-formed.

*The L*ORD* merely spoke, and the heavens were created.*
He breathed the word and all the stars were born.
He assigned the sea its boundaries and locked the oceans in vast reservoirs.
*Let the whole world fear the L*ORD*, and let everyone stand in awe of him.*
For when he spoke, the world began!
It appeared at his command.   Psalm 33:9 (NLT)

Creation and Science

The biblical doctrine of creation, including the Dominion Mandate*, encourages the observation of nature – an activity that is central to the scientific method and was foundational in the development of modern science.

> * The Dominion Mandate is described in the Supplemental Information at the end of *The Eternal State*, point fourteen of the BMW Doctrinal Statement.

God is both the sole Creator and the sole Sustainer of the universe (Colossians 1:17). God's consistency in sustaining the cosmos makes science possible. Stated differently, science is possible only because of the consistent, ongoing, sustaining work of the Creator.

When properly employed, science and technology are wonderful gifts of our Creator God!

Why Is Creation An Important Doctrine?

If evolution is true (and it isn't), then man is just a highly evolved animal and can be treated accordingly. This theory has been used as justification for horribly mistreating people. In Appendix 2 of the *New Defender's Study Bible*, Dr. Henry Morris lists some of the fruits of evolutionism:

Harmful Philosophies		Evil Practices	
Communism	Nazism	Abortion	Drug Culture
Racism	Imperialism	Promiscuity	Slavery
Atheism	Humanism	Pornography	Genocide
Materialism	Amoralism	Chauvinism	New-Agism
Scientism	Pantheism	Euthanasia	Pollution
Monopolism	Anarchism	Bestiality	Satanism
Occultism	Social Darwinism	Homosexuality	Criminality
Behaviorism	Freudianism	Cannibalism	Witchcraft

Ingrid Newkirk, president of PETA (People for the Ethical Treatment of Animals), said "A rat is a pig is a dog is a boy. They are all mammals." Ms. Newkirk's statement is incorrect. Man is not an evolved animal; he was created in fully human form from the beginning. Man was created in the image of God, animals were not.

According to Dr. Henry Morris, animals have a soul but not a spirit. The soul (Hebrew *nephesh*, Greek *psuche*) is the mind, the consciousness, the intellect, the will. Both man and animals have a soul (Genesis 1:21, 24; 2:7). Only man has a spirit. It is by means of our spirit that we fellowship with God and with other people. Our spirit discerns right from wrong, truth and falsehood, beauty and ugliness. Animals do not have these spiritual qualities.

A plant has a body. An animal has a body and a soul. Man is a tri-unity – he has a body, a soul, and a spirit (1 Thessalonians 5:23, Hebrews 4:12). Refer to the chart below.

	Body	Soul	Spirit
	physical	mental	spiritual
Greek / Hebrew	*soma*	*psuche* / *nephesh*	*pneuma* / *ruwach*
Visible	yes	no	no
Composition	physical structure	consciousness intellect will emotions mind	morality esthetics conscience
Applies To	Man		
	Animal		
	Plant		

Here's additional information regarding the differences between man and animals:

"What separates man from the animal kingdom? Although human genetics and human appearance are different from any animal, there are less apparent, but more important, reasons that determine the nature of man than just his genome.

"Genesis chapter one reveals that man was created in the image of God, a quality that separates him from the animals created on day six. This special creation explains why man's behavior is far more complex than any other living thing on the planet. Man reveals God's image in many ways. For example:

- He is able to imagine and create objects never seen before (art, buildings, etc.).

- He is able to show compassion for strangers.

- He is able to ponder his role and fate in creation.

"Man also differs from the other creatures in his relationship to God. Man was created to serve other men and God, a fact that forms the basis for society. Men are God's most treasured creation. God treasures man so much that He died to reconcile man to Himself. It is this value that God places on man that truly separates him from the rest of creation. What really distinguishes man from the animals is the decision each man will make in response to God's provision for salvation." Accessed at http://www.icr.org/special-creation/

What Happened To The Created Universe?

God created the universe and declared it to be "very good" (Genesis 1:31). That means it was perfect, flawless, everything functioned properly. God's "very good" couldn't and didn't include sin or death.

"There is absolutely no indication anywhere in the Scriptures that the living God—the God of life—created death. Nothing in the Bible suggests that death was a part of the good that God designed into His creation. Death in Scripture is separation from God. Death stops life. Death intrudes into and destroys everything. Death is *not* normal. ... No sin or death

A Survey of Major Biblical Doctrines – Creation

existed in all of creation—until the third chapter of Genesis." From the article *Genesis and the Character of God* by Dr. Henry Morris III, accessed at http://www.icr.org/article/6755/

The third chapter of Genesis records the fall of mankind into sin. As a result of the Fall, God imposed a curse of decay and death on His creation. Death is God's judgment for sin (Romans 5:12, 6:23).

God imposed the sentence of death, but in mercy He also provided His only Son – the Creator Himself, the Lord Jesus Christ – as an innocent sacrifice to pay the penalty for our sin and redeem us.

For more information regarding the fall of mankind and the results, refer to *Sinful Nature* on page 68.

16. Human Sexuality

"Sexual intimacy is a wonderful gift of God that is to be expressed only between a man and a woman within the love and bonds of marriage. Therefore, we believe that any other form of sexual intimacy is both immoral and a perversion of God's gift. (Genesis 2:24-25; Proverbs 5:18; 1 Corinthians 7:5; 1 Thessalonians 4:3-5; Hebrews 13:4; Leviticus 18:1-30; Proverbs 6:32; 1 Corinthians 6:18; Romans 1:26-27)"

Here's an index to the words and phrases in this note:

Definitions

Adultery is defined as the willful violation of the marriage contract by either of the parties, through sexual intimacy with a third party. Physical adultery can be committed only by a married person. In the Old Testament, adultery was punishable by death (Leviticus 20:10).

Fornication (Greek *porneia*) is a more broadly defined term referring to any act of illicit sexual intimacy. It thus includes adultery, homosexuality, and other forms of sexual perversion.

Homosexuality is defined as sexual intimacy with another person of the same sex.

Immorality, in the present context, is described as any form of illicit sexual behavior including, but not limited to, those described above.

The Gift of Sexual Intimacy

God gave us the good gift of human sexual intimacy for two purposes: procreation and pleasure – in a monogamous, lifetime marriage of a man and woman (Genesis 2:24-25, Proverbs 5:18, Song of Solomon).

Sexual intimacy is for married people only, and only within the bonds of marriage.

Prohibitions Against Sexual Sin

We are commanded to abstain from sexual immorality:

God's will is for you to be holy, so stay away from all sexual sin. 1 Thessalonians 4:3-5 (NLT)

God will judge adulterers:

Give honor to marriage, and remain faithful to one another in marriage. God will surely judge people who are immoral and those who commit adultery. Hebrews 13:4 (NLT)

The Apostle Paul was very explicit:

Do not be deceived: no sexually immoral people,... adulterers, male prostitutes, homosexuals, ...will inherit God's kingdom. 1 Corinthians 6:9-10 (HCSB)

The seventh commandment forbids adultery (Exodus 20:14).

The Holy Spirit, writing through the Apostle Paul, tells us

But among you there must not be even a hint of sexual immorality, or of any kind of impurity, or of greed, because these are improper for God's holy people Ephesians 5:3 (NIV)

One of the strongest reasons for avoiding sexual sin is that our body is the temple of the Holy Spirit:

...do you not know that your body is a temple of the Holy Spirit within you, whom you have from God? You are not your own, for you were bought with a price. So glorify God in your body. 1 Corinthians 6:19-20 (ESV)

Note the ramifications of the verses above:

- Our body is where the Holy Spirit has chosen to dwell. Whatever we do, He is in us. So any act of sin or immorality desecrates His holy temple.

- Our body belongs to God, it is His by right of creation and by right of redemption. The Apostle Paul reminds us that *You are not your own, for you were bought with a price.* That price, of course, was the blood of the Lord Jesus Christ. Someday we will have to give an account of how we used our body.

- God created our bodies to bring glory to Him: *So glorify God in your body.* Sexual sin does the opposite.

Results of Sexual Sins

Sexual sin is unique in that it touches the very core of our being, the means by which the zenith of God's creation procreates. All parties affected by sexual sin are harmed thereby – and the circle of offense and harm is very large indeed. There is no way to escape the consequences of sexual sin:

Can a man carry fire next to his chest and his clothes not be burned? Or can one walk on hot coals and his feet not be scorched? So is he who goes in to his neighbor's wife; none who touches her will go unpunished. Proverbs 6:27-29 (ESV)

Sexual sin is self-destructive: physically, emotionally, spiritually. The adulterer destroys his or her own soul:

But the man who commits adultery is an utter fool, for he destroys himself. Proverbs 6:32 (NLT)

Sexual immorality is a sin against one's own body. It often results in disease, "and it deeply affects our personality which responds in anguish when we harm ourselves physically or spiritually" (NLT note).

Run from sexual sin! No other sin so clearly affects the body as this one does. For sexual immorality is a sin against your own body. 1 Corinthians 6:18 (NLT)

Sexual intimacy is more than a physical union, it is also a spiritual union, a bonding. The Christian who is sexually intimate with someone other than his or her spouse actually makes Christ a part of the union:

Do you not know that your bodies are members of Christ Himself? Shall I then take the members of Christ and unite them with a prostitute? Never! Do you not know that he who unites himself with a prostitute is one with her in body? For it is said 'The two will become one flesh'. 1 Corinthians 6:15-16 (NIV)

Our merciful God will forgive sexual sin, but the multi-faceted devastation and pain that results from the sin are long-lasting, and often permanent.

Homosexuality

Homosexuality is strictly forbidden in Scripture; it is described as a detestable sin, a term reserved for the most abominable of sins (Leviticus 18:22). The Old Testament penalty for homosexual acts was death (Leviticus 20:13).

Homosexual activity may result in horrible, debilitating, even terminal, diseases. The Apostle Paul said that homosexuality was the result of God abandoning the people who suppressed His truth:

So God abandoned them to do whatever shameful things their hearts desired. As a result, they did vile and degrading things with each other's bodies. They traded the truth about God for a lie. So they worshiped and served the things God created instead of the Creator himself, who is worthy of eternal praise! Amen. That is why God abandoned them to their shameful desires. Even the women turned against the natural way to have sex and instead indulged in sex with each other. And the men, instead of having normal sexual relations with women, burned with lust for each other. Men did shameful things with other men, and as a result of this sin, they suffered within themselves the penalty they deserved. Since they thought it foolish to acknowledge God, he abandoned them to their foolish thinking and let them do things that should never be done. Romans 1:24-28 (NLT)

Widespread homosexual activity is what caused God to rain down fire and brimstone to destroy Sodom and Gomorrah (Genesis 19:4, 5, 12, 24).

Avoiding Sexual Sin

We live in a sex-saturated society where purity of heart and life are impossible to maintain without the filling of the Holy Spirit (Galatians 5:16, Ephesians 5:18).

Satan knows the power of the human sex drive. That drive is said to be second only to the survival instinct. One of Satan's favorite – and most successful – temptations is to sexual sin.

Prayer is always the first, and most effective, defense against any type of sin.

God has promised that we will not be tempted beyond our ability to, with His help, withstand it, and that He will make a way of escape. But we must avail ourselves of the escape provision.

The temptations in your life are no different from what others experience. And God is faithful. He will not allow the temptation to be more than you can stand. When you are tempted, he will show you a way out so that you can endure. 1 Corinthians 10:13 (NLT)

Regarding the avoidance of sexual sin, someone has wisely said, "don't trust your head or your heart, take to your heels." The Bible frequently admonishes us to flee, run from, temptation and sin. Solomon advised men to *remove your way far from* (the prostitute), *and do not go near the door of her house* Proverbs 5:8 (NKJV).

All sin originates in the mind (James 1:13-16). That's why it is so important that we control our thought life, and be very selective in what we read, what we listen to, where we go, what we watch, and with whom we associate.

The Old Testament character Job made a covenant with this eyes that he would not look lustfully on a woman (Job 31:1). That's a good principle for all men. In today's culture, we can't entirely avoid women who dress immodestly, but we can refuse to engage in those lengthy gazes that fuel the fires of desire.

Second Corinthians 10:5 tells us that we are to "bring into captivity every thought to the obedience of Christ." Arrest those sinful thoughts, treat them like criminals, like the intruders they are. Remember that God doesn't command us to do anything we cannot do with His help.

For more guidelines on maintaining personal holiness, refer to *Separation and Unity*, the study note for point seventeen of the BMW Doctrinal Statement.

Remember that sexual sins – like all sins – are not beyond the reach of God's forgiveness. But forgiveness doesn't necessarily mean the results of the sin are cancelled.

17. Separation and Unity

"We believe the saved should be **separated** *unto the Lord Jesus Christ, necessitating* **holy living** *in all personal and ecclesiastical associations and relationships. We believe we are responsible to identify* **false teaching** *and dangerous movements where they relate to the conduct of the Mission's ministries. We believe separation is required in those instances where people, groups, and organizations whose doctrinal position is the same as the Mission's engage in contradictory practices which compromise the faith. (Romans 12:1-2; 14:13; 1 Corinthians 6:19-20; Titus 2:14; James 4:4-5; 1 Peter 2:9; 1 John 2:15-17; Matthew 18:15-17; Romans 16:17; 1 Corinthians 5:7-11; 2 Corinthians 6:14-18; Ephesians 4:1-6; 2 Thessalonians 3:11-14; 2 Timothy 3:1-5; Titus 3:10; 2 John 9-11)"*

The words appearing in **bold** text in the paragraph above are explained in this study note. Here's where to find those words – and more – in this note:

This point of the Doctrinal Statement addresses two opposites: separation and unity. As we'll see, we are to be separate from the world (and other things), and united with our brothers and sisters in Christ – the people with whom we will spend eternity.

Separation

"Separation" is from a Greek word whose root also yields these words: "holy," "sanctified," "set apart" and "saint."

As Christians, we are called to be separate from

- The world

- Sin

- Sinning believers

- False teachers

- Improper alliances

- Doctrinally sound people or groups who engage in contrary practices that compromise the faith

After we discuss each of these points – which define and describe a separated life – we'll be prepared to discuss why we should live separated lives.

Separate From The World*

> * There is an excellent description of this term ("world") in the first point of the Supplemental Information at the end of this study note. I suggest reading it before proceeding.

As members of God's spiritual family, we are called to be "in the world but not of the world." We are not to imitate the world system or adopt its ways.

This world and what it offers are not of God. They are man-centered, not God-centered. They are temporal, not eternal. They are short-lived and soon fade away. We are not to love the world in the sense of treasuring what it offers, ascribing to it undue value and importance – we are to be separate from it. Here's how the Apostle John described what the world offers:

> *Do not love this world nor the things it offers you, for when you love the world, you do not have the love of the Father in you. For the world offers only a craving for physical pleasure, a craving for everything we see, and pride in our achievements and possessions. These are not from the Father, but are from this world. And this world is fading away, along with everything that people crave. But anyone who does what pleases God will live forever* 1 John 2:15-17 (NLT)

Because the world is not God-oriented, we are not to be conformed to the world, molded into its ways and values. Instead, we are to present our bodies – our entire lives – to God as living sacrifices. This is the ultimate act of worship.

> *I appeal to you therefore, brothers, by the mercies of God, to present your bodies as a living sacrifice, holy and acceptable to God, which is your spiritual worship. Do not be conformed to this world, but be transformed by the renewal of your mind*, that by testing you may discern what is the will of God, what is good and acceptable and perfect.* Romans 12:1-2 (ESV)

> * Studying God's Word is how we "renew (our) mind."

We'll look at Romans 12:1-2 again under the topic of Holy Living.

Because we live in a sinful world, there is no way to separate ourselves totally from all sinful influences, but we don't have to yield to the temptation to sin. That's God's promise. Here's what He wrote through the Apostle Paul:

> *The temptations in your life are no different from what others experience. And God is faithful. He will not allow the temptation to be more than you can stand. When you are tempted, he will show you a way out so that you can endure.* 1 Corinthians 10:13 (NLT)

Did you notice that this verse doesn't leave us any excuse when we succumb to temptation? God promises that He will not allow a temptation greater than we can endure – and He also promises to provide a way of escape. We'll continue this discussion under the heading *Holy Living*.

Being separate from the world doesn't mean we are to sequester ourselves in a convent or monastery. Our commission from the Lord Jesus Christ is to evangelize (Matthew 28:19-20), not withdraw.

Separate From Sin

What is sin? Here's a quote from Dr. John MacArthur, excerpted from the January, 2007, issue of *Decision* magazine:

"Sin is any lack of conformity to the moral character of God or the law of God*. We sin by thinking evil, speaking evil, acting evil, or omitting good."

> * Thus, sin is not being conformed to, not being aligned with, God's standards of right and wrong. Where are those standards revealed? In His Word!

The subject of sin is discussed in detail in *The Person And Work Of The Holy Spirit*, the study note for point four of the BMW Doctrinal Statement.

Being separate from sin means we don't allow sin to be our master. We don't willingly, purposely engage in those things that are sinful.

> *Let not sin therefore reign in your mortal body, that ye should obey it in the lusts thereof. Neither yield ye your members as instruments of unrighteousness unto sin: but yield yourselves unto God, as those that are alive from the dead, and your members as instruments of righteousness unto God. For sin shall not have dominion over you: for ye are not under the law, but under grace.* Romans 6:12-14 (KJV)

In the above verses, the Apostle Paul is admitting that we can continue to sin after salvation: He starts this passage with *Let not sin therefore reign* – in other words, don't allow sin to reign. He recognizes the possibility of sin reigning in a Christian's life and admonishes us not to allow that to happen. This verse also tells us that we must not yield (submit) our bodies unto sin; instead, we must yield ourselves to God.

The subject of victory over sin is further discussed in *Salvation and Security*, the study note for point six of the BMW Doctrinal Statement, and under the *Holy Living* topic later in this study note.

Separate From Sinning Believers

The church is to discipline those of its members who are practicing habitual sin. This discipline may include not fellowshipping with them.

Dr. Erwin Lutzer, pastor of Moody Church, stated that one reason the church is powerless today is that it doesn't discipline its sinning members. The failure to discipline a sinning church member has negative consequences for the member, for the congregation, and for those outside the church.

We must exercise caution when confronting a sinning brother or sister lest Satan also tempt us to the same sin.

Dear brothers and sisters, if another believer is overcome by some sin, you who are godly should gently and humbly help that person back onto the right path. And be careful not to fall into the same temptation yourself. Galatians 6:1 (NLT)

The Lord Jesus Christ Himself outlined the procedure for dealing with another Christian who sins against you personally:

If another believer sins against you, go privately and point out the offense. If the other person listens and confesses it, you have won that person back. But if you are unsuccessful, take one or two others with you and go back again, so that everything you say may be confirmed by two or three witnesses. If the person still refuses to listen, take your case to the church. Then if he or she won't accept the church's decision, treat that person as a pagan or a corrupt tax collector. Matthew 18:15-17 (NLT)

More regarding sinning brothers and sisters in Christ:

When I wrote to you before, I told you not to associate with people who indulge in sexual sin. But I wasn't talking about unbelievers who indulge in sexual sin, or are greedy, or cheat people, or worship idols. You would have to leave this world to avoid people like that. I meant that you are not to associate with anyone who claims to be a believer yet indulges in sexual sin, or is greedy, or worships idols, or is abusive, or is a drunkard, or cheats people. Don't even eat with such people.
1 Corinthians 5:9-11 (NLT)

But avoid foolish controversies, genealogies, dissensions, and quarrels about the law, for they are unprofitable and worthless. As for a person who stirs up division, after warning him once and then twice, have nothing more to do with him, knowing that such a person is warped and sinful; he is self-condemned. Titus 3:9-11 (ESV)

Separate From False Teachers

How do we identify false teachers? The principal indication that a person is a false teacher is that he or she doesn't teach the truth about the Lord Jesus Christ – they teach "another Christ" (2 Corinthians 11:4), a different Christ than presented in the Bible.

Some cults teach that Jesus was "a god" created by God the Father. That's not the Jesus of the Bible. Some teach that Jesus was only a prophet. That's not the Jesus of the Bible. Some teach that Jesus was an archangel who became a man. That's not the Jesus of the Bible. Some teach that Jesus was once a man who became God. That's not the Jesus of the Bible. Jesus is not a man who became God – He is God who became man*. He became one of us that He might taste death for everyone and provide salvation for us (Hebrews 2:9).

> * God became man at the incarnation of the Lord Jesus Christ. Refer to *The Person and Work of Christ*, point three of the BMW Doctrinal Statement.

False teachers have plagued the Church since its birth. The Apostle John wrote his first epistle (1 John) to combat Gnosticism and Mysticism. These heresies are still present today in various forms. "Gnosticism" comes from the Greek word *gnosko* which means "to know." Gnostics claim to possess an elevated knowledge, a "higher truth" known only to a certain few. Gnosticism teaches that salvation is gained through the acquisition of divine knowledge which frees one from the illusions of darkness. Additional information regarding Gnosticism and Mysticism is available in point three of the Supplemental Information at the end of this study note.

In more recent times, one of the predominant forms of false teaching has been the "Word of Faith" movement, described in point two of the Supplemental Information at the end of this study note.

The paragraphs below are from the book, *Perhaps Today*, by Tim LaHaye and Jerry Jenkins.

"... in the last days there will be an increase of false teachers who will be incredibly believable. Some will even use supernatural signs and wonders to deceive the best of Christians. These deceivers will accompany their false doctrines with miracles and thus deceive millions. Remember this: Satan has the power to perform miracles. He can reverse those sicknesses he has brought on people. In the Tribulation, he will so intensify his deceptive practices that he will appear to duplicate the miracles of Jesus.

"Satan has always been a liar and deceiver. But in the last days his deceptions will increase. In our day there has been an incredible increase of false teachers both inside and outside the church. Although the tactics and antics of these false teachers are not new, their activities in occultism, demonism, Satan worship and horoscopes are certainly becoming popular.

"In such a time, Christians need to continue to study God's Word in the fellowship of a good Bible-teaching church."

How are we to relate to false teachers? Stay away from them!

And now I make one more appeal, my dear brothers and sisters. Watch out for people who cause divisions and upset people's faith by teaching things contrary to what you have been taught. Stay away from them. Romans 16:17 (NLT)

In Apostolic times, churches were in homes. John warned believers not to invite false teachers into their house churches. This admonition has application today: We are not to knowingly invite false teachers to speak at our churches.

If anyone comes to your meeting and does not teach the truth about Christ, don't invite that person into your home or give any kind of encouragement. Anyone who encourages such people becomes a partner in their evil work. 2 John 10-11 (NLT)

The best defense against a counterfeit is a firsthand, personal knowledge of the authentic. This is true of Bible doctrine. The better you know the authentic (correct) doctrine, the easier it is to spot false teaching. How much time do you spend studying God's Word?

In his June 15, 2012, newsletter, Dr. John MacArthur lamented that the greatest threat to the Church today is "lack of discernment." Spiritual discernment is the skill of separating truth from error. Believers who lack spiritual discernment are susceptible to accepting heretical teaching.

Studying God's Word is the preventative! As Dr. MacArthur states, "there's only one source for understanding the truth, one source for creating that grid through which everything filters and becomes clear: rightly interpreting the truth."

Separate From Improper Alliances

Don't be a partner with an unbeliever in vital areas of life such as business and marriage. Does this mean we can't be friends with, or be employed by, unbelievers? Of course not!

Do not be bound together with unbelievers; for what partnership have righteousness and lawlessness, or what fellowship has light with darkness? Or what harmony has Christ with Belial*, or what has a believer in common with an unbeliever? Or what agreement has the temple of God with idols? For we are the temple of the living God; just as God said, I will dwell in them and walk among them; and I will be their god, and they shall be my people. "Therefore, come out from their midst and be separate" says the Lord.
2 Corinthians 6:14-16 (NASB)

> * In the New Testament, *Belial* is a synonym for Satan. The word "belial" means "worthless."

In the Old Testament, at various times God warned the Israelites not to marry "foreigners" (non-Israelites) because He knew the result would be that the foreign wives would draw their husbands away from serving the one true God. When the warnings were ignored, the Israelites suffered the consequences, becoming involved in idolatry. The same is true today. Check the statistics. Marrying outside one's faith predisposes the marriage to failure, spiritually and otherwise.

Here's a very telling description of people in the "last days." We are told to "turn away" from such people. We are not to emulate their ways, not do what they do, go where they go. But we should be friends and evangelize them.

You should know this, Timothy, that in the last days there will be very difficult times. For people will love only themselves and their money. They will be boastful and proud, scoffing at God, disobedient to their parents, and ungrateful. They will consider nothing sacred. They will be unloving and unforgiving; they will slander others and have no self-control. They will be cruel and hate what is good. They will betray their friends, be reckless, be puffed up with pride, and love pleasure rather than God. They will act religious, but they will reject the power that could make them godly. Stay away from people like that! 2 Timothy 3:1-5 (NLT)

Separate From Doctrinally Sound People Or Groups Who Engage In Contrary Practices That Compromise The Faith

Groups holding a similar doctrinal position don't necessarily agree on all matters regarding the practice of our faith. That's understandable and permissible. But when individuals or groups drift from doctrinal purity, support questionable organizations, or participate in questionable activities that weaken or bring shame on the faith, biblically we must distance ourselves from them.

Why Should We Live Separated Lives?

- Because God commands us to do so (2 Corinthians 6:16-18) – and that is reason enough! Why did He ask us to live separated lives? Because He loves us and knows it's best for us.

- As a testimony. We are ambassadors for Christ – we represent Him (2 Corinthians 5:20). That's an awesome privilege and a serious responsibility! Are you a winsome Christian? Based on observing your life, what do people think of the Lord Jesus Christ, the One you represent?

  People are watching our lives. Because the Holy Spirit indwells us and we have a new nature, we should be noticeably different from the people of the world. Different, not odd!

  > *Dear friends, I warn you as "temporary residents and foreigners" to keep away from worldly desires that wage war against your very souls. Be careful to live properly among your unbelieving neighbors. Then even if they accuse you of doing wrong, they will see your honorable behavior, and they will give honor to God when he judges the world.* 1 Peter 2:11-12 (NLT)

- So that we don't learn the ways of the world. We may not intend to learn those ways, but after repeatedly walking in them, they may become a habit. Paul admonished us not to be conformed to the ways of the world (Romans 12:2). God's desire for us is that we be conformed to the image of His Son (Romans 8:29) – now and eternally – and He is working in our lives to accomplish that.

Holy Living (Personal Holiness)

According to 2 Timothy 1:9, we have been called to a holy life. What constitutes a "holy life"? Is it living as a monk or nun? Does it mean we walk around looking like we just bit into a lemon, or loudly reciting scripture verses, or shouting condemnation at those whose religion and/or lifestyle are different than ours? Does it mean we dress strangely?

All of the above (and more) have been done in the name of "religion" and, unfortunately, some in the name of Christianity.

When applied to us, "holy" means "set apart for God's service." It doesn't mean "sinless." Thus, holy living is living a life set apart for God's service, dedicated to Him – it doesn't require a sinless* life. Thankfully! While we are on earth, we will continue to sin because of the sin nature within. Does that give us an excuse for sinning? Absolutely not! Remember 1 Corinthians 10:13, quoted earlier? God promises to provide a way of escape from every temptation.

> *   The subject of sinless perfection is discussed in *Salvation and Security*, the study note for point six of the BMW Doctrinal Statement.

Is victory over sin possible? Yes, thank God it is! It's outlined in the sixth chapter of Romans. For more information, refer to *Salvation and Security*, the study note for point six of the BMW Doctrinal Statement.

Holy living starts in the mind. Our minds control our actions. Sin also starts in the mind. The Apostle James wrote this by inspiration of the Holy Spirit:

> *Let no one say when he is tempted, "I am being tempted by God"; for God cannot be tempted by evil and He Himself does not tempt anyone. But each one is tempted when he is carried away and enticed by his own lust. Then when lust has conceived it gives birth to sin and when sin is accomplished it brings forth death. Do not be deceived my beloved brethren.* James 1:13-16 (NASB)

Holy living includes walking in the Spirit and allowing Him to control our lives (Ephesians 5:18, Galatians 5:16). Walking in the Spirit is not the same as being indwelled by the Holy Spirit. For additional details refer to *The Person and Work of the Holy Spirit*, the study note for point four of the BMW Doctrinal Statement.

The Bible explicitly tells us not to do certain things. Thus, a holy life, a life set apart for God's service, must exclude those things. The ten commandments (a.k.a. the *decalog*, literally "ten words") provide a starting point. We are not to worship other gods, take God's name in vain, covet, murder, etc.

Christians who would live a holy life are not to engage in murder, robbery, theft, adultery, fornication, homosexual behavior, lying, etc. The Christian who gets involved in these activities certainly doesn't lose his or her salvation, but needs to confess those sins (1 John 1:9) and repent of them to restore fellowship with God.

There are other activities for which the Bible doesn't provide such explicit guidance, but does provide some basic principles. Some people say these activities are in a "gray area " – not black or white. They are also known as "neutral issues" because the Bible is neutral (doesn't take an explicit position) on them.

Depending on your upbringing and/or church teaching and/or culture, neutral issues can include such things as going to movies, using tobacco products, consuming alcohol, dancing, gambling – even such things as shopping on Sunday and washing your car or mowing your lawn on Sunday. Later in this study note we'll provide some guidelines for evaluating neutral issues.

Here's a well-known passage regarding what we should (and by inference, shouldn't) do with our physical bodies:

> *... do you not know that your body is a temple of the Holy Spirit who is in you, whom you have from God, and that you are not your own? For you have been bought with a price: therefore, glorify God in your body.* 1 Corinthians 6:19-20 (NASB)

The two verses above follow a passage that deals with sexual immorality. From several other passages, we know that such activity is indeed wrong. But 1 Corinthians 6:19-20 has a wider, more general application. It teaches that doing anything detrimental to my physical body (tobacco, alcohol, drugs, promiscuity, unhealthy lifestyle) is wrong – and thus must be avoided if I am to live a life that glorifies God, a holy life.

Here's a verse we've seen before. It has application here too.

> *I urge you therefore, brethren, by* (because of) *the mercies of God, to present your bodies* a living and holy sacrifice, acceptable* (well pleasing) *to God, which is your spiritual service of worship. And do not be*

conformed to this world, but be transformed by the renewing of your mind, that you may prove what the will of God is, that which is good and acceptable and perfect. Romans 12:1-2 (NASB)

> *   All of life's activities.

In the passage immediately above, Paul tells us that presenting our bodies is a "spiritual service of worship"! The KJV says presenting our lives to God is our "reasonable service." The word *reasonable* is a translation of the Greek word *logikos* from which we get our word *logic*. Thus, in light of what Christ has done for us, it is only logical that we would serve Him by presenting ourselves as living sacrifices.

Presenting your body – your life, your most precious possession – to God as a living sacrifice is the ultimate act of worship. How is this done? By praying these verses back to God and telling Him you're giving Him every aspect of your life as a living sacrifice! Then put it into practice: seek His direction in everything you do (Proverbs 3:5-6); seek, with the help of the Holy Spirit, to glorify God in every area of your life (1 Corinthians 10:31).

In Romans 12:2 (above), Paul tells us not to be "conformed to this world" – not to allow the world system to shape us, force us into its mold. How can the world system force us into its mold? One way is by getting us to think and behave the way unsaved people do, getting us to accept the ethical and moral standards of unsaved people of the world.

Do we live like the people of the world? Do we talk like them (profanity, obscenity, gossip, lies, etc.), watch the same filthy movies and TV shows, read the same smutty books and magazines, visit the same pornographic internet sites, spend our time and money as they do? Remember, holy living starts in the mind. What are we putting into our minds? Are we allowing the world to shape us? Your spiritual health is determined by what you feed your soul.

The Apostle Paul said that instead of being conformed, we are to be "transformed." "Transformed" is *trans* (meaning "change") plus *formed*. We are to be re-shaped, re-molded, changed to a different form than that which we used to be, that which we observe in the unsaved people of the world. This transformation is an ongoing process, not a once-for-all-time event.

We're also told how to effect this spiritual transformation: by the renewing of our minds, changing our thought patterns and our will to make them more Christlike. This is accomplished by the study of God's Word.

Someone said we are to "think God's thoughts after Him." That can only be accomplished if we know His thoughts as a result of studying His Word. There is no substitute for studying God's Word!

> *Blessed is the man who walks not in the counsel of the wicked, nor stands in the way of sinners, nor sits in the seat of scoffers; but his delight is in the law of the Lord, and on his law he meditates day and night. He is like a tree planted by streams of water that yields its fruit in its season, and its leaf does not wither. In all that he does, he prospers.* Psalm 1: 1-3 (ESV)

R. T. Kendall, former pastor of Westminster Chapel, London, wrote this regarding the Bible's role in living a holy life:

> "The Bible is the Holy Spirit's greatest product. He wrote it. If you want to experience the power of the Spirit to live a holy life, get to know and love the Bible more than you do anything else in the world."

Does living a holy life mean we will have a dull, unenjoyable life? The Lord Jesus Christ didn't think so. Consider His words:

> *I came that they* (Christians) *may have and enjoy life, and have it in abundance – to the full, till it overflows.* John 10:10b (Amplified Bible)

Here's a note from the *New Defender's Study Bible* regarding the abundant life:

> "The 'abundant life' does not consist in an abundance of possessions (Luke 12:15). Rather, it consists of an 'abundance of grace' (Romans 5:17, 20), an abundance of 'every good work' (2 Corinthians 9:8), an abundance of 'consolation' (2 Corinthians 1:5), an abounding 'love' (1 Thessalonians 3:12), an 'abounding … work of the Lord' (1 Corinthians 15:58), and 'abounding' and thankful 'faith' (Colossians 2:7)."

The happiest, most peaceful, contented, joyful, excited people in the world should be Christians. Why? Think about what God has done and is doing for us – and what's ahead!

Gray-Area Or Neutral Activities

There are many activities – commonly referred to as "gray area" or "neutral" activities – for which the Bible doesn't provide explicit guidance, but does provide basic principles for evaluation. Some of those principles are the basis for the "will it" questions below. For a given activity, if the answer to any *italicized* question is "yes," you should not be involved with that activity.

- Will it not violate the clear teaching of God's Word?
  Will it violate the clear teaching of God's Word?

- Will it be profitable for me – build me up, strengthen me – spiritually? (1 Corinthians 6:12)
  Will it be detrimental for me – tear me down, weaken me – spiritually?

- Will it not enslave (master) me? (1 Corinthians 6:12, 10:23)
  Will it enslave me, become my master, become an addiction?

- Will it not violate my God-given conscience? (Romans 14:5-23)
  Will it violate my conscience?

- Will it bring glory to God? (Romans 14:10-12 ; 1 Corinthians 10:31)
  Will it bring dishonor to the One who redeemed me, He who bought me with the price of His blood?

- Will it edify other believers – build them up and not cause them to "stumble" spiritually? (Romans 14:13-15; 20-21 , 1 Corinthians 8:9-13, 10:23-33)
  Will it result in fellow believers stumbling, weakening their spiritual life?

- Will it be a good witness to the unsaved? (1 Corinthians 10:31-33)
  Will my actions and words cause unbelievers to think poorly of Christians and our Savior?

- Will it not be harmful to my physical body, the temple (sanctuary) of the Holy Spirit?
  (1 Corinthians 6:19-20)
  Will it harm my body, that which belongs to God and for which He paid a high price?

Remember: As Christians, we are a royal priesthood – our lives are to proclaim God's praises in word and deed.

> *… you are a chosen people. You are royal priests, a holy nation, God's very own possession. As a result, you can show others the goodness of God, for he called you out of the darkness into his wonderful light.* 1 Peter 2:9 (NLT)

Unity

"Christian unity" means that, as Christians, we're united around the Lord Jesus Christ and by certain doctrinal beliefs. As people who have been born into God's spiritual family by faith in Christ, we're united by that common faith.

The term "unity" is not unique to Christianity. Other groups and organizations also have common beliefs that unite their members. For example, if you belong to a political action group, you're united politically with others by common beliefs and goals.   Another example: families are united around certain core values.

Here's the Apostle Paul's plea for unity, and the reason why he made that appeal:

> *Therefore I, a prisoner for serving the Lord, beg you to lead a life worthy of your calling, for you have been called by God. Always be humble and gentle. Be patient with each other, making allowance for each other's faults because of your love. Make every effort to keep yourselves united in the Spirit, binding yourselves together with peace. For there is one body and one Spirit, just as you have been called to one glorious hope for the future. There is one Lord, one faith, one baptism, and one God and Father, who is over all and in all and living through all.* Ephesians 4:1-6 (NLT)

According to the passage above, Christian unity, including both doctrinal and spiritual unity, incorporates seven units:

- **One body,** composed of all the individual members that make up a body, as stressed by Paul
  (1 Corinthians 12:12)

- **One Spirit,** who indwells each believer and has baptized them into that body (1 Corinthians 12:13)

- **One hope,** centered on Christ's return to complete His work of redemption (Ephesians 1:14; Titus 2:13)

- **One Lord,** Jesus Christ, who has purchased each believer with His own blood (Ephesians 1:7; 1 Peter 1:18-19)

- **One faith**, that body of truth which has been "once [for all] delivered unto the saints" (Jude 3)

- **One baptism**, by which we have all been identified with and united with Christ*
(1 Corinthians 12:13)

> * Some people believe this refers to water baptism. It doesn't – because (1) 1 Corinthians 12:13 is the baptism of the Holy Spirit, and (2) not all believers are water baptized.

- **One God** and Father of us all

Unity doesn't mean we shouldn't confront error when it's taught or preached. The following two paragraphs are from the pen of Sean McDowell:

"There is a trend in the church today to elevate unity above truth. Many are willing to set aside essential doctrines for the sake of harmony. … As shown in the Sermon on the Mount, Jesus saw the value in dividing over essential doctrine because it saves people from the consequences of false teaching.

"True unity (in our churches) comes not when we sacrifice true doctrine, but when we focus on the core truths of the Gospel. Thus, the real question is not if we teach doctrine, but what doctrines do we teach, how do we teach them, and do we live them out in our relationships. For the sake of our youth and the vitality of the church, we must not cave in to the pressure to stop teaching doctrine. The proper response to the attack on doctrine is not to retreat, but to march forward with an even greater resolve, unity, and love." From *The Doctrine Debate: Why Doctrine Matters More Than Ever*, printed in the *Christian Research Journal*, Volume 31 Number 1

The McDowell article above incorporates the term "essential doctrines." These are biblical doctrines (teachings) that are vital to the Christian faith. In his article *Essential Christian Doctrines* (*Christian Research Journal*, Volume 28, Number 6), Dr. Norman Geisler stated that in terms of making salvation possible, essential doctrines include

- Human depravity

- Christ's virgin birth

- Christ's sinlessness

- Christ's deity

- Christ's humanity

- God's unity

- God's triunity

- The necessity of God's grace

- The necessity of faith in Christ's atoning death

- Christ's bodily resurrection

- Christ's bodily ascension

- Christ's present high priestly service

- Christ's second coming, final judgment (heaven and hell), and reign

Other essential doctrines include these points regarding Scripture:

- Inerrancy

- Infallibility

- Inspiration (Verbal and Plenary)

- Closed Cannon

These points are explained and expanded in *The Holy Scriptures*, the study note for point one of the BMW Doctrinal Statement.

The essential doctrines listed above are the foundation for our unity. They distinguish true Christianity from cultic spin-offs, and are nonnegotiable for followers of Christ. These doctrines are matters over which we *should* divide from those who do not ascribe to them.

Supplemental Information

1. The World System

The "world system" involves a concern for external appearances more than inner content and quality. As used in the New Testament, "world" does not refer to nature *per se*, but to the world-system, to society and human culture. The world system is outwardly religious, scientific, cultured and elegant. Inwardly it seethes with national and commercial rivalries.

The material below was written by Lambert Dolphin, PhD.

The general characteristics of "the world" as the term is used in the Bible when referring to the fallen "world system" may be described roughly as follows. The world:

- Ignores eternal values and invisible realities.

- Produces conformity to cultural norms or traditions of men; stifles individuality.

- Makes use of force, greed, ambition and warfare to accomplish objectives.

- Offers financial reward at the cost of one's soul.

- Cares little for the worth of the individual or his uniqueness.

- Promotes myths and illusions which appeal to human vanity and pride.

- Diverts attention from spiritual values by appeals to pursue pleasure, pride (vainglory), or to power.

- Permissive sexual, moral and ethical values to encourage self-indulgence.

- Superficiality of life and appeal to immediate pleasure rather than long-term goals.

- Offers false philosophies and value systems to support its goals. The root problem is pride.

- Exalts man, his abilities and his supposed "progress" – for example, through the myth of Social Evolution.

- Glosses over and hides suffering, death, poverty, the depravity of man, and our accountability to God.

- Seeks to unify mankind under an atheistic humanistic or pantheistic ("one world religion") banner.

- Emphasizes relativism and pluralism and denies biblical absolutes.

- Teaches human progress and advancement through better education or social welfare.

2. Word-Faith (Word of Faith) Movement

The quote below (three paragraphs) is excerpted from an article in the July, 2007, edition of *Christianity Today*.

> "While Christians of all types and times have relied on God's material provision, the kind of blessings that (prosperity gospel) preachers often promise – such as divine expectation of abundant wealth, runaway professional success, and unassailable physical and emotional health – spring from a relatively recent, American brand of religious thought.

> "The earliest proponents of positive thinking were spiritual innovators like Phineas P. Quimby and Mary Baker Eddy, founders of the New Thought movement and Christian Science, respectively. By the turn of the 20th century, Essek William Kenyon, a pastor and founder of Bethel Bible Institute, had incorporated similar ideas into his preaching on the finished work of Christ. Kenyon wrote that Christians could make a 'positive confession' to bring emotional and physical desires into being. 'What I confess,' he is purported to have said, 'I possess.'

> "In the 1930's, Kenneth Hagin added Kenyon's teachings to his Pentecostal beliefs to create what would become the Word-Faith movement. An Assemblies of God pastor, Hagin taught Christians that they could get rich by mustering enough faith. 'Say it, do it, receive it, tell it,' he said. He touted a 'Rhema* doctrine,' which held that words spoken in faith must be fulfilled, spawning slogans like 'name and claim it.' In the 1960's, a young associate of Oral Roberts, Kenneth Copeland, began teaching that faith is a 'force' which, when

confessed out loud, brings material results. Within a couple decades, Word-Faith had grown into a sizeable offshoot of charismatic faith."

    * *Rhema* means "sayings of God."

Word-Faith also teaches that if anything bad happens to you – sickness, financial setbacks, family troubles – it's because you didn't have enough faith or you have a secret sin. Contrast this teaching to what happened to Jesus, the apostles, Job, and others – they suffered greatly despite their faith and obedience to God.

Whether explicitly or implicitly, Word-Faith encourages greed and selfishness. The tenth commandment (Exodus 20:17) tells us that we are not to covet. And the Apostle Paul said …

    I have learned to be content whatever the circumstances Philippians 4:11 (NIV)

Word-Faith inverts our role and purpose as Christians. It encourages us to make God our servant rather than seeking how we might serve and please Him.

Hank Hanegraaff ("The Bible Answer Man" from the Christian Research Institute) connects the Word-Faith movement to occult movements:

> "Occult movements such as New Age, New Thought, and neo-pagan witchcraft have long held that the power to create one's own reality lies within oneself, that thoughts and words are imbued with creative power that directly and dramatically affect the real world in which we live, and that we can use creative visualization to speak, think, or even feel things into existence. These tenets of an occult worldview, a variation of which has sadly been promoted under the guise of Christianity by the heretical Word of Faith movement, are the essence of what is now being widely touted as *The Secret*. This essence is summed up by Mike Dooley, contributing author of *The Secret*, in three words: 'Thoughts become things'."

In addition to those mentioned above, Word-Faith teachers include Benny Hinn, T. D. Jakes, Joel Osteen, Rod Parsley, Morris Cerullo, Fred Price, Kenneth Hagin Jr., Creflo Dollar, Paul and Jan Crouch, John Avanzini, Robert Tilton, Joyce Meyer, Reinhard Bonnke.

Paul Crouch's Trinity Broadcasting Network (TBN) is a major supplier of Word-Faith programming.

For additional information, I recommend two books by Hank Hanegraaff: *Christianity in Crisis* (1993) and *Counterfeit Revival* (1997). (I don't agree with Hanegraaff on all matters, but these two books are solid.)

3. Gnosticism and Mysticism

First, let's understand that the frequently used term "Christian Gnosticism" is an oxymoron. True Christianity and Gnosticism are mutually exclusive systems of belief. The principles of Gnosticism contradict what it means to be a Christian.

Much of the material below was excerpted from an article accessed at
http://www.gotquestions.org/Christian-gnosticism.html

"Gnosticism is based on a mystical*, intuitive, subjective, inward, emotional approach to truth which is not new at all. It is very old, going back in some form to the Garden of Eden, where Satan questioned God and the words He spoke and convinced Adam and Eve to reject them and accept a lie. He does the same thing today as he 'prowls around like a roaring lion looking for someone to devour' (1 Peter 5:8). He still calls God and the Bible into question and catches in his web those who are either naïve and scripturally uninformed or who are seeking some personal revelation to make them feel special, unique, and superior to others.

> * "Mystical belief systems are collections of ideas that have arisen out of emotion, out of self-authenticated ideas unrelated to objective fact or evidence. Mysticism is a system of beliefs and ideas which are the product of my own personal intuition which I assume transcends ordinary understanding. To put it simply, it is sheer speculation believed to be reality." From a sermon by Dr. John MacArthur

"Gnosticism was perhaps the most dangerous heresy that threatened the early church during the first three centuries. Influenced by such philosophers as Plato, Gnosticism is based on two false premises. First, it espouses a dualism regarding spirit and matter. Gnostics assert that matter is inherently evil and spirit is good. As a result of this presupposition, Gnostics believe anything done in the body, even the grossest sin, has no meaning because real life exists in the spirit realm only.

"Second, Gnostics claim to possess an elevated knowledge, a 'higher truth' known only to a certain few. Gnosticism comes from the Greek word gnosis which means 'to know.' Gnostics claim to possess a higher knowledge, not from the Bible, but acquired on some mystical higher plain [sic] of existence. Gnostics see themselves as a privileged class elevated above everybody else by their higher, deeper knowledge of God.

"On the matter of salvation, Gnosticism teaches that salvation is gained through the acquisition of divine knowledge which frees one from the illusions of darkness.

"The Gnostics believe that Jesus' physical body was not real, but only 'seemed' to be physical, and that His spirit descended upon Him at His baptism, but left Him just before His crucifixion."

And from Dr. John MacArthur:

"Gnosticism is the belief that one must have a '*gnosis*' (from Greek *gnosko*, 'to know') or mystical, inner knowledge obtained only after one has been properly initiated. Only a few can possess this mystical knowledge, limiting the number of those 'in the know.' Naturally, the idea of having inside information is very appealing and makes the 'knower' feel important, special and unique in that he/she has a special experience with God that no one else has. The 'knower' believes that the masses are not in possession of spiritual knowledge and only the truly 'enlightened' can experience God."

Gnostic beliefs were/are a "mixed bag." We've already been introduced to some of these beliefs; here are more examples:

• All Gnostics rejected either the true deity or true humanity of the Lord Jesus Christ.

• Most Gnostics believed that Jesus was married to Mary Magdalene, and fathered children by her.

- Gnosticism teaches that Jesus was an illegitimate child. He was not born in Bethlehem, nor was His mother, Mary, a virgin.

- Gnostics deny that Jesus performed miracles. His acts of healing were psychosomatic in nature.

- In lifestyle, some Gnostics were ascetics; some were extremely self-indulgent.

- All Gnostics denied the bodily resurrection of Christ, and provided various reasons why there was no resurrection.

- Most Gnostics believed that God has two distinct personas – the good, unknowable, transcendent god; and the evil, knowable, creator god. Some Gnostics denied that there was a creator at all.

- Gnostics believe creation contains both good and evil. The creator caused certain aspects of the creation to be evil from the beginning. Light, spirit, and knowledge represent what is good, while darkness, matter, flesh, and ignorance represent all that is evil.

- Gnosticism teaches that salvation comes through secret knowledge. And while the spirit is redeemable, the flesh is not. Therefore, there is no such thing as the resurrection of the body.

Gnostic Writings

Some of the writings listed here were found in 1945, in an earthenware vessel buried in a cave near the northern Egyptian city of Nag Hammadi. They are variously referred to as "The Nag Hammadi Library," "The Nag Hammadi Scrolls," and "The Nag Hammadi Codices." This "library" was supposedly the result of faithful efforts of Gnostic monks to save the truth about Jesus Christ from the persecution of non-Gnostic Christians.

Most of the Gnostic writings below were written in the second and third centuries A.D.; some even later. Gnostic writings do not antedate the books that constitute the canon of Scripture. (Revelation, the last book of our Bible, was completed c. 96 A.D.) Some people claim that the Gnostic "gospels" are the "lost books of the Bible." They aren't.

- The Gospel of Peter

- The Gospel of the Ebionites*

- The Gospel of the Egyptians

- The Gospel of Thomas

- The Gospel of Mary Magdalene

- The Gospel of Truth

- The Gospel of the Savior

- Apocryphon (secret writing) of John

- Apocryphon of Peter

- Apocryphon of Adam

- Apocryphon of Mark

- Apocryphon of Ezekiel

- Apocryphon of James

- Acts of Peter and the twelve Apostles

  * Ebionism is the view that Jesus was fully human, but not divine. Ebionites denied the deity of Christ. Ebionism viewed Jesus as a normal human being who was simply empowered by God. Ebionism is rejected by a multitude of Scriptures. http://www.gotquestions.org/Docetism-Apollinarianism-Ebionism-Eutychianism.html

The Nag Hammadi scrolls are forgeries. The Apostle Philip did not write the Gospel of Philip. The Apostle Peter did not write the Gospel of Peter. The Gospel of Thomas was not written by the Apostle Thomas. These scrolls were fraudulently written in the apostles' names to give them legitimacy in the early church. The only "value" in the Nag Hammadi scrolls is that they provide insight into what early heretics taught and practiced.

In his book *Jesus: Why the world is still fascinated by Him*, Dr. Tim LaHaye describes Gnostic literature:

"Gnostics believe their texts represent the real core of Christian truth as originally conceived, but due to the 'sinister institution of the organized church' this truth has been concealed from the public. Therefore, what most Christians hold today as biblical truth, they say, is a flawed invention that has managed to suppress the 'real truth' of Gnosticism for twenty centuries. If the contents of these Gnostic documents are indeed true, then a thorough makeover of Christianity is surely needed. But are they true?

"Gnostic proponents claim that all historians, theologians, and believers down through the centuries have been duped, and that the millions of lives around the world that have been dramatically changed for the better as a result of a faith in Christ have been a mistake. The inspiration behind the world's greatest works of art; the motivation to build hospitals; the humanitarian assistance provided by Christian groups; the elevation of women as a result of Christ's teachings; the archaeological evidence for the Bible on display in the museums of the world; the reverence for Jesus – could all this be the result of one big, deceptive conspiracy?"

One of John's reasons for writing his first epistle was to combat Gnosticism in the early church. Many of the early church fathers actively contended against Gnosticism. Beginning in 155 A.D., Justin Martyr, a Christian apologist (defender), wrote a series of books defending the Christian faith against Gnosticism. Other apologists followed, including Irenaeus, Tertullian, Clement of Alexandria, and Origen.

Modern-Day Gnostic Writers

So you will recognize them for who they are, here are the names of a few Gnostic writers and the documents they produced.

- Walter Bauer (*Orthodoxy and Heresy in Earliest Christianity*)

- Michael Bigent (*Holy Blood, Holy Grail; The Jesus Papers*)

- Dan Brown (*The DaVinci Code*)

- Rhonda Byrne (*The Secret*)

- John Crossan and other members of the Jesus Seminar

- Bart Ehrman (*The Lost Gospel of Judas Iscariot: A New Look at Betrayer and Betrayed*)

- Elaine Pagels (*Beyond Belief: The Secret Gospel of Thomas; The Gnostic Gospels; Revelations: Visions, Prophecy, and Politics in the book of Revelation*)

- James Tabor (*The Jesus Dynasty*)

Bibliography

Books

Boice, James Montgomery, 1979, *Does Inerrancy Matter?*, Oakland, CA, International Council on Biblical Inerrancy

Bridges, Jerry, 2006, *The Pursuit of Holiness*, Colorado Springs, CO, NavPress

Edwards, Jonathan, 1854, *Charity and Its Fruits*, New York, Robert Carver and Brothers

Fruchtenbaum, Arnold G., 2004, *The Footsteps of the Messiah, Revised Edition,* San Antonio, TX, Ariel Ministries

Hanegraaff, Hank, 1992, *Christianity in Crisis*, Eugene, OR, Harvest House Publishers

Hanegraaff, Hank, 1997, *Counterfeit Revival*, Eugene, OR, Harvest House Publishers

Henry, Matthew, 1961, *Commentary*, Grand Rapids, MI, Zondervan Corporation

Hitchcock, Mark, and Ice, Thomas, 2007, *Breaking the Apocalypse Code*, Costa Mesa, CA, The Word for Today

Hodge, A. A., 1976, *Evangelical Theology*, Carlisle, PA, Banner of Truth

International Council on Biblical Inerrancy, 1978, *The Chicago Statement on Biblical Inerrancy*

LaHaye, Tim F., 2009, *Jesus, Why The World Is Still Fascinated By Him*, Colorado Springs, CO, David C. Cook

LaHaye, Tim F, and Jenkins, Jerry B, 2001, *Perhaps Today: Living Every Day In The Light Of Christ's Return*, Wheaton, IL, Tyndale House Publishers

Little, Paul E., and Nyqist, James F., 2008, *Know What You Believe*, Downers Grove, IL, InterVarsity Press

Longman III, Tremper, and Garland, David E., 2005, *The Expositor's Bible Commentary; Hebrews ~ Revelation*, Grand Rapids, MI, Zondervan Corporation

MacArthur, John, 2013, *Strange Fire: The Danger of Offending the Holy Spirit with Counterfeit Worship*, Nashville, Tennessee, Nelson Books

MacArthur, John, 2013, *The Glory of Heaven; The Truth about Heaven, Angels and Eternal Life (Second Edition)*, Wheaton Illinois, Crossway

MacArthur, John, 2015, *Why Believe The Bible?*, Grand Rapids, MI, Baker Books

Morris III, Henry M., 2008, *5 Reasons To Believe in Recent Creation*, Dallas, TX, Institute for Creation Research

Morris III, Henry M., 2003, *After Eden: Understanding Creation, the Curse, and the Cross,* Green Forest, AR, Master Books, Inc.

Morris, Henry M., 1987, *The Bible Has the Answer,* El Cajon, CA, Creation -Life Publishers Inc., Master Books Division

Morris, Henry M., 2004, *For Time and Forever,* Green Forest, AR, Master Books, Inc.

Murray, John, 1960, *The Epistle to the Romans,* Grand Rapids, MI, Eerdmans Publishing Company

Packer, J. I., 1993, *Concise Theology: A Guide To Historic Christian Beliefs,* Carol Stream, IL, Tyndale House Publishers

Packer, J. I., 2012, *Evangelism and the Sovereignty of God,* Downers Grove, IL, Intervarsity Press

Packer, J. I., 1993, *Knowing God,* Downers Grove, IL, Intervarsity Press

Ramm, Bernard, 1998, *Protestant Biblical Interpretation,* Grand Rapids, MI, Baker Book House

Romaine, William, 1826, *A Sermon on the Self-existence of Jesus Christ,* Chatfield and Coleman

Ryrie, Charles C., 1972, *A Survey of Bible Doctrine,* Chicago, IL, Moody Press

Ryrie, Charles C., 1999, *Basic Theology,* Chicago, IL, Moody Press

Ryrie, Charles C., 2007, *Dispensationalism, Revised and Expanded,* Chicago, IL, Moody Press

Sidders, Greg, 2011, *The Invitation, The Not-So-Simple Truth about Following Jesus,* Westwood, NJ, Revell Company

Smeaton, George, 1882, *The Doctrine of the Holy Spirit,* Edinburgh, T&T Clark

Vine, W. E., 1966, *An Expository Dictionary of New Testament Words,* Westwood, NJ, Revell Company

Walvoord, John F. and Zuck, Roy B., 1984, *The Bible Knowledge Commentary,* Wheaton, IL, Victor Books

Wiersbe, Warren, 2009, *Be Faithful,* Colorado Springs, CO, David C. Cook

Zacharias, Ravi, 2012, *Why Jesus? Rediscovering His Truth in an Age of Mass Marketed Spirituality,* Nashville, TN, FaithWords

Bibles

Morris, Henry M., 2005, *The New Defender's Study Bible* [King James Version], Arlington, VA, World Publishing Company

Zodhiates, Spiros, 1990, *Hebrew-Greek Key Word Study Bible, New American Standard Bible,* Chattanooga, TN, AMG Publishers

Magazines / Periodicals

Acts & Facts, Institute for Creation Research, Dallas, TX

Bibliotheca Sacra, Dallas Theological Seminary, Dallas, TX

Christian Research Journal, Christian Research Institute, Charlotte, NC

Christianity Today, Christianity Today International, Carol Stream, IL

Days of Praise, Institute for Creation Research, Dallas, TX

Decision Magazine, Billy Graham Evangelistic Association, Minneapolis, MN

General Index

Scripture Index